The New Wider World

Second Edition COURSEMATE

for **WJEC A** *GCSE Geography*

Cathie Brooks and Sue Taylor

Skills unit developed by
Simon Ross

Nelson Thornes
a Wolters Kluwer business

Contents

Introduction   iii

Unit 1: The fragile world

Section 1A: Ice, rivers and the sea
1 Ice 1
2 Rivers features and flooding 8
3 Coastal features and flooding. 17

Section 1B: Weather, climate and tourism
4 Weather and climate 25
5 Tourism 34

Section 1C: Towards sustainable development of energy and other resources
6 Sustainable development of energy and other resources 42
7 Environmental change: Dissertification and global warming . 51

Unit 1
8 The fragile world – decisions 60

Unit 2: The interdependent world

Section 2A: Economic activities and their consequences
9 Farming and industry................................. 66
10 Shopping 77

Section 2B: The influence of economic and social change on urban development
11 The consequences of urban development in the UK....... 82
12 Global urban development............................ 94

Section 2C: Global citizenship and interdependance
13 Patterns of world development and population change.... 102
14 Global communities.................................. 113

Unit 2
15 The interdependant world – decisions 120

Units 1 and 2
16 Skills 126
Index 138

Introduction

About this book

This New Wider World Coursemate matches the content of *The New Wider World* to your own GCSE Geography specification, and follows the same order. It is a pocket companion for your course and provides a summary of the core information you will need to know and revise for your GCSE/Standard Grade Geography examinations.

How the specification is structured

The specification consists of two units, each divided into three sections:

Unit 1	**The fragile world – physical systems and environmental issues**
	1A Ice, rivers and the sea (note: *either* rivers or *sea*)
	1B Weather, climate and tourism
	1C Towards sustainable development of the environment
Unit 2	**The interdependent world – economic activities, global inequalities and places**
	2A Economic activities and their consequences
	2B The influence of economic and social change on urban development
	2C Global citizenship and interdependence

How the specification is assessed

The examination consists of three components.

1. Exam: Paper 1 — Foundation Tier 1¾ hrs / Higher Tier 2 hrs — 37.5%
2. Exam: Paper 2 — Foundation Tier 1¾ hrs / Higher Tier 2 hrs — 37.5%
3. Coursework: Geographical investigation — 25%

Paper 1: assesses Unit 1: 1A, 1B, 1C.

Paper 2: assesses Unit 2: 2A, 2B, 2C.

In each paper three questions assess Sections A, B, C. The fourth question is a decision-making exercise (DME) combining concepts from across Sections A, B, C.

Geographical skills are assessed within the examination questions and coursework.

Coursework: The topic for investigation can come from any section of the specification. Students may submit **one** full investigation or **two** smaller pieces of work.

How your Coursemate is organised

Your Coursemate follows the same structure and order as the topics in your specification. Most of the information is from *The New Wider World*, so your book acts as a companion to both *The New Wider World* and your own specification. Your Coursemate is organised in the following way:

- The **unit** and **chapter headings** match those used in the specification.
- The **page references** to *The New Wider World* at the beginning of each chapter tell you which pages in the textbook your Coursemate refers to.
- The numbered **Key questions** relate to those that appear in your specification, and the numbered headings and content of your Coursemate are organised around these.
- **Key words to know** – these are the key geographical words and terms you need to know and be able to use.
- **Check this!...** – doing these questions will check that you know and understand the key concepts in each chapter.
- **Back to...** is a cross-reference to *The New Wider World* for finding more information. It can also be a cross-reference to other information in your Coursemate.
- **Case Studies** are based on the case studies and place studies in *The New Wider World*, and **Case Study Extras** are new case studies written especially for your specification. Where relevant these will: refer you back to the textbook for more information; tell you how to get the best from your case study; provide links to other topics; provide updates to the case study, which may be accessed via a link from the Nelson Thornes Coursemate website at www.nelsonthornes.com/NWWCoursemates
and include questions that encourage you to learn the case study so that you can use it well in your examination.
- **Exam practice** – these questions are similar to those you will meet in the examination. You can check your answers by going to *The New Wider World* Coursemate website at www.nelsonthornes.com/NWWCoursemates.
- Each exam practice question is followed by an **exam tip** to provide help and advice on answering the question.

At the end of this book you will find a chapter on **geographical skills**. This gives information on the basic geographical skills you will need for the interpretation, presentation and analysis of geographical information and data throughout your Geography course and in your examinations.

> All references to *The New Wider World* in your Coursemate are to the Second edition.

Unit 1: The fragile world

⇨ *The New Wider World*, pp246–247; 316–323

Ice

1 What is the nature of weathering and mass movement?

Weathering

Weathering is the disintegration (breaking up) and decomposition (decay) of rocks **in situ** – that is, in their place of origin. Weathering, unlike erosion, does not involve the movement of material.

Physical weathering

Physical weathering is the disintegration of rock into smaller pieces by physical processes without any change in the chemical composition of the rock. It is most likely to occur in areas of bare rock where there is no vegetation to protect the rock from extremes of weather.

Freeze–thaw is one example of physical weathering which occurs in cold climates where temperatures move above and below freezing point and where exposed rock contains many cracks (Figure 1.1).
- Water enters the cracks during the day.
- During the colder night the water turns into ice, expands and exerts pressure on the surrounding rock.
- When temperatures rise, the ice melts and the pressure is released.

Repeated freezing and thawing widens the cracks and causes pieces of rock to break off.

KEY QUESTIONS

1. What is the nature of weathering and mass movement?
2. How do glaciers erode, transport and deposit material?
3. What landforms give the upland glaciated landscape its character, and how are these landforms created?

Key words to know

In situ
Physical weathering
Freeze–thaw

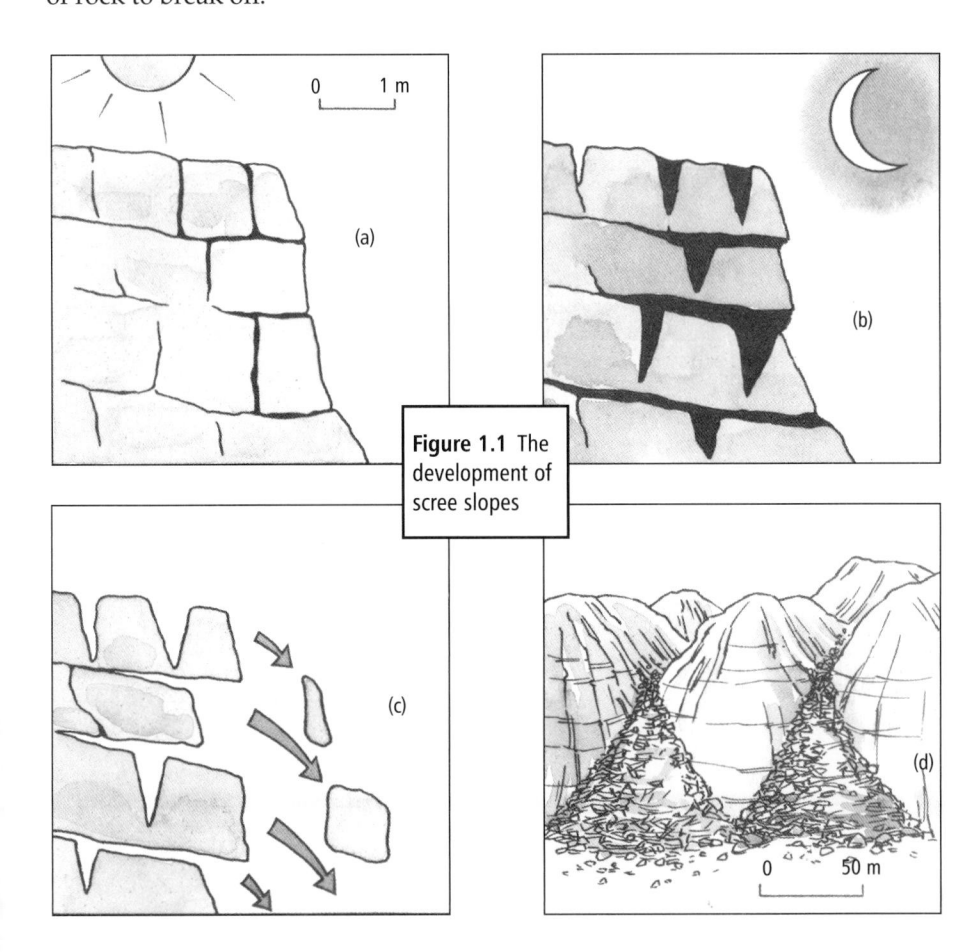

Figure 1.1 The development of scree slopes

Back to ...

The New Wider World **p246** Figure 15.8 which shows a photograph of a scree slope.

Key words to know

Scree
Chemical weathering
Mass movement
Soil creep
Terracettes

Scree slopes are made of these loose, sharp rocks, which have fallen down a cliff, often down a narrow gully, to form a fan shape at the foot of the cliff. As material is weathered by freeze–thaw it falls on top of the existing scree and so the scree slope gradually becomes higher and spreads further out into the valley floor (Figure 1.1).

Chemical weathering

Chemical weathering is the decomposition of rock caused by a chemical change within the rock. It is more likely to occur in warm, moist climates. As rainwater passes through the atmosphere and soil it picks up carbon dioxide and becomes a weak form of carbonic acid. Rainwater reacts particularly with limestone which is a rock composed mainly of calcium carbonate. The limestone is changed into a soluble product. This slowly dissolves and is removed in solution by running water.

Mass movement

Mass movement is the downhill movement of weathered material under the action of gravity. This movement, which occurs on all slopes, transports rocks and soil.

Figure 1.2 Processes and evidence of soil creep

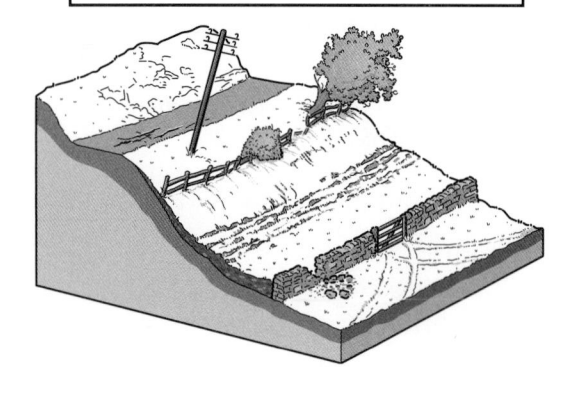

Soil creep is the slowest process of mass movement. It occurs in moist climates on low angled, vegetated slopes with a soil layer.

- The low angle of slope and vegetation cover encourage the rainwater to seep into the soil providing lubrication for downhill movement.
- But the low slope angle and the binding effect of the vegetation roots make this downhill movement a very slow process, typically less than 1 cm a year.

Terracettes, or small wrinkles on a grassy slope, are produced by this process.

Check this!...

1. What is the difference between physical and chemical weathering?
2. Describe the scree slope in Figure 15.8 on p246 of *The New Wider World*.
3. Copy Figure 1.1 and add labels to your diagrams to show how a scree slope develops as a result of freeze–thaw.
4. Copy Figure 1.2. Use the phrases in the box to annotate (label) this diagram. Use a different colour for a) processes of soil creep and b) evidence of soil creep.

Grass roots binding the soil
Terracettes
Leaning telegraph pole
Covering of moist soil
Soil piled up behind wall causing it to break
Curved tree trying to grow straight on moving soil
Direction of soil movement

2 How do glaciers erode, transport and deposit material?

Glaciers

The landscape in mountain areas in the UK has similar glaciated features to those shown in the photograph in Figure 19.2 on p316 of *The New Wider World*, indicating that most of the mountains of the UK were once covered by ice. During the **Ice Age** snow fell on these mountains. After a time snow gradually compacts into ice, especially on north-facing slopes where the ground is sheltered from the sun. As the ice builds up it spreads out and moves downhill, usually down an already existing river valley. Some **glaciers** are over 1 km thick.

Erosion

There are two main processes of glacial **erosion**:
- **Plucking** results from glacial ice melting then refreezing on to solid rock. As the glacier moves away it pulls with it pieces of rock.
- **Abrasion** is when the rock fragments carried by a glacier rub against and, like sandpaper, wear away the sides and floor of the valley. It is similar to corrasion by a river, but on a much larger scale.

Transport

- In glacial regions temperatures fall below freezing at night but it is warmer during the day. The landscape is one of steep, bare rock containing water from the melting snowfall. These are the ideal conditions for freeze–thaw. The shattered blocks of rock from the rock faces above the glacier fall on to the moving glacier below which then carries the fallen blocks along *above the ice*.
- As the glacier moves down the valley it plucks fragments away from the parts of the valley floor over which it is moving. These fragments are frozen into the base of the glacier and transported as debris *below the* main body of *ice*.
- The rocks from above and below may be transported *within the ice*:
  - by more snow and ice covering the surface of the glacier thus burying the freeze–thaw material that was once on the top of the glacier
  - by large blocks slowly sinking into the glacier
  - by ice, containing debris, at the base of the glacier, being forced up into the main body of the glacier above.

The rock fragments carried in ice are not tumbled about as in a river. They remain frozen as jagged rocks in the slowly moving ice.

Deposition

Glaciers are like slow-moving down escalators with ice and rock fragments constantly moving forwards. The end or **snout** of the glacier occurs where the ice melts at the same rate as the glacier is moving forward. This melting is due to warmer conditions in the valley floor. As more and more ice melts the snout of the glacier looks dirty as it is now mainly made of rock with only small amounts of ice. The rock fragments are deposited on the valley floor when there is no ice left to

---

Back to …

The New Wider World **p316**
Figure 19.2. This photograph shows a glacier. How big is it? What sort of landscape is it in? What is it made of? What sort of climate is needed for a glacier to exist?

Key words to know

Ice Age
Glacier
Erosion: Plucking
    Abrasion
Transport
Deposition
Snout

Ice

Key words to know
Moraine
Corrie
Arête
Rock lip
Tarn

support them. These rock fragments can be likened to boxes being carried on an escalator which get deposited at the foot of the escalator and then pile up. This deposit of rock fragments on the floor of a glaciated valley is called **moraine**.

3 What landforms give the upland glaciated landscape its character, and how are these landforms created?

Corries

Corries are deep, rounded hollows consisting of a rock basin with a steep back wall. Figure 1.3 shows how they are formed.

Arêtes

When two or more corries develop back to back (or side by side), they erode backwards (or sideways) towards each other. The land between them gets narrower until a knife-edged ridge, called an **arête**, is formed.

Figure 1.3 Formation of a corrie

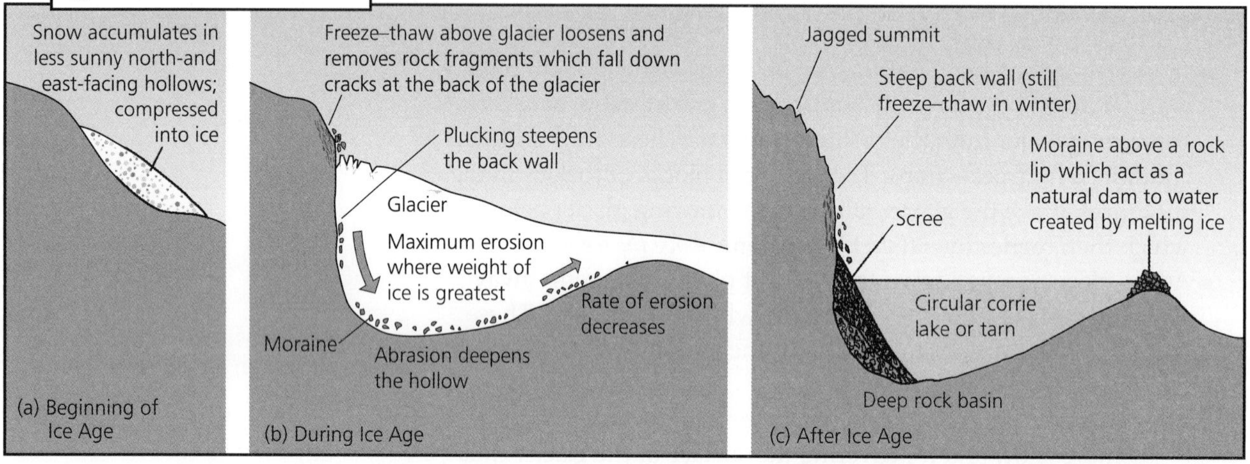

(a) Beginning of Ice Age
Snow accumulates in less sunny north-and east-facing hollows; compressed into ice

(b) During Ice Age
Freeze–thaw above glacier loosens and removes rock fragments which fall down cracks at the back of the glacier
Plucking steepens the back wall
Glacier
Maximum erosion where weight of ice is greatest
Rate of erosion decreases
Moraine
Abrasion deepens the hollow

(c) After Ice Age
Jagged summit
Steep back wall (still freeze–thaw in winter)
Moraine above a rock lip which act as a natural dam to water created by melting ice
Scree
Circular corrie lake or tarn
Deep rock basin

Figure 1.4 Arêtes
Arête
Arête
Corrie lake

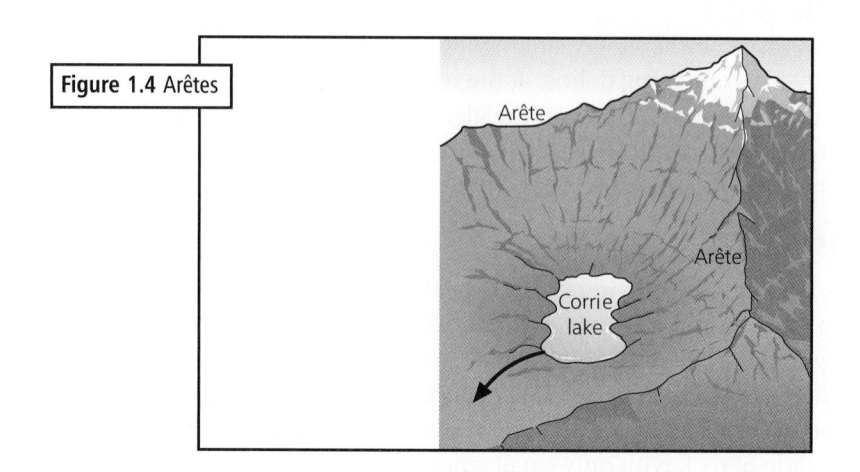

Glacial troughs and hanging valleys

Glaciers flowing out of corries and moving downhill from the mountains follow the easiest possible route which, in most cases, is an existing river valley. Unlike a river, however, the glacier often fills much of the valley and has much greater erosive power. This means that, instead of having to flow around obstacles, such as interlocking spurs, (Figure 1.5a) the glacier is able to widen, deepen and straighten the valley (Figure 1.5b). The result is the U-shaped cross-section of a **glacial trough**. As the glacier moves down the valley it removes the ends of interlocking spurs to leave steep, cliff-like, **truncated spurs**.

Key words to know

Glacial trough
Truncated spur
Hanging valley
Terminal moraine

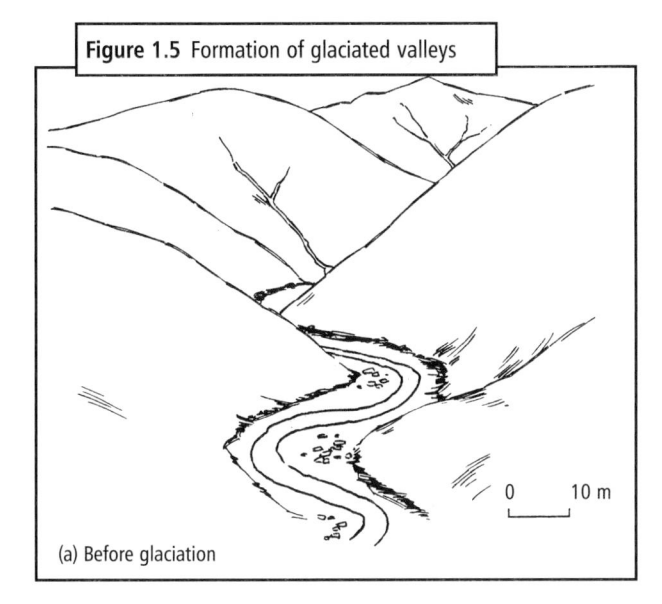

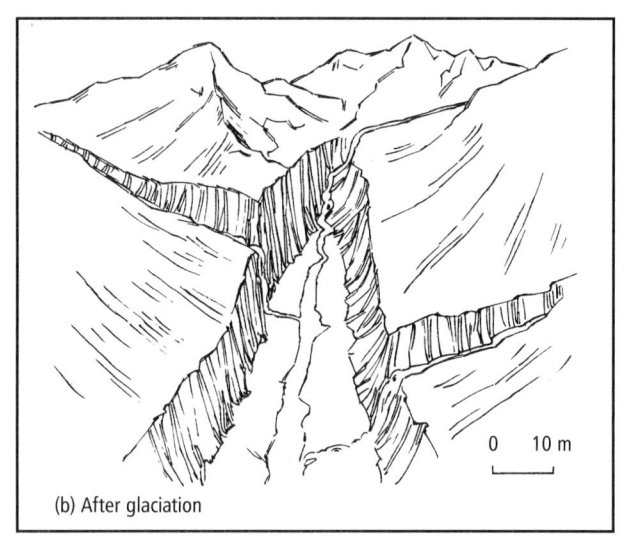

Figure 1.5 Formation of glaciated valleys

(a) Before glaciation

(b) After glaciation

Between adjacent truncated spurs are **hanging valleys**. Before the Ice Age, tributary rivers cut down their valleys to join, with a gradual, gentle gradient, the river on the main valley floor. During the Ice Age, the glacier in the main valley would be much larger than glaciers in the tributary valleys, and so it could erode downwards and sideways much more rapidly. The smaller glacier in the side valley would form a U-shaped valley which was not so deep. The tributary glacier would meet the main glacier near its upper surface. When the ice melted, the tributary valleys were left 'hanging' above the main valley. After the Ice Age the tributary river now flows firstly along the flat floor of the tributary U shape and then descends to the main river by a steep waterfall falling down the side of the main valley (Figure 1.5b).

Terminal moraine

The photograph in *The New Wider World* shows a **terminal moraine** being formed. Moraine is the name given to the rock fragments transported by the glacier and which are deposited when the ice melts. The jumble of loose rocks of different sizes marks the furthest point, or terminus, reached by the snout of a glacier. If the climate stays the same for a lengthy period the forward moving glacier will melt at the same place in the valley floor for a long time. More and more rock fragments will be brought by the forward moving glacier to this point of melting leaving a sizeable mound of terminal moraine *across* the valley.

Back to ...

The New Wider World
p319 Figure 19.11 which shows a terminal moraine in Greenland.

Key words to know

Ribbon lake

Ribbon lakes

Many glacial troughs in highland Britain contain long, narrow, **ribbon lakes** (Figure 1.5b). Ribbon lakes may be the result of erosion when a glacier over-deepens part of its valley, perhaps in an area of softer rock or due to increased erosion after being joined by a tributary glacier which adds more ice. They may also be formed by water being dammed up behind deposits of terminal moraine across the main valley. In some situations both the erosion and deposition mentioned above combine to create a ribbon lake.

Check this!...

1 Explain how corries are formed.

2 Look at Figure 19.14 on p320 of *The New Wider World*. Below are two columns, the first contains a series of grid references from the OS map, the second is a jumbled series of landforms found in glaciated uplands. Match the correct landform to each grid reference.

Grid reference	Landform
601558	Valley floor of a glacial trough
605538	Corrie lake, tarn
601540	Valley floor of a hanging valley
633513	Arête
642541	Back wall of a corrie

3 Look at Figure 19.8 on p318 of *The New Wider World*. Describe the upland glaciated landscape shown by the photograph.

4 You need to know one named example for all the glacial landforms above. You could learn the name of examples near to where you live, or those you have studied on a field trip, or the names of the landforms taken from the OS extract on p320 and field sketch on p323 of *The New Wider World*.

EXAM PRACTICE

a Study Figure 1.6.

  i Match the letters on the diagram with each of the following landforms:

Landform	Letter
Arête	
Tarn	
Corrie	
Ribbon lake	

(4)

  ii Copy the shape of the cross-section shown in Figure 1.6. On this cross-section draw a dashed line to show the likely cross-section of the main river valley before glaciation. (2)

  iii Compare the north and south side of the cross-section.
   1 Give **one** difference of shape.
   2 Suggest **one** reason for this difference. (3)

b i Name the **two** main processes of erosion that have changed the shape of the main glacial valley in Figure 1.6. (2)

  ii Explain how each of these processes works. (4)

  iii Explain why valley H was left hanging above the main glacial valley. (4)

c Figure 1.6 shows a ribbon lake. Using diagrams, explain how a ribbon lake is formed. Name an example of a ribbon lake. (6)

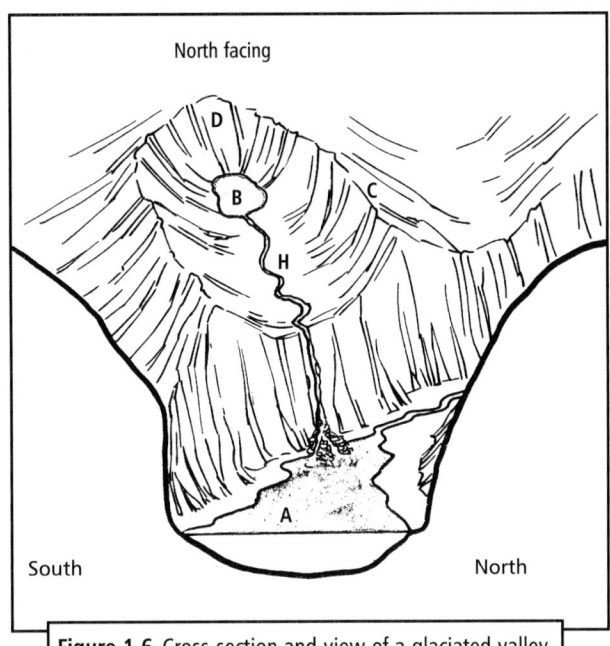

Figure 1.6 Cross-section and view of a glaciated valley

EXAM TIPS

It is often easier to explain the formation of a landform by using a diagram or diagrams that show changes through time, e.g. the formation of a corrie, p4. When you draw the diagram, keep it simple. The examiner is not looking for artistic skills. Use one-word labels to identify a feature and annotations (short notes) to explain the formation of a feature. Do not repeat the annotations in the written part of the answer. This will waste time. The examiner only marks the explanations once.

Back to …

The New Wider World website to check your answers to the Exam Practice question.

Ice 7

2 River features and flooding

The New Wider World, pp282–287; 291–292; 305; 307

Students can choose to study either rivers or coasts. (Chapter 3)

KEY QUESTIONS

1. How does a river erode, transport and deposit material?
2. What landforms give a river valley its distinctive character and how do process, structure and time shape these landforms?
3. How do physical and human factors contribute to river flooding and how can the effects be reduced?

1 How does a river erode, transport and deposit material?

River processes

If a river has plenty of energy (e.g. when it is falling down a steep slope, when it contains more water after heavy rainfall or after a tributary has joined) it will erode its channel, and it can carry (transport) material, but if it has little energy it cannot carry much and so will deposit its load (the material that is transported).

River erosion

A river **erodes** by four processes.
- **Solution**   Acids in the river dissolve rocks, such as limestone, which form the banks and bed.
- **Hydraulic action**   The sheer force of the river dislodges particles from the river's banks and bed.
- **Corrasion (Abrasion)**   Material transported by the river rubs against the banks which are worn away by a sand-papering action.
- **Attrition**   Boulders and other material, which are being transported along the bed of the river, collide and break up into smaller pieces.

Back to ...

The New Wider World **p282** Figure 17.12 for a diagram to show the methods of transportation.

River transportation

A river **transports** its load in four ways.
- **Solution**   Minerals dissolve in the river water. This needs the least amount of energy.
- **Suspension**   Fine particles are carried along in the flow of the river.
- **Saltation**   Particles rolling along the river bed meet an obstruction such as a larger stone. This causes them to bounce into the flowing river and only gradually sink. This is like a series of 'leap-frog' movements.
- **Rolling (Traction)**   The larger material, stones and boulders, carried by a river is rolled along the bed of the river channel. This needs the most energy.

The size and amount of material carried by each of these methods depends on the amount of energy in the river. In times of flood when there is much energy even large tree trunks can be moved by saltation. When there is less energy only very fine material is carried down the river, usually in suspension.

Key words to know

Erosion
Solution
Hydraulic action
Corrasion (Abrasion)
Attrition

Transport
Suspension
Saltation
Rolling (Traction)
Deposition

River deposition

Sediments are deposited when a river does not have enough energy to carry its load. **Deposition**, beginning with the heaviest material first, can occur:

- following a dry spell when the amount of water in the river drops
- where the current slows down, e.g. the inside of a meander bend
- where the river slows down as it enters the sea in an estuary or flows into a lake
- where the slope of the river bed (gradient) becomes more gentle.

Back to ...
The New Wider World **p283** Figure 17.13 for a photograph showing a V-shaped valley and interlocking spurs in the Peak District.

2 What landforms give a river valley its distinctive character and how do process, structure and time shape these landforms?

V-shaped valleys and interlocking spurs

A river flowing down steep slopes cuts downwards. This 'vertical erosion' leads to the development of steep-sided, narrow valleys shaped like the letter V. The valley sides are steep due to soil and loose rock being washed down the slopes following heavy rainfall. The river itself is forced to wind its way around protruding hillsides. These hillsides, known as **interlocking spurs**, overlap as you look up or down the valley.

Waterfalls and gorges

Waterfalls form when there is a sudden drop in the bed of a river. They may result from:
- erosion by ice, e.g. hanging valleys (see Figure 1.5 on p5)
- *structure*, e.g. a fault line (a line where the land on one side has been moved relative to the other side) may produce a steep slope resulting from earth movements
- *structure*, e.g. alternating hard and soft rocks in the river channel.

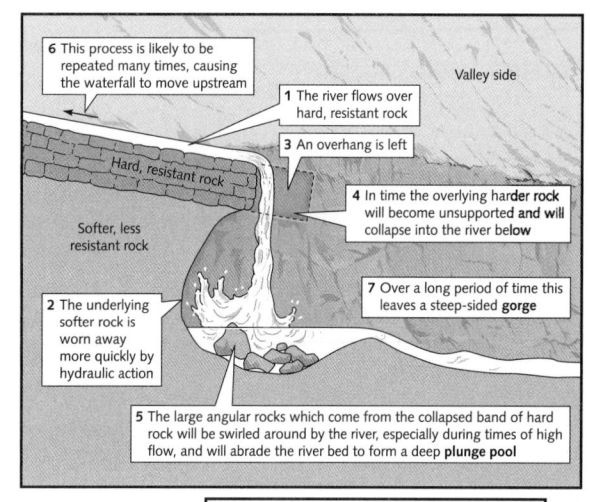

Figure 2.1 Formation of a waterfall and a gorge

Labels on figure:
1 The river flows over hard, resistant rock
2 The underlying softer rock is worn away more quickly by hydraulic action
3 An overhang is left
4 In time the overlying harder rock will become unsupported and will collapse into the river below
5 The large angular rocks which come from the collapsed band of hard rock will be swirled around by the river, especially during times of high flow, and will abrade the river bed to form a deep **plunge pool**
6 This process is likely to be repeated many times, causing the waterfall to move upstream
7 Over a long period of time this leaves a steep-sided **gorge**

Valley side; Hard, resistant rock; Softer, less resistant rock

Check this!...

1 Explain the erosion processes of:
   a) solution
   b) hydraulic action
   c) corrasion
   d) attrition.

2 Look at Figure 17.13 on p283 of *The New Wider World*. Describe the photograph of a typical V-shaped river valley and interlocking spurs.

3 Draw three labelled diagrams to show the changing shape through time of a river valley containing a waterfall. Use the following headings for your diagrams:
   Valley before waterfall formed.
   Formation of waterfall.
   Valley gorge after waterfall has moved upstream.

4 Look at Figure 17.38 on p292 of *The New Wider World*. Which of these four landforms: V-shaped valley; interlocking spurs; waterfall; gorge are found at the following grid references?
   a) 883314   c) 866283
   b) 897315   d) 903280

Key words to know

V-shaped valley
Interlocking spurs
Waterfall
Plunge pool
Gorge

Meanders and ox-bow lakes

Figure 2.2 Development of meanders and ox-bow lakes

(a) View from above

Key:
- Outer bend erosion
- Inner bend deposition
- Fastest current

Labels: Inside of bend with slip-off slope; Meander loop bends increasingly; Ox-bow lake; Meander core; Meander neck; Fastest current on outside of bend; Neck gets narrower; River cuts through the neck of land during a time of flood

(b) Cross-section

Key:
- Erosion
- Deposition
- Fastest current

Labels: Deposition Slip-off slope; Erosion River cliff; Deposition Slip-off slope; Direction of meander movement

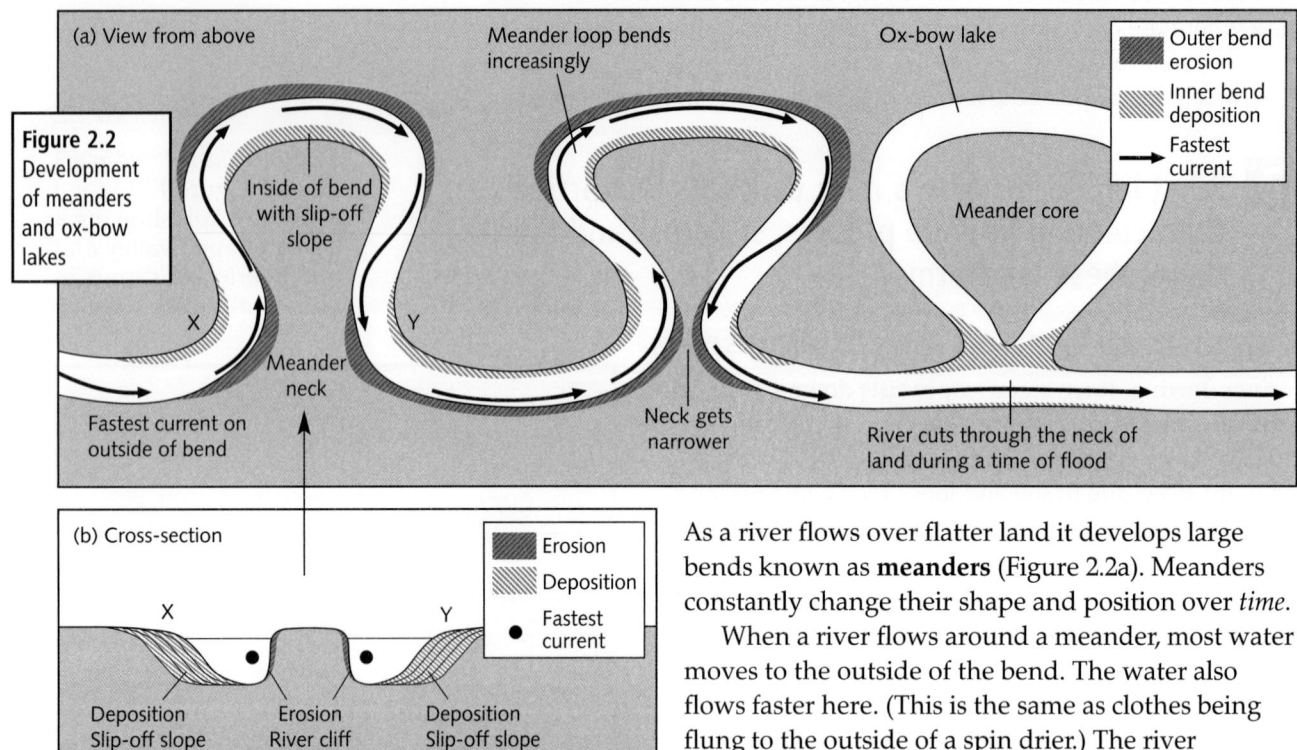

Key words to know

Meander
River cliff
Slip-off slope
Meander neck
Ox-bow lake
Floodplain

As a river flows over flatter land it develops large bends known as **meanders** (Figure 2.2a). Meanders constantly change their shape and position over *time*.

When a river flows around a meander, most water moves to the outside of the bend. The water also flows faster here. (This is the same as clothes being flung to the outside of a spin drier.) The river therefore has more energy on the outside of the bend, and so erodes the outside bank and bed and transports the material away. The bank is undercut, collapses and moves backwards to leave a small **river cliff** (Figure 2.2b).

Meanwhile on the inside of the bend there is less water. This water is flowing slower and has less energy so the river deposits some of its load here. The deposited material builds up to form a gently sloping **slip-off slope** (Figure 2.2b).

Continual erosion on the outside bends results in the **meander neck** (Figure 2.2a) getting narrower until, usually at a time of flood, the river cuts through the neck and shortens its course flowing straight down the valley. The fastest current is now flowing in the centre of the channel and deposition occurs on both banks of the river. The deposits block off the original meander leaving a crescent-shaped **ox-bow lake** (Figure 2.2a). This lake will slowly dry up, except during periods of heavy rain.

The river in a meander erodes sideways (lateral erosion) rather than downwards (vertical erosion) as in V-shaped valleys.

Floodplains

Floodplains are flat areas of land across a valley floor and may be tens of metres to tens of kilometres wide.

The river, as it meanders, erodes one bank and leaves deposits on the opposite bank. This results in the river moving sideways across the valley floor. The path that a river has taken in the past can often be seen by old meanders and ox-bow lakes showing up as water filled depressions after flooding. The valley floor is widened by this sideways movement. The valley sides at the edge of the floodplain are often marked by steeper **bluffs** which are the original slopes of the valley being undercut by an old meander.

At times of high flow, the river transports large amounts of material in suspension. If the river overflows its banks water will spread out across any surrounding flat land. The water is now much shallower and flows less quickly resulting in deposition on the valley floor. Each time the river floods a layer of silt is added leading to the development of a floodplain. Coarse material is deposited first forming a natural embankment, called a **levée**, next to the river.

> **Key words to know**
> *Bluff*
> *Levée*
> *Estuary*

Check this!...

1. Look at Figure 17.39 on p292 of *The New Wider World*.
   a) Describe the valley and river features between the two roads: grid references 024064 and 015024.
   b) Arun District Council is about to develop a new picnic site by the side of the R Arun. The Council is thinking of three sites: grid references 006050, 036085, 024068. Decide which site you consider to be the best for a new picnic site. Give reasons for your choice.

2. Draw a labelled diagram to show the formation of a floodplain.

3. You need to know the name of a location for the five sets of river landforms: V-shaped valley and interlocking spurs; waterfall and gorge; floodplain; meanders and ox-bow lake; estuary. You could learn the name of examples near to where you live, or those you have studied on a field trip, or the names of the landforms taken from the two OS extracts on p292 of *The New Wider World*.

Estuaries

Estuaries are found where a river meets the sea. An estuary is the tidal part of a river. When the tide is in at high water, the river mouth becomes very wide. When the tide goes out at low water large areas of mudflats are found either side of the meandering river. There may be a spit (sand bar) with sand-dunes stretching from one coastline, with salt marshes behind it.

There is much deposition of muddy material in estuaries because a chemical reaction between river water and seawater causes the mud particles to stick together, become bigger and sink.

> **Back to ...**
> *The New Wider World* **p305** Figure 18.19 for an OS extract showing part of the south coast of England and **p307** Figure 18.20 for a diagram showing the New Forest coastline.

Check this!...

1. Describe the features of the estuary shown at grid reference 309918 in Figure 18.19 on p305 of *The New Wider World*.

2. Compare the estuaries of the Lymington River and the Beaulieu River shown in Figure 18.20 on p307 of *The New Wider World*.

3 How do physical and human factors contribute to river flooding and how can the effects be reduced?

What are the physical causes of river flooding?
- Very heavy rainfall and long periods of rain resulting in saturated soil. Further rainfall then flows over land and into rivers rather than soaking into the ground.
- Water flowing over the surface rather than soaking in due to:
  - impermeable rocks
  - steep valley sides
  - removal of vegetation.
- Tributaries joining and increasing the flow of the river.
- Levées on wide floodplains, since once the river has spread over the floodplain it is trapped.

What are the human causes of river flooding?
- Bridges trap trees and other material temporarily causing surges of fast moving water.
- Draining agricultural land.
- Building on the floodplain. Tarmac stops water soaking in. Drains collect water and move it quickly to the river.
- Diverting the river from its natural course.

What are the effects of river flooding?
- Loss of life, especially in LEDCs since many people live on floodplains where fresh silt brought by floods creates fertile soils.
- Destruction of homes and buildings.
- Stress of clearing out polluted water and drying out damp homes and belongings.
- Costs of lost businesses, homes and belongings.
- Loss of crops and animals may mean starvation to people in LEDCs.
- Disease from polluted water, e.g. cholera in Bangladesh.
- Disruption of transport links. This may mean that rescuing people affected by the flood is difficult.

How may the effects of river flooding be reduced?
Some people consider that flooding should be allowed as a natural event, i.e. allow the river to follow its natural course and do not build on the floodplain.

Others suggest structures should be built or measures taken to prevent the water overflowing the channel, such as:
- construct levées
- widen bridges
- straighten or deepen the channel
- build dams to control the flow of the river
- improve early warning systems.

How successful are schemes for reducing river flooding?

- Lynmouth has been largely rebuilt since the devastating floods of 1952 and has since managed to cope with three high rainfall periods.
- In the UK some local councils have stopped giving planning permission for floodplain development.
- LEDCs remain very vulnerable to flood disasters since they have little money to spend on schemes.
- The Three Gorges Dam in China is the biggest in the world and will probably stop flooding but some consider the change to people's livelihoods – whole cities being rebuilt 500 m higher on the valley slopes with loss of lifestyle, jobs, ancient cultural sites, wildlife – too great a price to pay for the reduction of flooding.

Back to ...

The New Wider World **pp286–287** and **293–295** for further information on named examples of river flooding in Lynmouth, Devon and China.

Case Study Extra

Shrewsbury floods 1998

Back to ...

The New Wider World p35 Figure 3.3 for a photograph showing the meander at Shrewsbury.

a) Physical causes

- The source of the River Severn is at Plynlimon in Powys in Wales. Here the river drops in height quickly through steep-sided valleys – this means rainwater doesn't soak into the ground but has rapid runoff over the surface into the river. Below Llanidloes the Severn flows through hills and receives water from many tributaries. Water from the large River Vyrnwy joins the Severn near the English border. The river then meanders over a wide, flat floodplain to Shrewsbury.
- The source area receives heavy rain. In October 1998 135 mm of rain fell, 20 per cent of the average yearly rainfall.
- In the autumn of 2000, the worst flooding in 50 years flooded the town three times in six weeks.

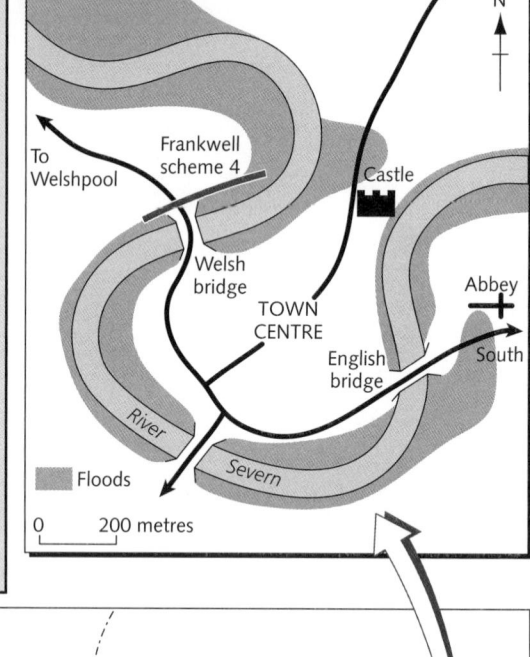

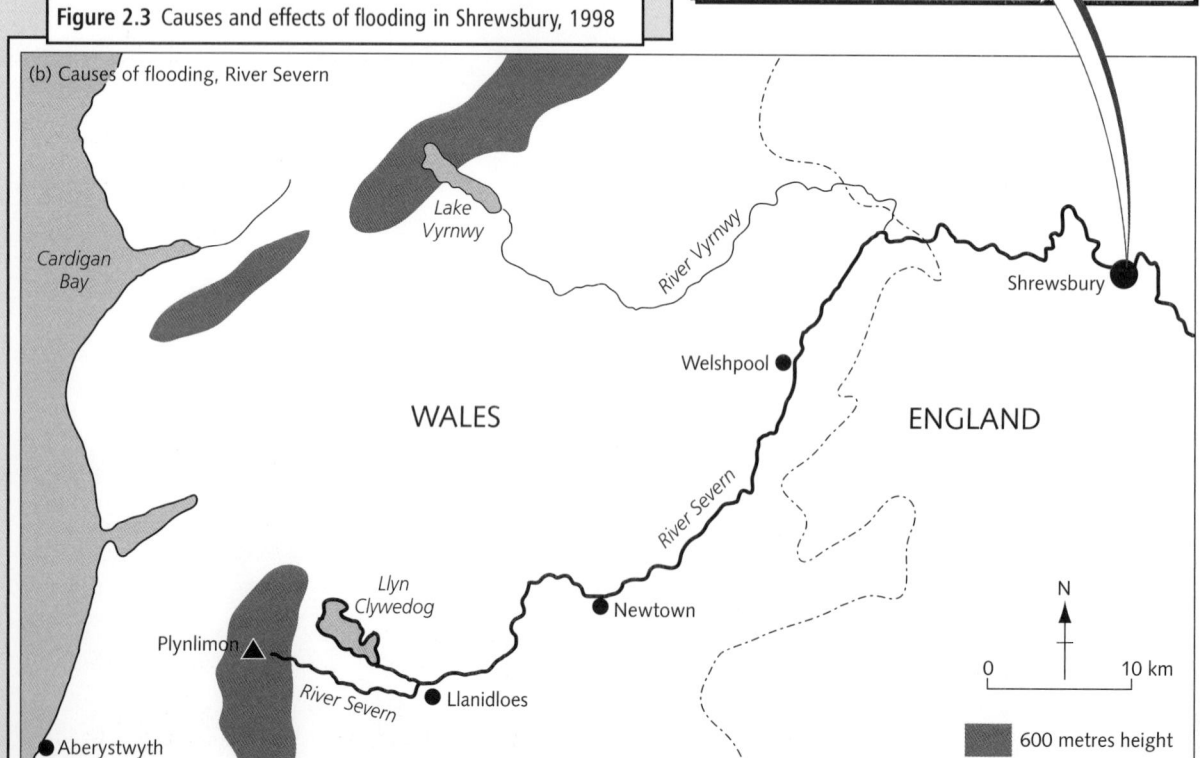

Figure 2.3 Causes and effects of flooding in Shrewsbury, 1998

b) Human causes
- Agricultural land on the floodplain above Shrewsbury has been drained and water is not allowed to flood naturally.
- The centre of the town is sited on a meander neck.
- Shrewsbury has become a large built-up area which has spread across the Severn floodplain.

c) Effects of flooding
- The extent of the 1998 flood is shown on Figure 2.3.
- The 1998 flood cost £4m. This included:
  - damage, to 400 buildings and belongings, claimed from insurance companies
  - farmers' loss of income since agricultural land took time to dry out
  - car parks and playing fields near the river could not be used so the council lost money
  - overtime payment to the emergency services, council workers and shop workers
  - loss of trade in the centre of Shrewsbury because the bridges were closed.
- Much stress was suffered by people having to clean out and dry off their flooded homes.
- There has been no reported loss of life because the floods are accurately predicted early by measurements of rainfall taken in the Welsh mountains and by automated water level measures.
- Health warnings about contamination by raw sewage in the flood water meant that people did not drink the water and thus did not become ill.

d) Schemes to reduce the effects of flooding in Shrewsbury

Scheme	Cost	Positive effects	Negative effects
1 Allow the river at the Welsh/English border to flood across the agricultural land	£18m	Would be effective in stopping flooding in Shrewsbury. Would create large areas of wetland which would attract birds.	Farmers do not want this plan.
2 Make the river deeper, 35 metres, as it flows through Shrewsbury	High, especially if the river had to be dredged regularly	There would be less flooding in Shrewsbury	Visually, the river would have wide muddy banks for most of the time when it wasn't in flood
3 Construct walls along the river in parts of Shrewsbury	£3.1m	Would be effective in the areas selected. Would not affect the water table.	Other areas would have an increase of 1 metre in times of flood. Some visual impact on the medieval townscape.
4 Provide defences of aluminium planks to be slotted into permanent posts only when the river floods. The Frankwell scheme is situated on the meander in the centre of Shrewsbury.	£3.8m	Not permanently spoiling the view of the river frontage which is of attractive medieval buildings	Only 74 properties will benefit from the defences

Figure 2.4 Flood reduction schemes in Shrewsbury

e) How successful are the schemes for control of river flooding in Shrewsbury?

The first three schemes were rejected by the people of Shrewsbury. People did not like them or were concerned about the cost. Grants were given for scheme 4 in 2001 and construction started in 2002. The temporary planks were put in place in Shrewsbury and downstream at Bewley, for the floods in February 2004. They were successful in diverting the flood water away from the urban areas.

Using your case study
Use the information in this case study as a named example to answer questions on:
- physical and human causes of river flooding
- effects of river flooding

- schemes for reducing river flooding
- evaluation of the success of the schemes.

Case study links

This case study has links with:
- Chapter 4 – the causes of floods are linked to depressions (and heavy rainfall)
- Chapter 11 – building on floodplains linked to urban development.

Update

For more information on flooding in Shrewsbury use the link on *The New Wider World Coursemate* website.

Learn it!

a) Explain the physical and human causes of river flooding in Shrewsbury.

b) Describe the effects of river flooding in Shrewsbury.

c) Describe the attempts or schemes to reduce river flooding and evaluate how successful they are.

Use examples and maps to illustrate your answer. You could annotate Figure 2.3 as a basis for your answer.

EXAM PRACTICE

Figure 2.5 Field sketch of an estuary

- Salt marsh
- Sand-dune
- Sand
- Mud

a i Look at Figure 2.5. Name the features A, E and F. (3)

ii Give **one** difference in the view of this estuary at high tide. (1)

iii Explain why there is much deposition in estuaries. (2)

b i Draw a labelled diagram to describe how material is transported by saltation in a river. (4)

ii Using diagrams, explain how ox-bow lakes form. (6)

c i Describe the physical and human causes of river flooding. Use an example or examples of real floods to illustrate your answer. (6)

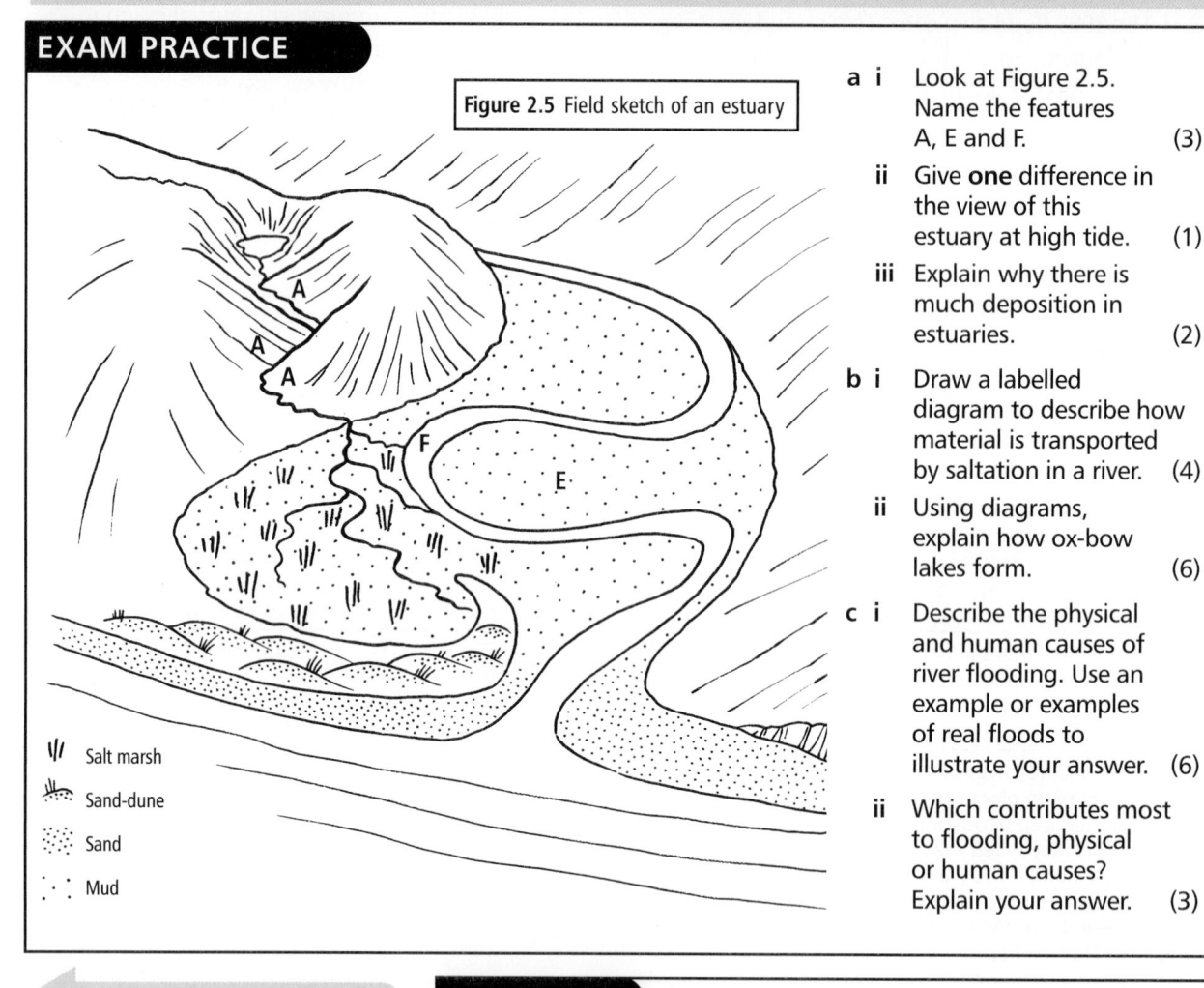

ii Which contributes most to flooding, physical or human causes? Explain your answer. (3)

Back to ...

The New Wider World website to check your answers to the Exam Practice question.

EXAM TIPS

A sketch map will help if you are answering a question that involves a place or real example. Make sure the map you draw is adapted to the question, e.g. do not draw a map which shows the location of structures to prevent flooding if the question asks about the causes of flooding. A map is not a drawing. It should show a plan view from above. If you are allowed an atlas in the exam room, use it for the outline shape of your map. Features that do not show up on a map are best described by writing, e.g. costs and stress of flooding. Always include a title, north arrow and, if possible, a scale.

⇨ *The New Wider World*, pp300–303; 305–311

Students can choose to study either rivers or coasts. (Chapter 2)

3 Coastal features and flooding

1 How does the sea erode, transport and deposit material?

The coast constantly changes due to the effects of land, air and sea processes. On many coastlines the dominant process results from the action of **waves**.

Waves

The largest waves are formed when winds are very strong, blow for a long time and cross wide areas of ocean. The maximum distance of water over which winds can blow is called the **fetch**.

KEY QUESTIONS

1. How does the sea erode, transport and deposit material?
2. What landforms give a coastline its distinctive character and how do process, structure and time shape these landforms?
3. How do physical and human factors contribute to coastal flooding and how can the effects be reduced?

Figure 3.1 Waves: Movement and types

(a) Wave movement
 1 Open sea
 2 Touching beach
 3 Breaking
 4 Movement on the beach

(a)
 1 Circular motion of water
 2 Circular motion interrupted when wave hits the beach
 3 Waves break since no water below crest of wave
 4 Swash
 4 Backwash

(a) Destructive waves
 • higher
 • further apart
 • found on steep beach

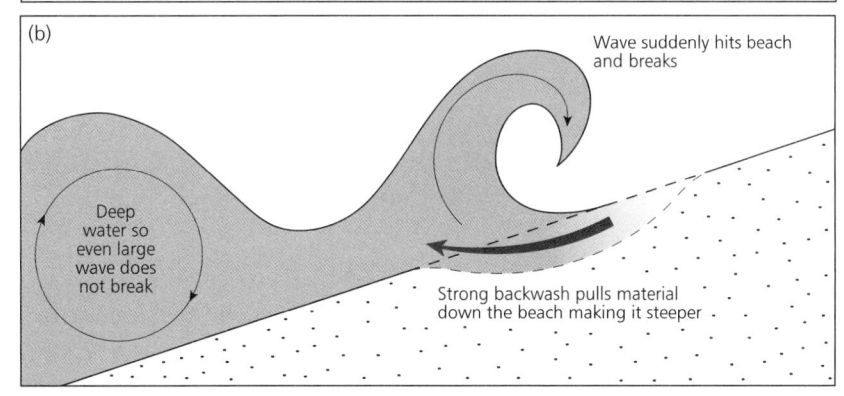

(b)
 Deep water so even large wave does not break
 Wave suddenly hits beach and breaks
 Strong backwash pulls material down the beach making it steeper

(c) Constructive waves
 • lower
 • more frequent
 • found on gentle beach

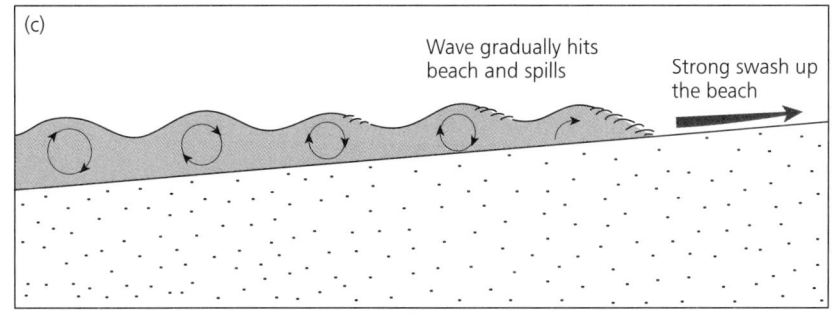

(c)
 Wave gradually hits beach and spills
 Strong swash up the beach

Coastal features and flooding   **17**

Key words to know

Wave: *Fetch*
Destructive wave
Constructive wave
Erosion: *Solution*
Hydraulic pressure
Corrasion (Abrasion)
Attrition

Coastal erosion

There are four processes of coastal **erosion.**
- **Solution**   Seawater chemically attacks the rocks of the beach and cliff.
- **Hydraulic pressure**   Inward moving waves compress air in cracks in a cliff.
- **Corrasion (Abrasion)**   Destructive waves hurl beach material against a cliff.
- **Attrition**   Swash and backwash cause rocks and boulders on the beach to bump into each other and to break up into small particles.

Coastal transportation

Although waves carry material up and down a beach, the major movement of beach material is along the coast by a process called **longshore drift** (Figure 3.3). Material is slowly moved along the coast in a zig-zag course. The effect of longshore drift can best be seen when **groynes**, which are a series of walls built down the beach to low tide level, prevent material from being moved along the beach.

Back to ...

The New Wider World
p302 Figure 18.9 for a photograph of groynes at Worthing, West Sussex.

Coastal deposition

The sea deposits its load where it doesn't have much energy. Deposition associated with constructive waves occurs where the coastline:
- is sheltered from strong prevailing winds
- has only a gentle breeze blowing
- has a shallow, gently sloping sea bed.

The material is deposited to form a **beach**. Beaches are not permanent features as their shape can be altered by waves every time the tide comes in and goes out. Shingle beaches have a steeper gradient than sandy beaches.

Key words to know

Longshore drift
Groynes
Beach
Headland
Bay
Cliff

2 What landforms give a coastline its distinctive character and how do process, structure and time shape these landforms?

Headlands and bays

Headlands and **bays** form along coastlines where the rock *structure* consists of alternating outcrops of resistant (harder) and less resistant (softer) rock. Waves are able to erode the areas of softer rock more rapidly to form bays. The resistant rock is left protruding out into the sea as headlands.

The headlands are now exposed to the full force of destructive waves, and become the target for erosion. **Cliffs** form around the resistant, higher ground of a headland. Over time headlands protect the adjacent bays where constructive waves build up the beach.

Back to ...

The New Wider World
p305 Figure 18.17, OS map of Swanage. The OS map shows the headlands of The Foreland, made of chalk and the headland of Peveril Point, made of limestone, protecting Swanage Bay, cut into softer clay.

Cliffs and wave-cut platforms, caves, arches and stacks

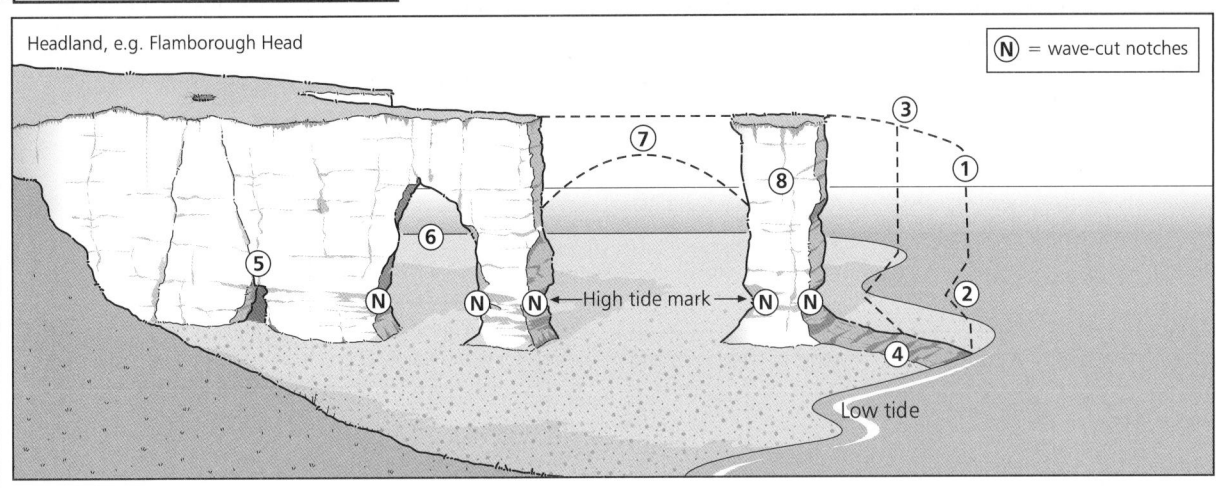

Figure 3.2 Development of landforms on a sea cliff over a long period of time

Headland, e.g. Flamborough Head

(N) = wave-cut notches

High tide mark
Low tide

① Wave erosion is greatest when large waves break against the foot of the cliff
② By hydraulic action the waves undercut the foot of the cliff to form a **wave-cut notch**
③ Over a period of time the notch enlarges until the cliff above it is left unsupported and collapses. As this process is repeated, the position of the cliff retreats (moves backwards) and may increase in height.
④ The gently sloping expanse of rock marking the foot of the retreating cliff is called a **wave-cut platform**. Wave-cut platforms are exposed at low tide but covered at high tide.
⑤ Cliffs are more likely to form where the coastline is made of hard rock. However, within these resistant rocks there are usually structural lines of weakness, such as a joint or a fault.
⑥ Solution, corrasion and hydraulic action by the waves will widen any weakness to form a **cave** at sea-level. Two caves might form along the weakness at either side of the headland. These caves will be widened and deepened until they join. The sea has cut through the headland to form an **arch**.
⑦ Waves will continue to erode the foot of the arch until its roof becomes too heavy to be supported.
⑧ When the roof collapses it will leave part of the former cliff isolated as a **stack**.

Check this!...

1 What is the difference between destructive and constructive waves?

2 Look at Figure 18.7 on p302 of *The New Wider World*. Describe the erosional landforms of the headland shown in the photograph.

3 Draw three labelled diagrams to show the changing shape through time of a cliffed coastline. Use the following headings for your diagrams:

Original position and shape of the cliff showing a cave developing.
Formation of an arch on the cliff.
Formation of a stack and the new position of the coastline.

4 Look at Figure 18.17 on p305 of *The New Wider World*. Swanage District Council is about to develop a new picnic site on the long distance coastal footpath. The Council is thinking of three sites at the following grid references:
036847
054825
024769

Decide, with reasons, which site you consider to be the best for a new picnic site.

Spits

A **spit** is described as a permanent landform resulting from marine deposition. It is long and narrow and made up of sand or shingle. One end is attached to the land, and the other juts out at an angle either into the sea or across a river estuary. Many spits have a hooked or curved end.

Spits form where:
- longshore drift moves large amounts of sand and shingle along the coast
- the coastline suddenly changes direction to leave a shallow, sheltered area of water.

Key words to know

Wave-cut notch
Wave-cut platform
Cave
Arch
Stack
Spit
Sand-dune
Salt marsh

Coastal features and flooding

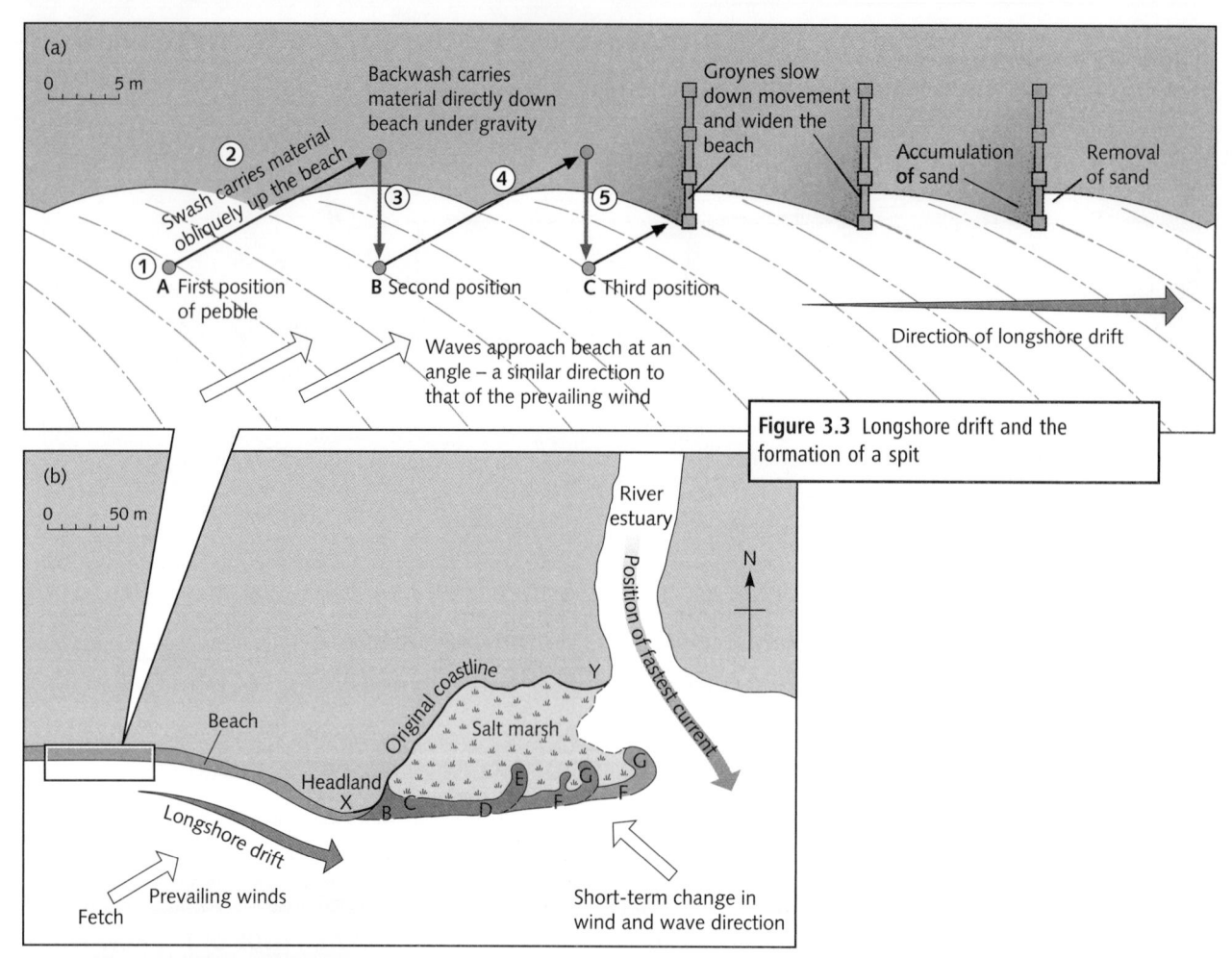

Figure 3.3 Longshore drift and the formation of a spit

Check this!...

1. Look at Figure 18.10 on p303 and Figure 18.19 on p305 of *The New Wider World*.
   a) Describe the spit shown by the photograph.
   b) Describe the spit shown by the OS map. Use the OS map to give the size and directions of the spit.

2. You need to know the name of a location for the seven sets of coastal landforms: headland and bay; cliffs; wave-cut platform; cave, arch and stack; beach; spit; estuary. You could learn the names of examples near to where you live, or those you have studied on a field trip, or the names of the landforms taken from the two OS extracts on p305 of *The New Wider World*.

In Figure 3.3 the fetch and prevailing winds are from the south-west so material is being moved eastwards along the coast by longshore drift.

In Figure 3.3b after headland X the direction of the original coastline changes to go north east towards Y.

- Larger material (shingle) is deposited in water sheltered by the headland (B).
- Longshore drift continues and further deposition of finer material (sand) allows the feature to build up slowly to sea-level (C) and to extend in length (D).
- Sometimes the wind changes direction. In this example it occasionally comes from the south-east. This causes the waves to alter their direction, to approach from the south-east. During this time some material at the end of the spit may be pushed inland to form a curved end (E).
- When the wind returns to blow from its usual direction the spit goes back to growing eastwards (F).
- The spit is unable to grow across the estuary as the river current carries material out to sea.

Spits become permanent when sand is blown up the beach, by the prevailing wind, to form **sand-dunes**. **Salt marsh** is likely to develop in the sheltered water behind the spit.

Estuaries

Estuaries are found where a river meets the sea. An estuary is the tidal part of a river. When the tide is in at high water, the river mouth becomes very wide. When the tide goes out at low water large areas of mudflats are found either side of the meandering river. There may be a spit with sand-dunes stretching from one coastline, with salt marshes behind it.

There is much deposition of muddy material in estuaries because a chemical reaction between river water and seawater causes the mud particles to stick together, become bigger and sink.

3 How do physical and human factors contribute to coastal flooding and how can the effects be reduced?

What are the physical causes of coastal flooding?

- Flat and low-lying coastal areas, e.g. river floodplain, estuary.
- Storm surges that may be several metres high. These result from depressions moving in from the Atlantic north-east towards the UK. The height of the sea slightly increases due to the low pressure. Waves created by the strong winds are also very high since they have had a long fetch.
- The predicted rise in sea-level through global warming, together with higher tides, more storm surges and increased coastal flooding.

What are the human causes of coastal flooding?

- The low-lying areas behind sand-dunes, sea-walls and dykes are more likely to flood if the coastal defences are not continually maintained.
- Draining fields for farming removes the water from the soil and thus reduces the volume of the soil so it shrinks. The height of the land may sink below sea-level (Fens).

What are the effects of coastal flooding?

- The land behind the coast becomes flooded with seawater. Debris and even boats may be carried far inland. Drains block and the water becomes polluted with sewage.
- Strong winds make rescue difficult. People may be trapped in upper storeys or even die as buildings collapse and are washed away.
- Sea defences or dunes trap the flood water which may need pumping away.
- Economically this has a major effect: homes cannot be lived in; buildings cannot be used; livelihoods are threatened – the seaside is often a tourist attraction with many constructions for entertainment on the sea shore, e.g. fun fairs, redeveloped dockland and marinas, e.g. Swansea. This adds to the number of people and amount of property at risk.
- The soil becomes contaminated with the salt from seawater which affects farming. Animals may be washed away.

How may the effects of coastal flooding be reduced?

- Building barriers across major estuaries.
- Building higher and stronger sea-walls and dykes.

> *Check this!...*
>
> 1 Look at Figure 18.19 on p305 of *The New Wider World*. Locate grid reference 309918. Describe the features of the estuary.
>
> 2 Look at Figure 18.20 on p307 of *The New Wider World*. Compare the estuaries of the Lymington River and the Beaulieu River.

Coastal features and flooding

Back to ...

The New Wider World **pp304** and **309** Figures 18.16 and 18.27 to see photographs of different types of coastal flood protection, and **pp310–313** for further information on named examples of coastal flooding in south-east England, the Netherlands and Bangladesh.

- Maintaining the shoreline by building stone groynes to prevent the removal of beach material.
- Improving weather forecasting and implementing early flood warning systems.

How successful are schemes for reducing coastal flooding?

- The Thames Barrier has proved very successful. The barrier is closed when early warning systems forecast an exceptionally high tide. Despite a rise in sea-level London has not been flooded since the completion of this construction in 1984.
- Concrete sea-walls, apart from being eyesores and destroying bird habitats, absorb, rather than deflect, wave energy and without constant maintenance and expense, they can be breached.
- Some people feel that nature should be allowed to take its course and those areas prone to flooding by the sea should be allowed to flood. Naturally, people who live and work in these areas disagree and want increased protection.

Case Study Extra

Towyn floods 1990

Figure 3.4 The Towyn floods 1990

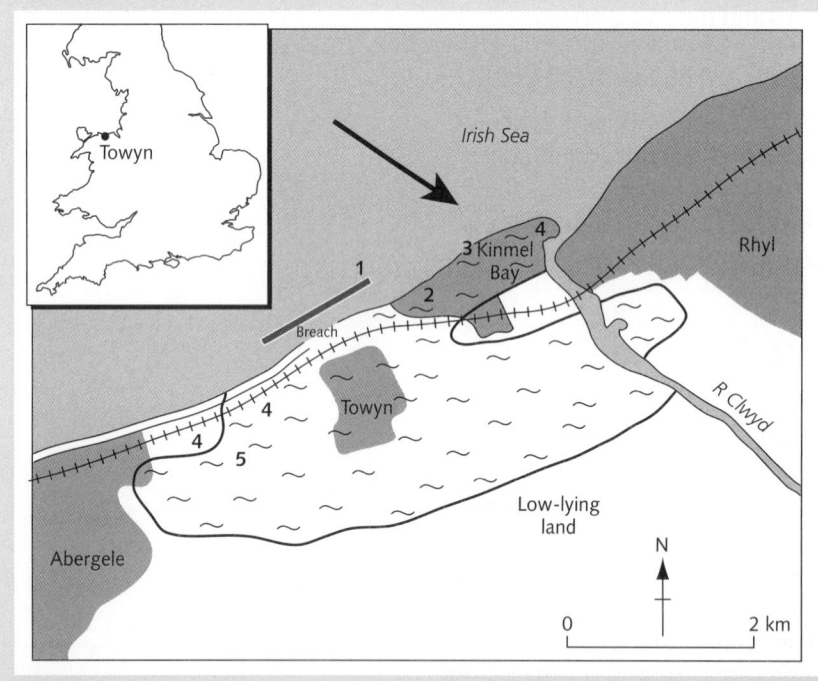

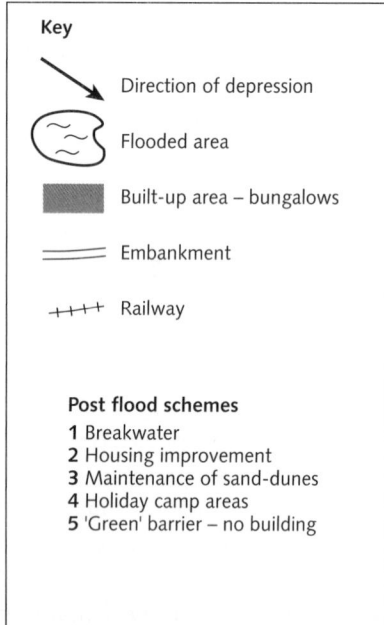

Key
- Direction of depression
- Flooded area
- Built-up area – bungalows
- Embankment
- Railway

Post flood schemes
1 Breakwater
2 Housing improvement
3 Maintenance of sand-dunes
4 Holiday camp areas
5 'Green' barrier – no building

The Towyn floods were caused by a number of physical and human factors.

a) Physical causes

- Towyn lies below the height of spring tides.
- On 26 February 1990, a deep depression, 951mb with winds gusting to 83 knots, moved from the north-west across the British Isles. This continued through the following morning giving very high wave heights.
- The highest tides of the year, 6.3 metres, occurred during the same period.

b) Human causes

- Marshland was reclaimed from the sea and an embankment built in 1800 by Rhuddlan Marsh Commissioners.
- The railway was built behind the embankment. The Railway Company took control of the embankment in 1880.

- The 1920s saw the development of bungalows for retired people on the flat land behind the embankment.

c) Effects of flooding

- 467 metres of the embankment were breached by the storm surge for three hours, flooding the area between the bank and the railway line.
- 10 km² in Towyn and Kinmel Bay were flooded to a depth of 1.8 metres, 2800 properties were flooded – 12 per cent of houses in Colwyn Bay area. Since the majority of housing was bungalows the damage was very great.
- Of the 5000 evacuated 31 per cent were elderly, 40 per cent had no insurance on their home contents and 6 per cent had no insurance on their home.
- Electricity supplies failed, stopping the sewerage pumps. This resulted in major contamination of flood water and a delay in pumping the water away. Silt left by the floods was contaminated by radioactivity 10 times higher than government safety limits. It is thought that this was due to the nuclear reprocessing plant at Sellafield, Cumbria on the edge of the Irish Sea.

d) Schemes to reduce coastal flooding in Towyn

- British Rail accepted full responsibility for the cost of replacing the embankment. Large 'armour' rocks were placed in layers across the breach, and gaps were filled with concrete. This was built up to the same height as the existing embankment.
- A rock breakwater was later built to protect the wall. This is a large ridge of rocks dumped off-shore to the height of high tide causing waves to break off-shore, away from the embankment.
- Colwyn Borough Council developed a planning policy for any new development in the area (Figure 3.4):
  - They developed a contour map showing pockets of low-lying land where development would be undesirable.
  - They created green barriers – areas where no building is allowed.
  - They released land for housing development in higher areas of the Borough but this is south of the A55, east of Abergele, and a special landscape area.
  - They grant planning permission only for houses or dormer bungalows with stairs.

e) How successful are the schemes for reducing coastal flooding?

- The flooding meant that many authorities in the area now work together to reduce the likelihood of flooding.
- The area has not suffered flooding since 1990 but many people are concerned that the embankment has not been raised much above its pre-flood level. They consider that possible effects of global warming raising sea-levels have not been addressed.

Using your case study

Use the information in this case study as a named example to answer questions on:
- physical and human causes of coastal flooding
- effects of coastal flooding
- schemes for reducing coastal flooding
- evaluation of the success of the schemes.

Case study links

This case study links with:
- Chapter 4 – the causes of floods are linked to depressions and storm surges
- Chapter 9 – building on coastal plains is linked to industrial development.

Update

For more information on the Towyn floods use the link on *The New Wider World Coursemate* website.

Learn it!

a) Explain the physical and human causes of coastal flooding in Towyn.

b) Describe the effects of coastal flooding in Towyn.

c) Describe the attempts or schemes to reduce coastal flooding and evaluate how successful they are.

Use examples and maps to illustrate your answer. You could annotate Figure 3.4 as a basis for your answer.

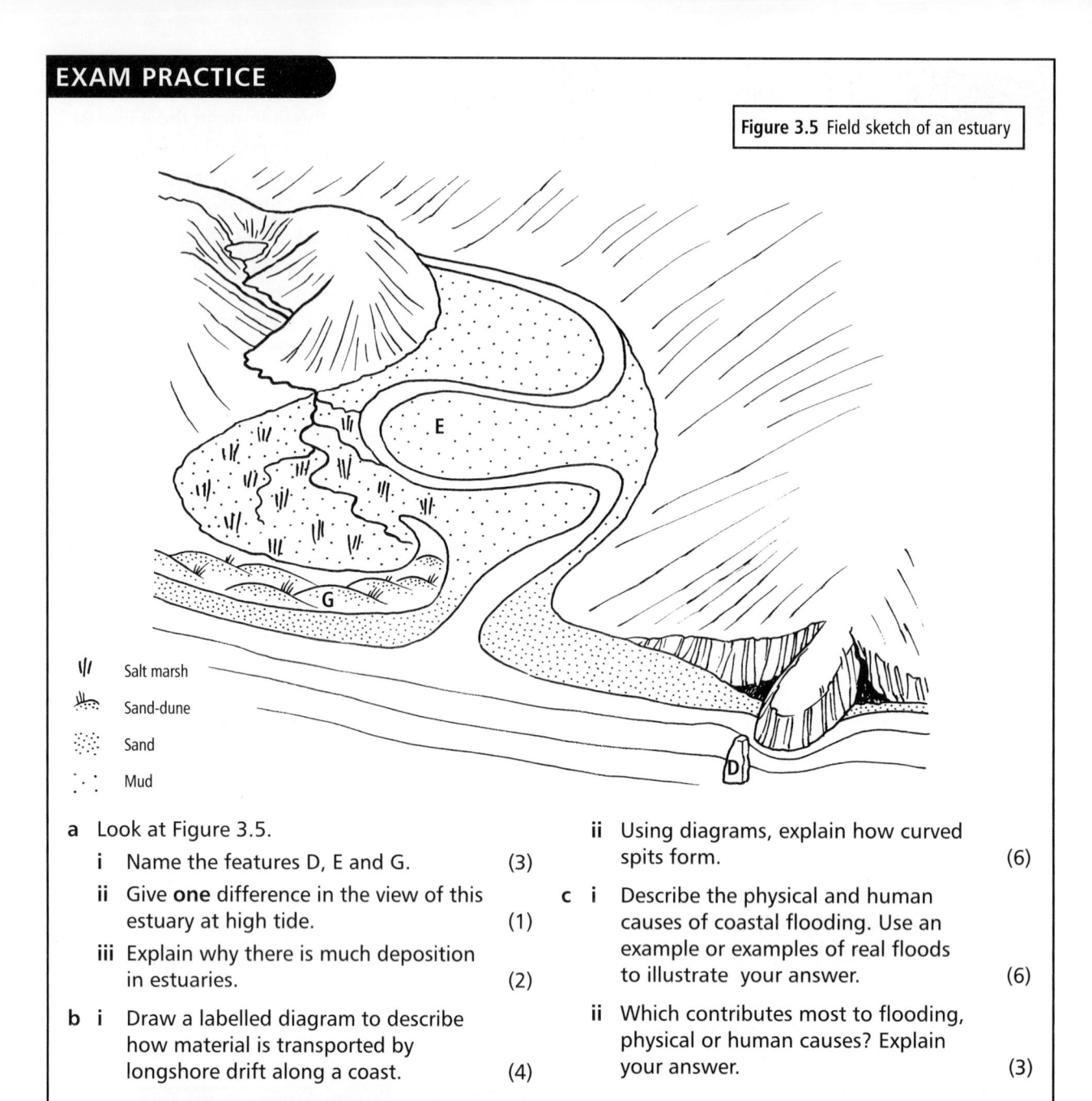

EXAM PRACTICE

Figure 3.5 Field sketch of an estuary

Key:
- Salt marsh
- Sand-dune
- Sand
- Mud

a Look at Figure 3.5.
  i Name the features D, E and G. (3)
  ii Give **one** difference in the view of this estuary at high tide. (1)
  iii Explain why there is much deposition in estuaries. (2)

b i Draw a labelled diagram to describe how material is transported by longshore drift along a coast. (4)

  ii Using diagrams, explain how curved spits form. (6)

c i Describe the physical and human causes of coastal flooding. Use an example or examples of real floods to illustrate your answer. (6)

  ii Which contributes most to flooding, physical or human causes? Explain your answer. (3)

Back to ...

The New Wider World website to check your answers to the Exam Practice question.

EXAM TIPS

A sketch map will help if you are answering a question that involves a place or a real example. Make sure the map you draw is adapted to the question, e.g. do not draw a map which shows the location of structures to prevent flooding if the question asks about the causes of flooding. A map is not a drawing. It should show a plan view from above. If you are allowed an atlas in the exam room, use it for the outline shape of your map. Features that do not show up on a map are best described by writing, e.g. costs and stress of flooding. Always include a title, north arrow and, if possible, a scale.

Weather and climate

1 What makes up the weather?

Weather is the hour-to-hour, day-to-day state of the atmosphere. It is short term and can vary over relatively small areas. Elements of the weather include:

- **air pressure** (the pressure exerted by the weight of the atmosphere). When air is cooled its molecules become packed more tightly, this means colder air is heavier and sinks giving **high pressure**. When air is warmed the molecules move further apart, air rises and gives **low pressure**. **Isobars** are lines of equal pressure value on a weather map.
- **temperature** (the measurement of the heat of the atmosphere). Temperature of air is measured in the shade.
- **precipitation** (this includes rainfall and snowfall). Air contains water vapour picked up from the sea or other bodies of water. Cold air cannot hold as much moisture as warm air so as air cools, (by being forced upwards, or by contact with cold ground) it reaches the dew point where the vapour turns to moisture, i.e. it condenses. **Condensation** may be in the form of **dew**, **mist**, **fog** or **clouds**. Further condensation gives rain.
- **cloud cover** (the amount, in ⅛ths, that the sky is covered by cloud. It does not measure the type of clouds). Clouds have a blanket effect. They reduce the amount of heat coming from the sun during the day and keep in the heat at night.
- **wind direction** and **wind speed** (the movement of air from high pressure areas to low pressure areas). Winds are always described by the direction from which the wind is blowing. Winds are strong if the pressure gradient (difference in value between high and low pressure) is high.
- **sunshine** (the number of hours the sun shines in a day).

KEY QUESTIONS

1. What makes up the weather?
2. How do different air masses affect the British weather?
3. How and why is the weather over the British Isles different in anticyclones and depressions?
4. What are the factors affecting climate?

Key words to know

Air pressure
High pressure
Low pressure
Isobar
Temperature
Precipitation
Condensation
Dew
Mist
Fog

Figure 4.1 Weather map symbols

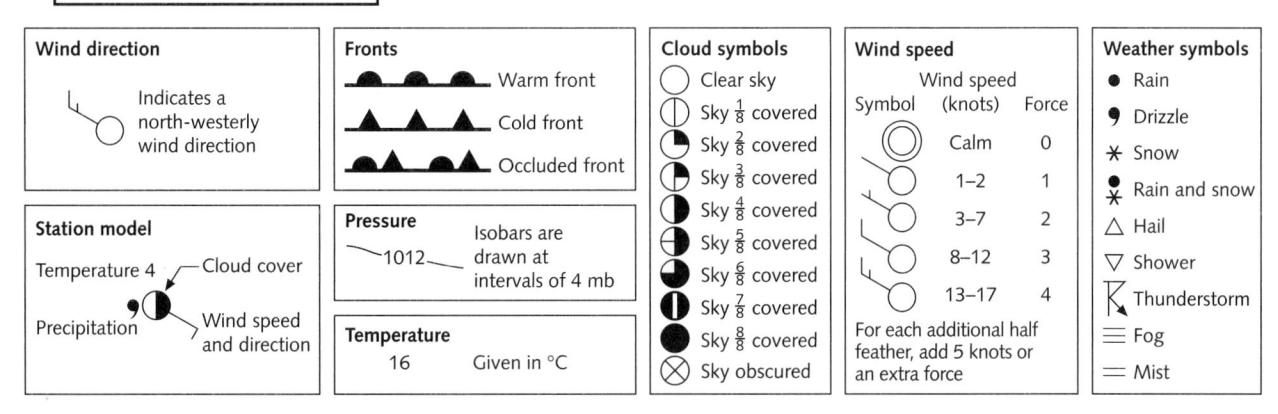

Wind direction
Indicates a north-westerly wind direction

Station model
Temperature 4 — Cloud cover
Precipitation — Wind speed and direction

Fronts
Warm front
Cold front
Occluded front

Pressure
1012 — Isobars are drawn at intervals of 4 mb

Temperature
16 — Given in °C

Cloud symbols
○ Clear sky
Sky ⅛ covered
Sky ⅖ covered
Sky ⅜ covered
Sky ⁴⁄₈ covered
Sky ⅝ covered
Sky ⁶⁄₈ covered
Sky ⅞ covered
Sky ⅞ covered
⊗ Sky obscured

Wind speed

Symbol	Wind speed (knots)	Force
	Calm	0
	1–2	1
	3–7	2
	8–12	3
	13–17	4

For each additional half feather, add 5 knots or an extra force

Weather symbols
● Rain
, Drizzle
✶ Snow
Rain and snow
△ Hail
▽ Shower
⚡ Thunderstorm
≡ Fog
= Mist

Key words to know

Cloud
Wind direction
Wind speed
Sunshine
Syoptic chart
Satellite image
Air mass
Polar maritime (Pm)
Tropical maritime (Tm)
Tropical continental (Tc)
Polar continental (Pc)

The state of the weather at any given time is shown on a weather map. **Synoptic charts** (weather maps) produced by the Meteorological Office use official symbols to show weather conditions at specific weather stations (Figure 4.1). Five weather elements are shown by symbols. But atmospheric pressure is obtained by interpreting the isobars.

Satellite images are photographs taken from space and are used for weather forecasting. Depressions can be seen on satellite images as masses of swirling cloud (see Figure 4.5a). An anticyclone is shown on Figure 4.3a.

2 How do different air masses affect the British weather?

An **air mass** forms when air remains stationary over an area, e.g. the Azores in the North Atlantic, for several days. During this time the air takes up the temperature and humidity (amount of moisture in the air) properties of that area. When air masses move towards Britain they bring the weather from their place of origin with them. Britain is affected by four main air masses at different times.

Polar maritime (Pm) air from the north-west. Cold and wet. Very common over Britain. Gives cool conditions with heavy showers or longer periods of rain.

Polar continental (Pc) air from the east and north-east. Cold and dry.
Very cold in winter when it is most likely to occur. Usually gives dry weather. Eastern Britain may get snow (moisture collected from passage over North Sea).

Tropical maritime (Tm) air from the south-west. Warm and wet.
Very common over Britain. Warm in summer and mild in winter.
Often long periods of steady rain or drizzle with hill fog/low clouds.

Tropical continental (Tc) air from the south and south-east. Hot and dry.
Only occurs in summer when it gives very hot (heat-wave) and dry (drought) conditions. Can last several days and often ends with thunderstorms associated with heat-waves.

Figure 4.2 Air masses affecting the British Isles

Check this!...

1 Study the weather symbols in Figure 4.1. Describe the weather in Figure 4.5b on p27:
   a) in the Atlantic
   b) in the south east of England.

2 Give the lowest pressure value on Figure 4.5b and the highest pressure value on Figure 4.3b.

3 Which Figure, 4.3b or 4.5b, has the highest wind speed? Is strong wind associated with close isobars (a steep pressure gradient) or widely spaced isobars (a gentle pressure gradient)?

3 How and why is the weather over the British Isles different in anticyclones and depressions?

Key word to know
Anticyclone

Anticyclones (high pressure systems)

Description of weather conditions
- Clear skies and no rain.
- Winds are light. At times they may even be non-existent and give periods of calm.
- Winds blow in a *clockwise* direction.
- Settled conditions.

There are differences between summer and winter **anticyclones**.
Summer The absence of cloud gives very warm, sunny conditions during the day. At night, when clear skies allow some of this heat to escape, temperatures can fall rapidly and dew and mist may form.
Winter Although temperatures remain low during the day, the weather is likely to be dry and bright. Nights can be very cold. Frost and fog are common and may persist all day.

Explanation of the weather associated with anticyclones
- Anticyclones are high pressure air masses where the air sinks downwards. As the air descends it warms. Warm air can hold more moisture than cold so it rarely rains.
- There is very little difference in the value of the air pressure from one part of the anticyclone to another (see Figure 4.3b). Thus there are only very light winds.
- Because the air is sinking and winds are light anticyclones can remain stationary for several days.
- Clear skies and calm conditions allow heat to be lost at night. This means that air next to the ground cools. Condensation can occur. There is less cooling in the summer so there is dew and perhaps mist but in the colder conditions of winter, with its longer nights, there is more condensation giving foggy conditions.

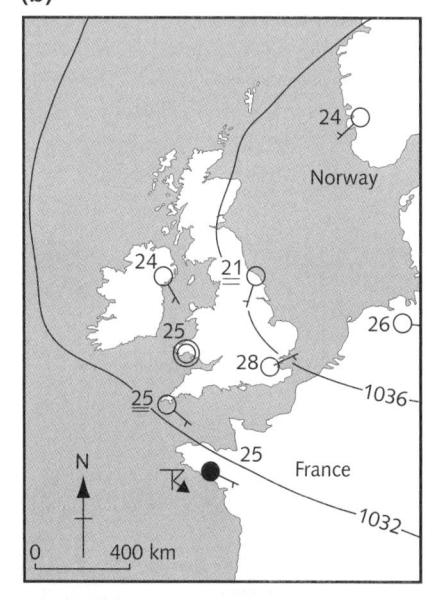

Depressions (low pressure systems)

Description of weather conditions
- Cloudy skies and rain.
- Winds can be very strong. At times they may even be storm force.
- Winds blow in an *anticlockwise* direction.
- Unsettled conditions. **Depressions** usually approach from the west so the weather in one place will change from **A** to **D** as shown at the base of Figure 4.4.

Back to ...
The New Wider World **p206**
Figure 12.16 showing a winter anticyclone

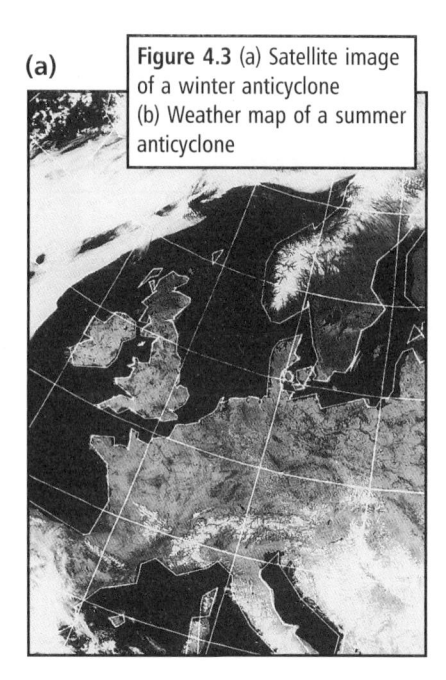

Figure 4.3 (a) Satellite image of a winter anticyclone
(b) Weather map of a summer anticyclone

Weather and climate   27

Figure 4.4 Weather in a depression

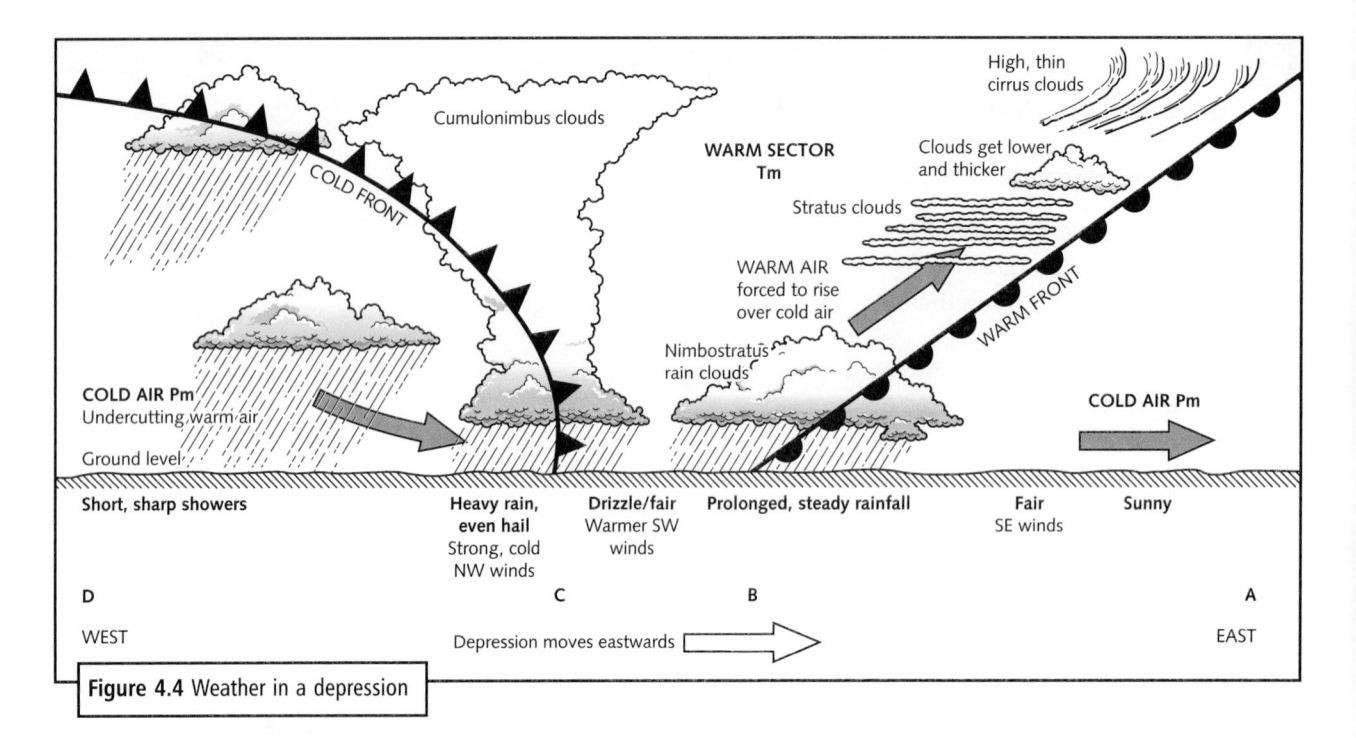

Key words to know

Depression
Front
Warm front
Warm sector
Cold front
Occluded front

Explanation of the weather associated with depressions

- Depressions are areas of low pressure which form over the Atlantic Ocean when a warm, moist tropical air mass from the south, Tm, meets a colder, drier, heavier polar air mass from the north, Pm (see section on air masses on p26). The two different masses of air do not mix. The boundary between two air masses is called a **front**.
- The lighter, warmer air is forced to rise up over the dense cold air at a warm front. Rising warm air is cooled, it cannot hold so much moisture and some of its water vapour content condenses, producing cloud and frontal rain (Figure 4.4).
- The **warm front** is at the leading edge of the depression as it moves (Figure 4.4). This is followed by the **warm sector** consisting of the Tm air.
- The **cold front** follows where denser, colder air moving in behind, forces the warm air to rise. The cold front travels faster than the warm front, catching up with it to form an **occluded front**.
- Most depressions take between one and three days to pass over the British Isles.

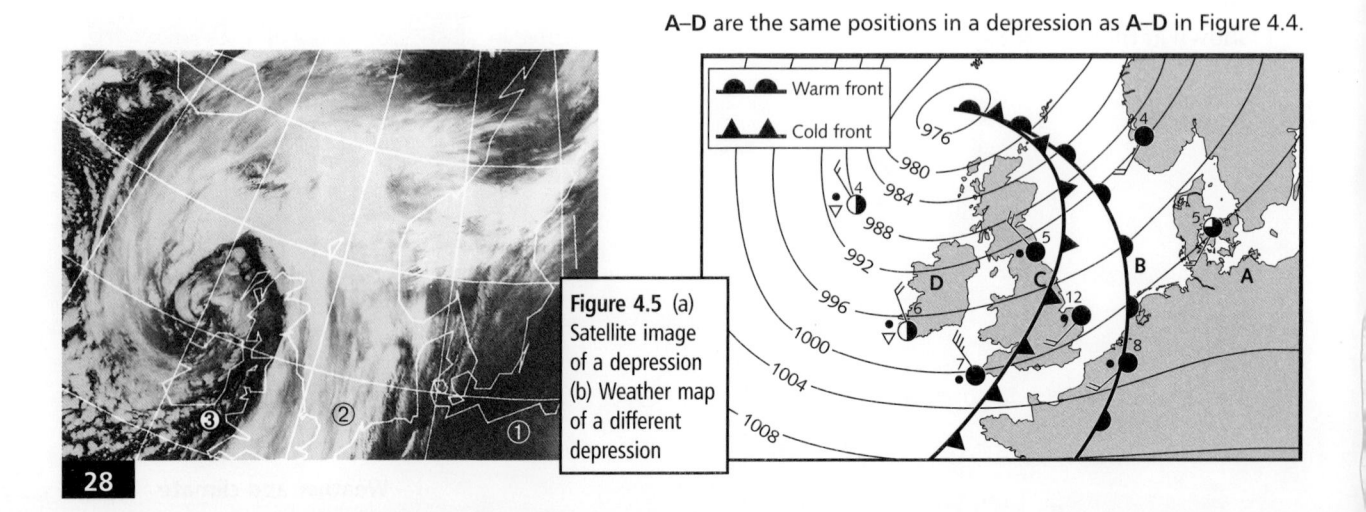

A–D are the same positions in a depression as A–D in Figure 4.4.

Figure 4.5 (a) Satellite image of a depression (b) Weather map of a different depression

> *Check this!...*
>
> 1 Look at Figure 4.5. Using the satellite image (4.5a), describe the cloud over position:
>   a) ①   b) ②   c) ③.
>
>   What parts of a depression are areas ② and ③?
>
> 2 Compare the weather experienced in Britain during anticyclones with that experienced during depressions.
>
> 3 Explain the weather brought by a depression.
>
> 4 Compare and contrast weather in summer and winter anticyclones.

4 What are the factors affecting climate?

Climate is the average weather conditions of a place taken over a period of time. It is the expected, rather than the actual, conditions. It is long-term and is often applied to sizeable parts of the globe, e.g. the Mediterranean climate.

How do latitude, altitude, aspect and continentality affect temperature and rainfall?

Latitude

Places nearer the Equator are much warmer than those nearer the Poles. The reasons are given in Figure 4.6.

Figure 4.6 Explanation of the effects of latitude

(a) Earth
(b) Sun's rays
(c) Atmosphere (dust, vapour)

1 Parallel and equal rays of heat and light from the sun
2 Equator (sun high in sky) X–Y a smaller area to heat up
3 Sun at a low angle, A–B a greater area to heat up
4 Rays have a shorter path through atmosphere at Equator (Q) than nearer poles (P) thus less heat is lost at Q

Altitude

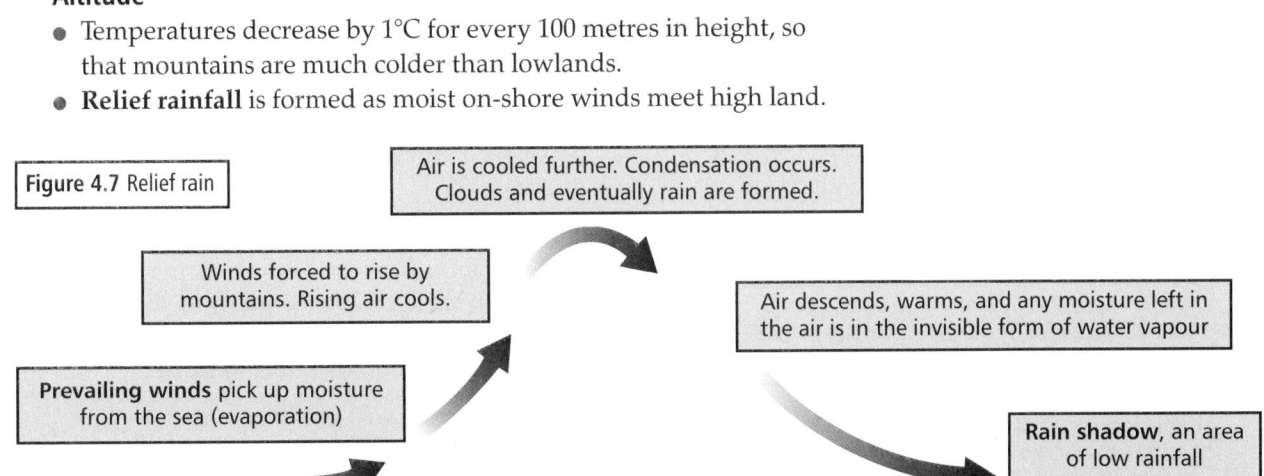

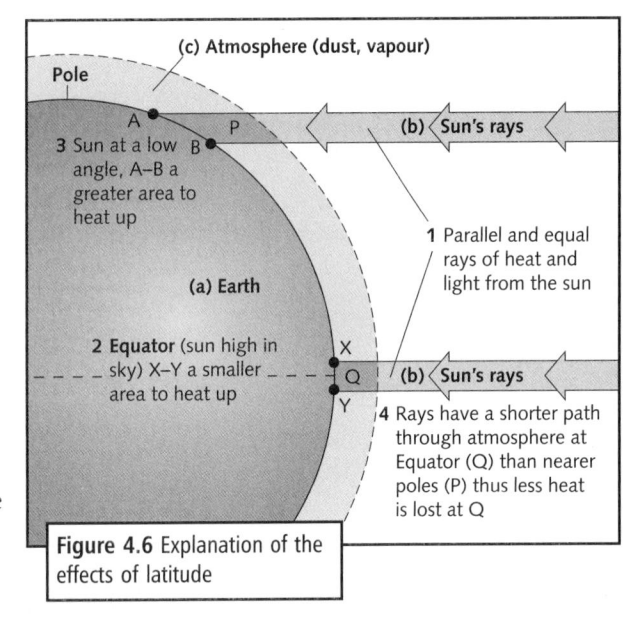

- Temperatures decrease by 1°C for every 100 metres in height, so that mountains are much colder than lowlands.
- **Relief rainfall** is formed as moist on-shore winds meet high land.

Figure 4.7 Relief rain

Prevailing winds pick up moisture from the sea (evaporation)

Winds forced to rise by mountains. Rising air cools.

Air is cooled further. Condensation occurs. Clouds and eventually rain are formed.

Air descends, warms, and any moisture left in the air is in the invisible form of water vapour

Rain shadow, an area of low rainfall

Weather and climate

Aspect

- **Aspect** is the direction a place or slope faces.
- Aspect affects how much sun a place gets and how strong the sun is.
- In Britain and the Mediterranean the sun is always to the south but at an angle in the sky, not overhead.
- The sun shines on the south facing slope and, when the sun is low in the sky, leaves the one facing north in shade.
- The south facing slope also has stronger sun since the sun's rays are hitting the slope at a higher angle (the same principle as the sun at the Equator in Figure 4.6).

Continentality

Continentality describes how much a region is influenced by the sea.

- An area like Britain that is small, surrounded by the sea and which has a long coastline has a moderate (small annual temperature range) climate that is strongly affected by the sea.
- Places towards the centre of continents and so further away from the sea have extreme (high annual temperature range) continental climate.

Causes of continentality

Distance from the sea Land heats up more quickly during the summer and cools down more rapidly in winter than the sea. So places towards the centre of continents have warmer summers and colder winters than those with a coastal location (e.g. British climate).

Ocean currents Ocean currents are either warm or cold. Warm currents tend to raise winter temperatures of coastal areas. The **North Atlantic Drift** is a warm current starting in the Gulf of Mexico which keeps the west coast of Britain much warmer in winter than other places in similar latitudes. Cold currents usually lower summer temperatures.

Prevailing winds Winds bring the weather characteristics of the area they come from. Winds that blow from the warm sea in winter will

---

Key words to know

Climate
Latitude
Altitude
Relief rainfall
Prevailing wind
Rain shadow
Aspect
Continentality
North Atlantic Drift

Check this!...

- A warm spell has closed the ski slopes in Scotland.
- Come to sunny Costa Brava this summer – we can guarantee the temperature will be hot enough to sunbathe and you needn't bring your umbrellas.
- The M4 was shut this morning due to many accidents caused by people driving too close to the car in front in the foggy conditions.
- Temperatures in the summer of 2003 were the third highest on record.
- Forest fires have destroyed large areas of southern France with some loss of life. The French police think they have been started deliberately but the strong winds and recent dry spell have made the fires very difficult to control.

1. Decide whether the statements on the left describe the weather or the climate.

2. Use a diagram to explain why the mountains of Wales have more rain than the eastern lowlands of England.

3. There are more corries (Chapter 1, p4) on north-facing slopes than south-facing slopes in the British Isles. Draw a diagram to show the effect of aspect, to explain why snow does not melt so quickly on north-facing slopes.

4. Describe and explain continentality.

raise temperatures and bring moist conditions (e.g. British climate). Those blowing from warm land in summer will also increase temperature but bring dry conditions (e.g. Mediterranean). However, winds that blow from the cooler sea in summer (British climate) will lower temperatures.

Case Study

British Isles, temperature and rainfall

Back to ...

The New Wider World p207 for the case study of seasonal and regional weather patterns in the British Isles.

Using your case study

Use the information in this case study to describe the general patterns of rainfall and temperature in the four areas of the British Isles shown in Figure 12.18 on p207 of *The New Wider World*.

Explain how: latitude; altitude; aspect; continentality and winds influence the climate of the British Isles.

Case study links

This case study links with Chapter 5 – how tourism of the Lake District is affected by climate.

Update

For more information on British Isles climate use the link on *The New Wider World Coursemate* website.

Learn it!

a) Describe the pattern of temperature and rainfall in the British Isles.

b) Explain the effects of the following on the climate of the British Isles:
latitude
altitude
aspect
continentality
prevailing winds.

Case Study

Mediterranean, temperature and rainfall

Back to ...

The New Wider World p164 Figure 10.15 to see climate graphs for Costa del Sol, and p215 for information on the Mediterranean climate.

Using your case study

Use the information in *The New Wider World* to describe the climate of Malaga, on the Mediterranean coast of Spain.

Use p215 to explain why the summers are hot and dry with winds blowing from the dry land of the Sahara and why winters are warm and moist.

Confine your description and explanation to the area north of the Mediterranean Sea.

Case study links

This case study links with Chapter 5 – how Mediterranean EU tourism is affected by climate.

Update

For more information on Mediterranean climate use the link on *The New Wider World Coursemate* website to access the BBC website and look under Geography.

Learn it!

a) What is the temperature and rainfall pattern of the Mediterranean?

b) Draw a sketch map to show the area of Mediterranean climate in Europe. Add labels to explain the factors affecting the temperature and rainfall.

c) Explain how latitude, altitude, aspect, continentality and prevailing winds affect the climate of a European Union area bordering the Mediterranean.

Weather and climate

EXAM PRACTICE

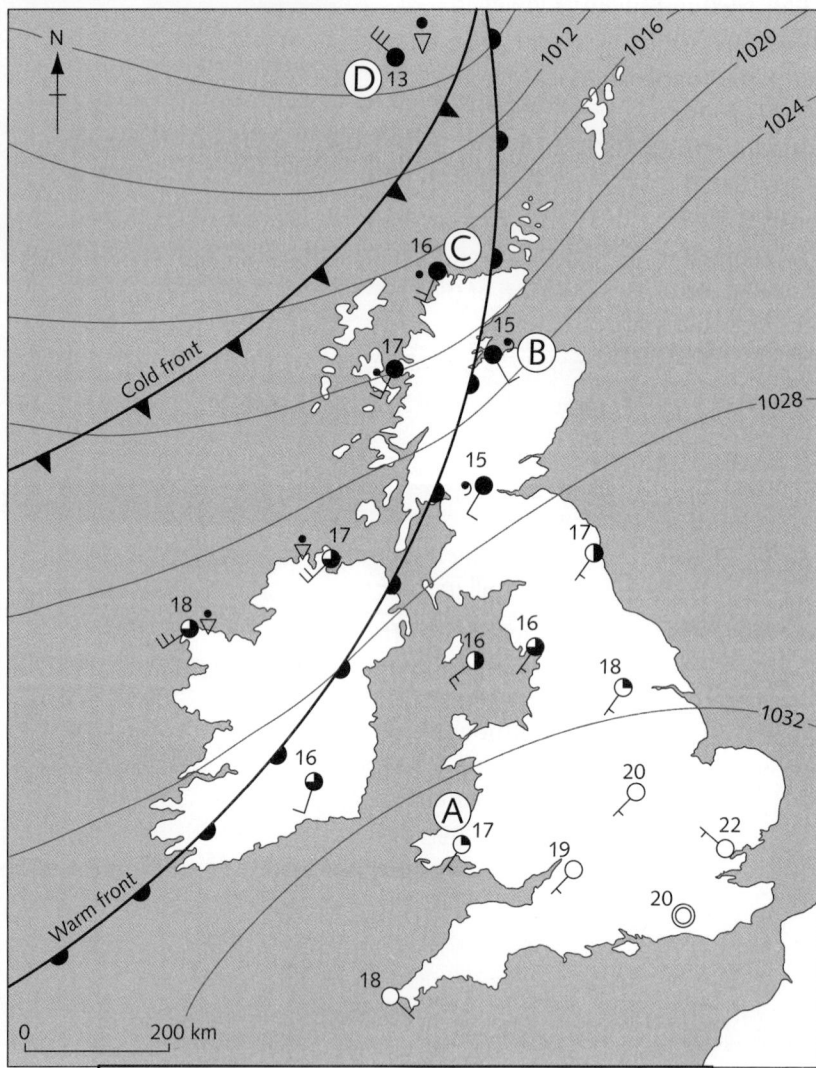

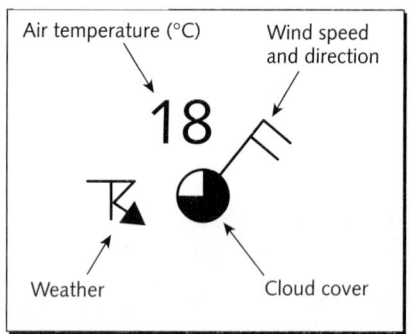

Figure 4.8 Weather map of the British Isles

a Study Figure 4.8. (Use points of the compass to answer questions ai and ii.)

  i Give the area of the British Isles where the pressure is:
  1 highest
  2 lowest. (2)

  ii Give the area of the British Isles where the winds are:
  1 strongest
  2 calm. (2)

  iii Name the pressure system to the south-east of the British Isles. (1)

  iv Name the part of the depression that is over C. (1)

b Write a weather report for a news bulletin to describe the weather at:

  A
  B (6)

c Copy the diagram below which is a cross-section of the depression in Figure 4.8 showing positions Ⓑ, Ⓒ and Ⓓ. Explain the weather conditions at B, C and D by adding annotations (notes) to the diagram. (6)

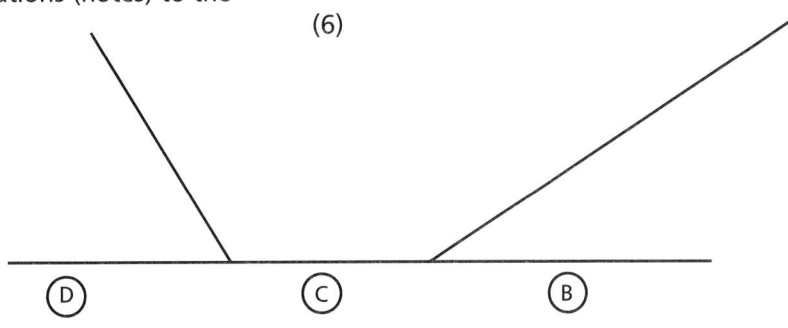

d Describe and explain the temperature and precipitation patterns of the climate of an EU area bordering the Mediterranan Sea. (6)

EXAM TIPS

Command words are very important. If you do not follow the command you may be writing about the wrong thing. Command words include:
- 'name', 'state', 'list' – asking you to write a single word or phrase
- 'describe' – asking you to write about what a diagram or graph shows, or what a place looks like
- 'explain' – asking you to show an understanding of the causes or how something works.

For example in question d 'describe' – warm, give values, etc., 'explain' – show how factors affecting climate work, e.g. how temperature is affected by wind direction, etc.

It may help you to underline the command words when you first read a question.

Back to ...

The New Wider World website to check your answers to the Exam Practice question.

5 Tourism

KEY QUESTION

1 What factors account for the nature of tourism?

Key words to know
Culture
Amenities

1 What factors account for the nature of tourism?

Attractive landscape	Suitable climate	Interesting plants and animals
Does the area have: • mountains • lakes • sea • beaches • volcanoes?	Does the area have: • sunny weather • snow in the winter • dry summers • warmer weather December to March?	Does the area have: • distinctive vegetation, e.g. cacti • unusual birds, e.g. migrating birds • wild animals, e.g. tigers • visible underwater life?

Figure 5.1 What are the physical factors affecting tourism in an area?

Cultural features	Built amenities	The interests and age of the tourists
Does the area have: • an interesting history • many old buildings • an unusual architecture • different customs, food, drink?	Does the area have: • suitable accommodation, e.g. 5-star hotels, caravans • built activities, e.g. shops, theme parks, theatres • modern transport, e.g. motorways, a nearby airport?	Does the area cater for: • children, e.g. beach • teenagers, e.g. activities • the 18–30 age group, e.g. night life • family holidays, e.g. purpose built resorts • retired people, e.g. cruises?

Figure 5.2 What are the human factors affecting tourism in an area?

What are the environmental impacts of tourism?

Environmental impacts include the effects of tourism on the physical and human environment.

Around **Building of large high-rise hotels, apartments, villas, roads & airports**:

- Increased demand for food maintains the local agriculture & fishing industries unless tourists only want 'imported food'.
- Increased employment & money spent in the region reducing migration, but this may be very seasonal & create unemployment for much of the year.
- Major demand for water which means building water storage facilities.
- Increased cultural links.
- Demand for better services from tourists: drainage; sanitation; transport; power supply, means that the locals can benefit from these also.
- Loss of local way of life, jealousy of the lifestyle of the tourist.
- Damage to natural environment: beach cafés; ski pylons; pollution by boats on lakes; views lost; litter.
- Increased traffic congestion leading to pollution & accidents.
- Increased demand for second homes which increases housing cost for locals and leaves the area without life for much of the year.
- Much of the development is funded by big companies who then take much of the profit out of the region.

Figure 5.3 Environmental impacts of tourism

The New Wider World, pp160–161; 164–5; 172–5

34

How has tourism changed?

The table below shows how:
- tourists and their lifestyle
- tourist destinations and the type of holiday
- the structure of the tourist industry

have changed.

Back to ...
The New Wider World **pp160–161** for more information on recent trends and changing patterns of tourism.

Change	Reason for change
Greater wealth	– increases in salary – people receive holiday with pay.
Greater mobility	– increase in car ownership with greater freedom to choose where and when to go for the day, or for longer. In 1951, 5 % had a car in the UK. By 2000, this was 74 %.
Improved **accessibility** and transport facilities	– more and better roads, especially motorways and urban by-passes, have reduced driving times between places – improved and enlarged airports – reduced air fares – **package holidays** – organisation of mass tourism by transnational companies.
More **leisure** time	– shorter working week – longer paid holidays (UK 3 weeks a year, USA still only 1 week) – flexi-time and more people working from home – more part-time workers – an ageing population, retiring early and still active – more holidays taken as weekend/short breaks and longer more distant destinations.
Changing holiday activities	– decline in the 'beach holiday' – increase in active holidays (skiing, water sports, mountain biking, health/sport resorts) – increase in theme parks – most rapid growth in mid-1990s has been in 'cruise holidays' – increase in self catering – increase in 'green' tourism.
Changing destinations	– away from seaside towns in the UK to package holidays in Europe to long haul locations, USA or southern hemisphere.
Advertising and ease of booking	– holiday TV programs – magazines and brochures – Internet.

Figure 5.4 The changing nature of tourism

How may sustainable tourism be developed?

Sustainable tourism is the development of tourism which will benefit the community in the area visited but will not spoil this area for future tourists. There are many different ways to develop sustainable tourism.

- Extend the holiday season so that the number of people in an area are more spread out over time. Thus fewer built amenities are needed with employment over more of the year. For example, Spanish carnivals in September.
- **Ecotourism**. Small groups staying in local homes visit areas to view natural features and local cultures, e.g. small groups scuba diving in the Mediterranean.
- Repair the damage created by past tourism, e.g. redevelopment of tourist centres to remove vandalised areas, clean up the polluted environment, build footpaths, e.g. in the Lake District.

Key words to know

Accessibility
Package holidays
Leisure
Sustainable tourism
Ecotourism
Honeypot

Tourism

Back to ...

The New Wider World **p163** Figure 10.12 which gives strategies for sustainable tourism in National Parks in the UK.

- Restrict the number of visitors, e.g. in the Lake District, by limiting car parking space.
- Create car parking outside an area and allow public transport access only, e.g. in the Lake District.
- Increase the number of activities across an area so that there are fewer '**Honeypots**' (areas where many people gather because most of the activities are there). For example, development of cultural sites away from the beaches in the Mediterranean.

Check this!...

1. Collect a holiday brochure from a travel agent. Decide where you would like to go on holiday. Give your reasons for wanting to visit this place.

2. The following are included in the top attractions of the Lake District, a tourist area in north-west England. Sort the list of attractions into a table with two columns headed 'physical attractions' and 'human attractions'.

   Wordsworth's Dove Cottage
   Lake Windermere
   John Ruskin museum
   Skiddaw mountain
   Penrith Castle
   Hill top farm – world of Beatrix Potter's animals
   Brewery Arts Centre
   Wastwater screes
   Ravensglass and Eskdale steam railway
   Lanthwaite wood and red squirrels
   Blencathra ridge
   Windermere Steamboat museum
   Helvellyn arête
   Acorn Bank garden

3. Decide whether each of the environmental impacts in Figure 5.3 on p33 is a positive or negative impact.

4. The Lake District is an area of great natural beauty which is under intense pressure because it has many day visitors. The following plans were submitted to the Lake District National Park Sustainable Development Fund in 2003. Which plan(s) would you grant money to? Give your reasons.

Harnesses and wooden arches for horses to be used to haul timber that has been cut down. This will keep a local tradition alive.

Development of a cycle centre in Windermere, a local honeypot. This will encourage people to move around the area on bikes.

Garden restoration of a country hall. This will provide an eco-educational experience and develop organic produce for the local area.

Case Study

The Lake District National Park, north-west England

Back to ...

The New Wider World pp172–175 for the case study of the Lake District National Park in north-west England, a small region in the British Isles

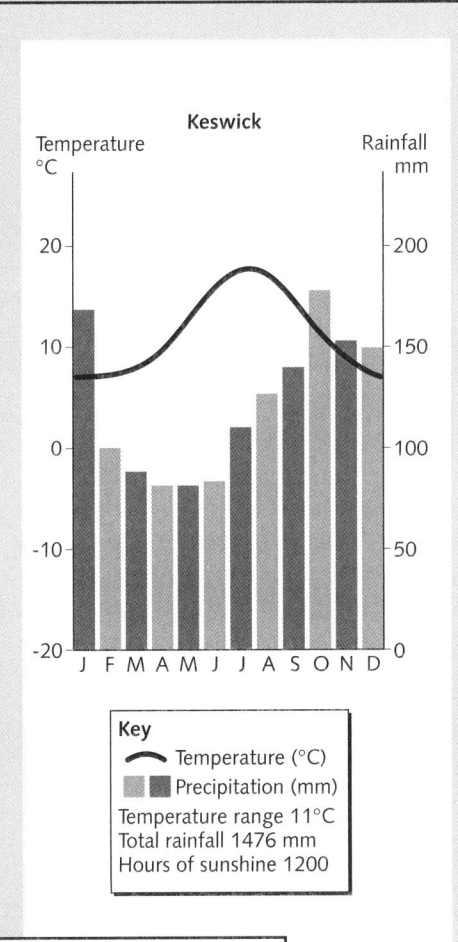

Key
- Temperature (°C)
- Precipitation (mm)

Temperature range 11°C
Total rainfall 1476 mm
Hours of sunshine 1200

Figure 5.5 Climate graph, Keswick, Lake District

Using your case study

Use the information in this case study and Figure 5.5 to answer questions:

1. **How do the physical and human factors affect the type of tourism in the Lake District?**
   a) Physical factors – describe the: landscape (use Figure 19.15, on p320 of *The New Wider World* to help you); climate (see Figure 5.5); and ecosystems.
   b) Human factors – describe the: cultural features; most visited places; type of accommodation; reasons for the visits.

2. **How has the pattern of tourism changed in the region?**
   - Late eighteenth century – tourism began advertised by poets, Wordsworth and Coleridge.
   - End of the nineteenth century – increase in tourism, big houses were built on lake shores by wealthy industrialists, working classes had a shorter working week and one week paid holiday, the railway came to Windermere bringing day trippers.
   - Twentieth century – increasing car ownership and improved motorways increased the number of day visitors from a wider area. By 1994 there were 12 million visitors per year, (10 million were day visitors).

3. **What are the environmental impacts of tourism in the region?**
   - Quote figures for: arrival by car; numbers of walkers creating footpath erosion; level of second home ownership.
   - Identify the honeypot areas.

4. **What attempts have been made to develop sustainable tourism in the area?**
   Describe the National Park Authority Aims to develop sustainable tourism and reduce the impacts of tourists on the natural environment through landscaping and traffic management.

Case study links

This case study provides links with:
- Chapter 1 – glaciation provides the correct words to use when describing the Lake District – a glaciated area
- Chapter 4 – British Isles climate, provides information on the climate of the region (north-west)
- Chapter 9 – link between tourism and farming in hill sheep areas
- Chapter 13 – ageing population structure affects the type of tourism.

Update

For more information on tourism in the Lake District use the link on *The New Wider World Coursemate* website.

Learn it!

Learn your case study.
a) Where is the Lake District?
b) Draw a sketch map of the Lake District based on Figure 10.35 on p172 of *The New Wider World*.
c) Use examples to describe its physical nature and human amenities.
d) Describe the changing pattern of tourism.
e) Explain how the environment is affected by tourism.
f) Explain what is meant by sustainable tourism and how the region is trying to keep the area attractive for future visitors.

Case Study

The Costa del Sol, Spain

Back to ...
The New Wider World pp164–165 for the case study of the Costa del Sol, a small region in the EU bordering the Mediterranean Sea.

Using your case study
Use the information in this case study to answer questions:
1. **How do physical and human factors affect tourism in the Costa del Sol?**
   a) Physical factors – describe the: landscape; climate (of Malaga).
   b) Human factors – describe the: cultural places; built environment; type of tourism.
2. **How has the pattern of tourism changed in the region?**
   Describe the four stages in tourism.
3. **What are the environmental impacts of tourism in the region?**
   Describe the impact of tourism on landscape and the built environment.
4. **What attempts have been made to develop sustainable tourism in the area?**
   Describe the developments in the stagnation period and the role of the Spanish Government.

Other attempts by the Spanish government to improve this area include:
- stricter planning/building controls to ensure buildings blend with the environment by using local styles, building materials, colour
- spreading tourism away from honeypots by building new golf courses, theme parks, nature parks, green areas away from main centres, bike hire
- developing cultural excursions to historical sites, reviving local crafts – lace making, leather and pottery, local food outlets
- reducing noise levels, e.g. bars must close at a given time.

Case study links
This case study provides links with:
- Chapters 2 and 3 – river and coastal landscapes
- Chapter 4 – Mediterranean climate.

Update
For more information on tourism in the Costa del Sol use the link on *The New Wider World Coursemate* website.

Learn it!

a) Where is the Costa del Sol?
b) Draw a sketch map of the Costa del Sol, based on Figure 10.13 on p164 of *The New Wider World*.
c) Describe its physical nature and human amenities.
d) Describe the changing stages of tourism.
e) Explain how the environment is affected by tourism.
f) Explain what is meant by sustainable tourism and how the region is trying to keep the area attractive for future visitors.

EXAM PRACTICE

(a)

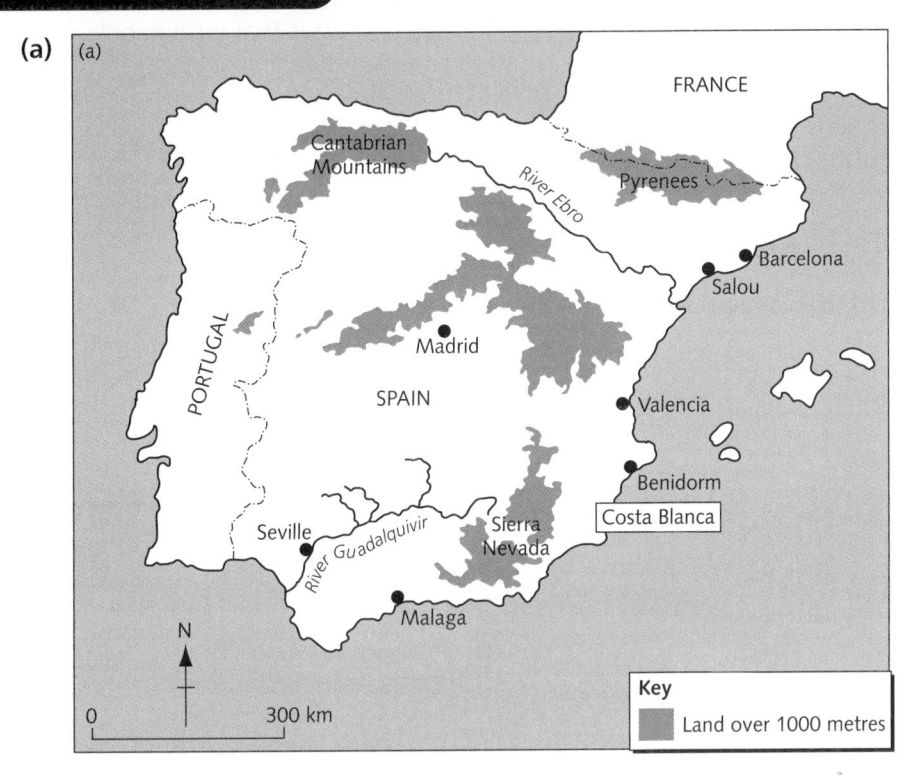

Figure 5.6 Benidorm: (a) Location and photographs in (b) 1963 and (c) 1980

Tourism

a Benidorm on the Costa Blanca has been a favourite holiday destination for UK tourists since the early 1960s. It has been Spain's most important holiday resort for the package holiday business. By the 1980s Benidorm had a poor image so the Spanish government stepped in to try to revive the region.

  i Study photograph (b) in Figure 5.6. Give **three** physical factors other than climate that originally attracted tourists to this area. (3)

  ii Study photographs (b) and (c) in Figure 5.6. Give **two** ways that local people will have changed their employment from 1963 to 1980. (2)

  iii Study photograph (c). Give **three** advantages, other than employment, that this scale of tourism would bring to Benidorm. (3)

Figure 5.7 'Benidorm dives downhill'

"We'd never eat Spanish food."
"No way!"
"We eat chips and burgers – just like at home."
"This resort is just SO tacky."
"Those lager louts are everywhere."
"Well, you get what you pay for."
"They haven't finished building our hotel yet!"
"I'll never come back here again."
"We party all night long – that's what we're here for."
"We booze all night and fry in the sun all day."
"They keep us awake all night with their carry-on."
"We never bother with the cultural tours."
"...and all that loud music."

b i Study Figure 5.7. Describe the type of tourist attracted to Benidorm in the 1980s. (4)

  ii Copy and complete the 'vicious circle' diagram (Figure 5.8), to show how tourism can ruin an area. Insert the numbers of the statements opposite in the boxes in the correct order.

1 Developers build new tourist facilities.
2 Development isn't controlled by the government.
3 Many tourists are put off.
4 Tourists rush to book because it is so cheap.
5 The resort's natural attractions get ruined.
6 The tour operators need to slash prices further. (5)

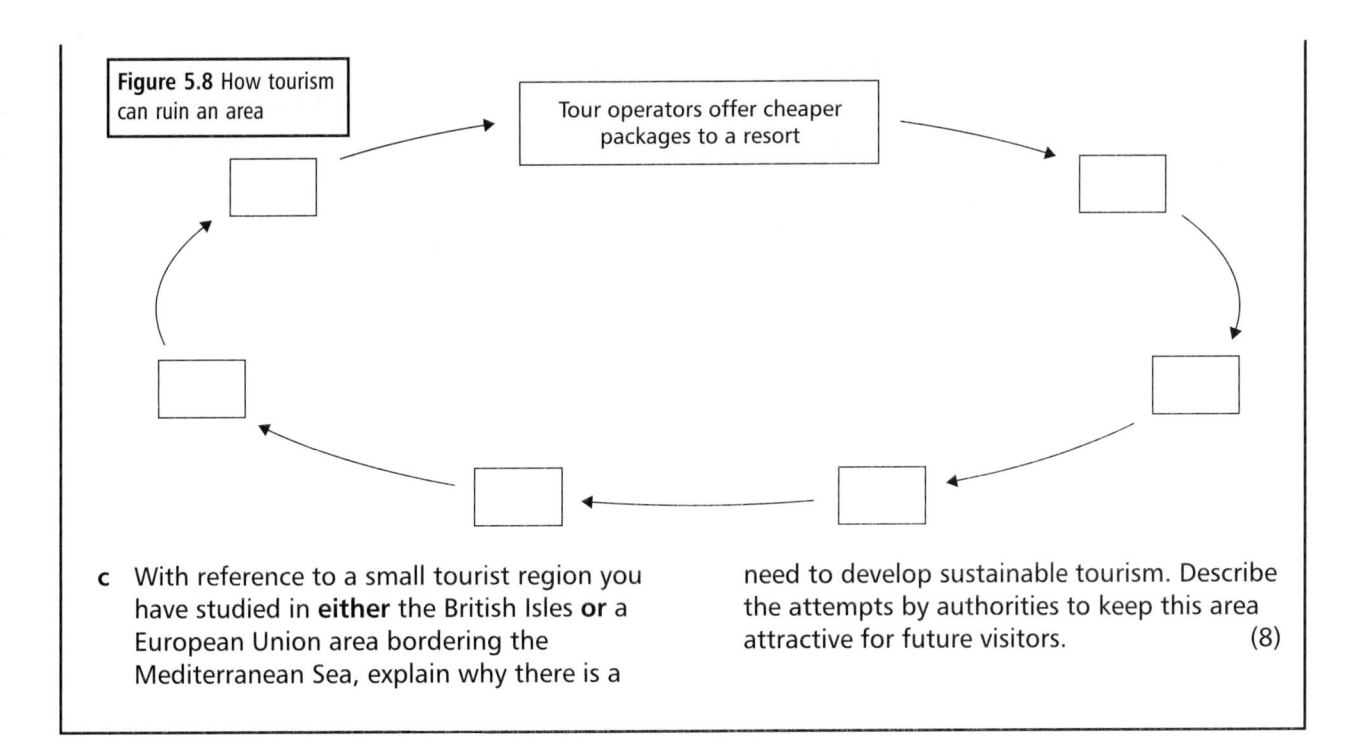

Figure 5.8 How tourism can ruin an area

Tour operators offer cheaper packages to a resort

c With reference to a small tourist region you have studied in **either** the British Isles **or** a European Union area bordering the Mediterranean Sea, explain why there is a need to develop sustainable tourism. Describe the attempts by authorities to keep this area attractive for future visitors. (8)

EXAM TIPS

The last section of some questions will have a choice. Read the whole question before you make your choice to ensure you choose the one you can answer best.

There is often more than one part to the extended questions at the end. Make a small plan at the start of your answer with key words for each command. This will stop you having to think about what comes next and you can concentrate on what you are writing. Don't spend too much time on writing a plan.

For example, your plan for your answer in question c about the Lake District could be:
- 'explain why there is a need for sustainable tourism' – *10 million day visitors by car, quiet, walking, congestion, hill erosion. Need to get back to attractive countryside.*
- 'describe the attempts by authorities to keep area attractive': *repairing footpaths, traffic plan.*

Back to ...

The New Wider World website to check your answers to the Exam Practice question.

Tourism 41

6 Sustainable development of energy and other resources

The New Wider World, pp118–125; 128–131

KEY QUESTIONS

1. What is the 'sustainable development of resources'?
2. What are the issues in the sustainable development of energy?
3. What factors need to be considered in the location of wind farms?
4. The development of resources in one part of the world may be the result of a changing demand from other countries.
5. How can these resources be sustainably developed?

Key words to know

Natural resources
Renewable
Sustainable
Human and economic resources
Non-renewable

1 What is the 'sustainable development of resources'?

Study Figure 6.1 below for the different types of resources.

Natural resources can be defined as features of the environment which are needed and used by people.

Renewable resources can either be:
- continuous, i.e. they can be used over and over again, or
- **sustainable**, which means resources are able to be maintained at the same level if left to nature. However, if these sustainable resources are used carelessly or are over-used by people, then either:
  - their value may be reduced, e.g. soils lose their fertility and are eroded, or
  - their existence is threatened, e.g. over-fishing.

Check this!...

1. What is the difference between non-renewable and renewable resources?
2. Define the term 'sustainable resources'.
3. What type of resources are:
   a) gold
   b) soil
   c) tidal current
   d) wood
   e) money?

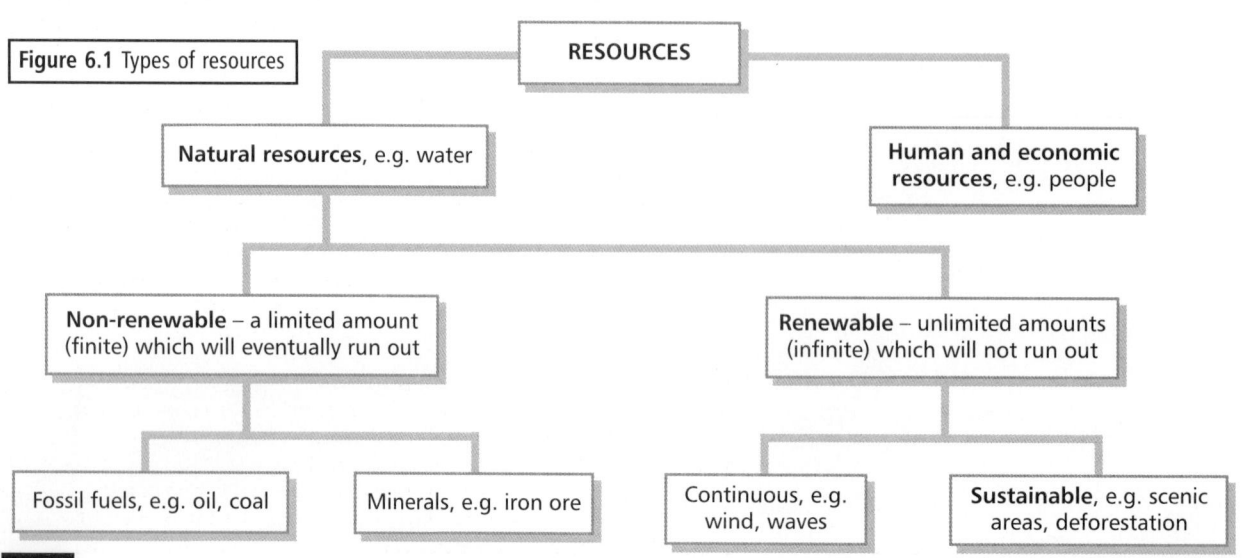

Figure 6.1 Types of resources

```
                        RESOURCES
                       /         \
        Natural resources,        Human and economic
        e.g. water                resources, e.g. people
        /         \
Non-renewable – a limited amount      Renewable – unlimited amounts
(finite) which will eventually run out  (infinite) which will not run out
   /         \                              /         \
Fossil fuels,   Minerals,            Continuous, e.g.   Sustainable, e.g. scenic
e.g. oil, coal  e.g. iron ore        wind, waves        areas, deforestation
```

42

2 What are the issues in the sustainable development of energy?

Key words to know
Energy resources
Coal
Oil
Gas
Nuclear
Hydro-electric power (HEP)
Solar
Wind

British target: 10% of total energy supplies from renewable energy by 2010

Source	UK electricity production 2003
Coal	36 %
Gas	36 %
Oil	0.7 %
Nuclear	25.5 %
Hydro-electric power (HEP)	1.6 %
Other non-renewables	0.2 %

Figure 6.2 Sources for UK electricity production 2003 (total 343 billion kWh)

Non-renewable energy

You need to understand the arguments for and against the use of non-renewable sources in the supply of energy.

Figure 6.3 The arguments for and against non-renewable energy

Source	For	Against – a finite supply
Coal – used for generating electricity in coal fired power stations	• Reserves are likely to last for over 300 years. • Improved technology has: – increased the output per worker – allowed deeper mining with fewer workers – made conversion to electricity more efficient.	• The most easily accessible deposits have been used up and production costs have risen. There is increased competition from other types of energy. • Burning coal causes air pollution and, by releasing carbon dioxide, contributes to global warming. • Deep mining can be dangerous. • Opencast mining harms the environment. • Coal is heavy and bulky to transport.
Oil and natural **gas** – both used for electricity with many coal power stations now converted to gas-fired power stations. Used for transport and heating.	• Oil and gas are more efficient to burn, easier to transport and distribute (by pipeline and tanker), and less harmful to the environment than coal, with gas being even cheaper and cleaner than oil. • They are safer than nuclear energy.	• New fields are increasingly difficult to discover and exploit. • There could be very little oil and natural gas left by 2030. • Terminals and refineries take up much space and there is the danger of spillage, leaks, explosions and fire. • The burning of gas and oil releases nitrogen oxide and sulphur dioxide which contribute to acid rain. • Oil and gas are subject to political and military pressures with sudden international price changes.
Nuclear energy – used in nuclear power stations	• Only very limited raw materials are needed, e.g. 50 tonnes of uranium per year (compared with 540 tonnes of coal per hour needed for coal-fired electricity stations). • The process results in only small amounts of nuclear waste which can be stored underground. • Nuclear power is believed to contribute less than conventional fuels to the greenhouse effect and acid rain.	• It is not clear how safe it is. Nuclear waste can remain radioactive for many years. There have been leaks at Sellafield, (north-west coast, England) which reprocesses and stores nuclear waste. The Irish Sea is increasingly contaminated (see Towyn floods p23). • Nuclear power cannot be used for two of industry's major demands, heating and transport, as costs are too high. • The cost of decommissioning old power stations is extremely high.

Sustainable development of energy and other resources

Figure 6.4 The arguments for and against non-renewable energy

Renewable energy

You need to understand the arguments for and against the use of renewable sources in the supply of energy.

Source	For – an infinite supply	Against
Hydro-electric power (HEP) – electric power generated by turbines rotated by water running downhill, often from a storage area	• HEP is a relatively cheap form of electricity. • HEP creates only limited pollution. • Dams, built to store water for the HEP, also reduce the risk of flooding and water shortages.	• Dams are very expensive to build. • Large areas of hilly land and rural population may have to be flooded forcing people and animals to move. • Unsightly pylons can cause visual pollution, expensive to bury cables.
Solar power – electricity generated through solar panels	• Solar power is safe. • Solar power is pollution free. • It is efficient for small amounts, e.g. a house.	• Technology has not yet found a cheap and efficient way to construct a power station. • Weather is not always suitable in the British Isles.
Wind – electricity generated by wind turbines in wind farms	• Wind power is safe (no radioactive emissions) and clean (no chemical emissions). It does not contribute to global warming or acid rain. • It has little effect on local vegetation/can create local reefs that are ideal breeding grounds for fish if sited off-shore. • Winds are much stronger in winter, the same time as the peak demand for electricity. • After the initial expense of building a wind farm, the production of electricity from this source is relatively cheap for small users. • In Wales wind farms are often located on upland sheep farmland and can provide extra income of up to £5000 per turbine per year for the farmer. Nearby villages can also be given compensation, e.g. Cenmaes in Central Wales received £5000. • Individual turbines might be operated by a local company. • Some say the turbines are attractive and bring tourists. • The off-shore industry may require up to 20 000 jobs. • Britain could become an exporter of off-shore wind technology.	• Tops of hills and coastal areas (the best sites for wind farms) are also often the location of National Parks or Areas of Outstanding Natural Beauty. Groups of turbines spoil the scenic attraction of the countryside or sea view from long distance as well as nearby. • They can affect wildlife, especially birds. There is some concern for kites in Central Wales and seabirds in off-shore sites. • Electricity generated during high winds cannot be stored for use during calm periods. • It is an expensive (4 times the price of coal) and inefficient form of energy for national use. As many as 50 000 wind farms may be needed if Britain is to generate 10 per cent of its total energy supply from the wind. • Income from wind farms may go to large non-local companies. • 70 truckloads of cement are needed for the foundations for each turbine. This can affect the minor roads leading up to the sites/disturb the seabed and tidal currents. • Wind farms are noisy and can interrupt radio and TV reception for people living nearby. They can also affect property values. • Off-shore sites could affect shipping routes and interfere with radar signals.

Check this!...

1 What is the difference between total energy supplies and supplies for electricity?

2 Give the main arguments against the use of coal and oil in power stations.

3 How are these arguments different from the use of nuclear power?

4 Summarise the arguments for and against non-renewable energy.

5 Do you think that Britain should increase its proportion of renewable energy? Give your arguments.

3. What factors need to be considered in the location of wind farms?

On-shore wind farms

- A typical **wind farm** in Britain is made of 20–40 wind turbines which are 25–40 metres high, with 2 or 3 blades moved by wind speeds of over 8 metres per second. They need to be located in consistently windy areas of Britain. The blades are stopped for safety at times of very high winds. (*Climatic factors.*)
- The best place for a wind farm is on the top of a hill or mountain, or on the coast, where the prevailing winds can blow uninterrupted by other taller features. (*Physical factors.*)
- Each turbine creates enough energy for 250 homes. Wind farm companies contribute to the local economy through compensation but the main profits go outside the region. (*Economic factors.*)
- Turbines create a noise (a roaring mechanical drone) which is made worse if they are near background noise of heavy traffic or industry. Wind farms affect scenery, wildlife and, during construction, local roads. (*Social factors.*)

Off-shore wind farms

In 2003, in order to meet Government targets to increase the use of renewable energy in the UK to 10 %, a major building programme of off-shore wind farms began. **Off-shore wind farms** have been built in North Wales off the coast at Prestatyn (North Hoyle). The 30 turbines generated their first electricity in November 2003. It is claimed that when the site is fully operational it will generate enough electricity for 50 000 homes. A second site has been acquired at Rhyl Flats. Local people can buy electricity generated from these turbines through the company npower Juice.

In South Wales planning permission for a wind farm is being sought off Porthcawl (Scarweather Sands).

Why North Hoyle?
- Excellent wind resource.
- Low exposure to larger waves of prevailing south-west winds.
- Low water depth – 12 m with 9 m tidal range.
- Good seabed properties for foundations and cables.
- Strong electricity infrastructure near coast.
- Port facilities for construction and operations – Mostyn, Rhyl, Liverpool, Holyhead.

> **Back to ...**
> *The New Wider World* p124
> Figure 8.18 for a photograph of a wind farm in California, USA.

Key words to know
Wind farm
Off-shore wind farm

Figure 6.5 Location of North Hoyle and British off-shore wind farms

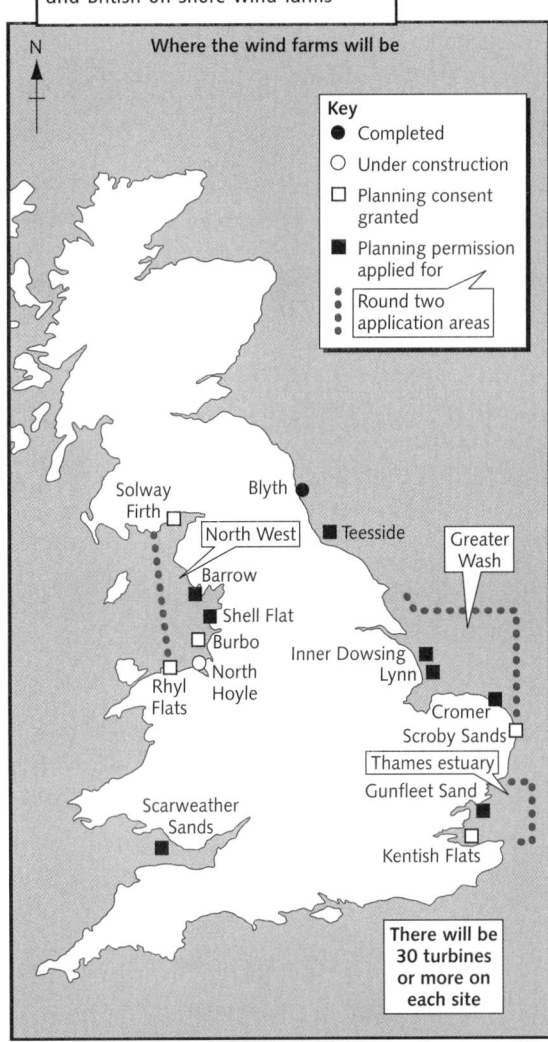

Key
- ● Completed
- ○ Under construction
- □ Planning consent granted
- ■ Planning permission applied for
- Round two application areas

There will be 30 turbines or more on each site

Check this!...

1. What are the physical, climatic, economic and social considerations in the location of wind farms?
2. The 2003 policy of the British government is to increase coastal wind power to have the biggest capacity in the world. Compose a letter to the Department of Trade and Industry to say whether you think more off-shore wind farms should be built. Give your arguments.

Sustainable development of energy and other resources

4 The development of resources in one part of the world may be the result of a changing demand from other countries

The demand for, and the use of, the world's resources is growing at an increasingly faster rate. This is mainly due to:
- population growth
- economic development, e.g. industrial and economic development as countries attempt to raise their standard of living and quality of life
- increasing wealth, especially in MEDCs
- technological advances
- changing fashions, e.g. change in type of food eaten.

Resources are not always found close to their demand. For example, there is a great demand for the tropical crop, coffee, in the UK where it cannot be grown.

5 How can these resources be sustainably developed?

There is a growing need to manage and protect the Earth's resources. **Sustainable development**, which is improving people's standard of living and quality of life without overusing resources or spoiling the environment, includes:
- developing renewable resources, e.g. tides
- recycling, e.g. glass
- controlling pollution, e.g. reducing emissions from vehicles
- conservation, e.g. wildlife
- greater efficiency in existing resource use, e.g. home insulation
- using appropriate technology, e.g. local building materials.

For this topic you may study any resource or activity that impacts on the environment, e.g. oil, timber, tourism in an LEDC.

Here we are looking at the fishing industry.

Back to ...

The New Wider World **pp128–131**, Energy and the environment – oil in Alaska; **pp169–171** tourism in LEDCs (West Indies and Kenya); **pp236–237** deforestation in the Amazon Basin are suitable case studies.

Key words to know

Sustainable development
Over-fishing

Fishing

What has caused the growth in demand for fish resources?

- Fish forms an important part of the European diet. A move towards healthier eating habits has led to a rise in demand.
- Fish is sometimes the only source of protein for people in LEDCs, where increases in population demand more fish supplies.

	Cod / haddock	Herring	Beef	Lamb
Protein (g)	4.9	4.8	4.9	4.5
Fat (g)	0.2	5.2	6.9	8.6
Calories (kcal)	21	66	75	95
Analysis per ounce based on raw edible portions of flesh.			

Figure 6.6 Fashion for lower fat diets

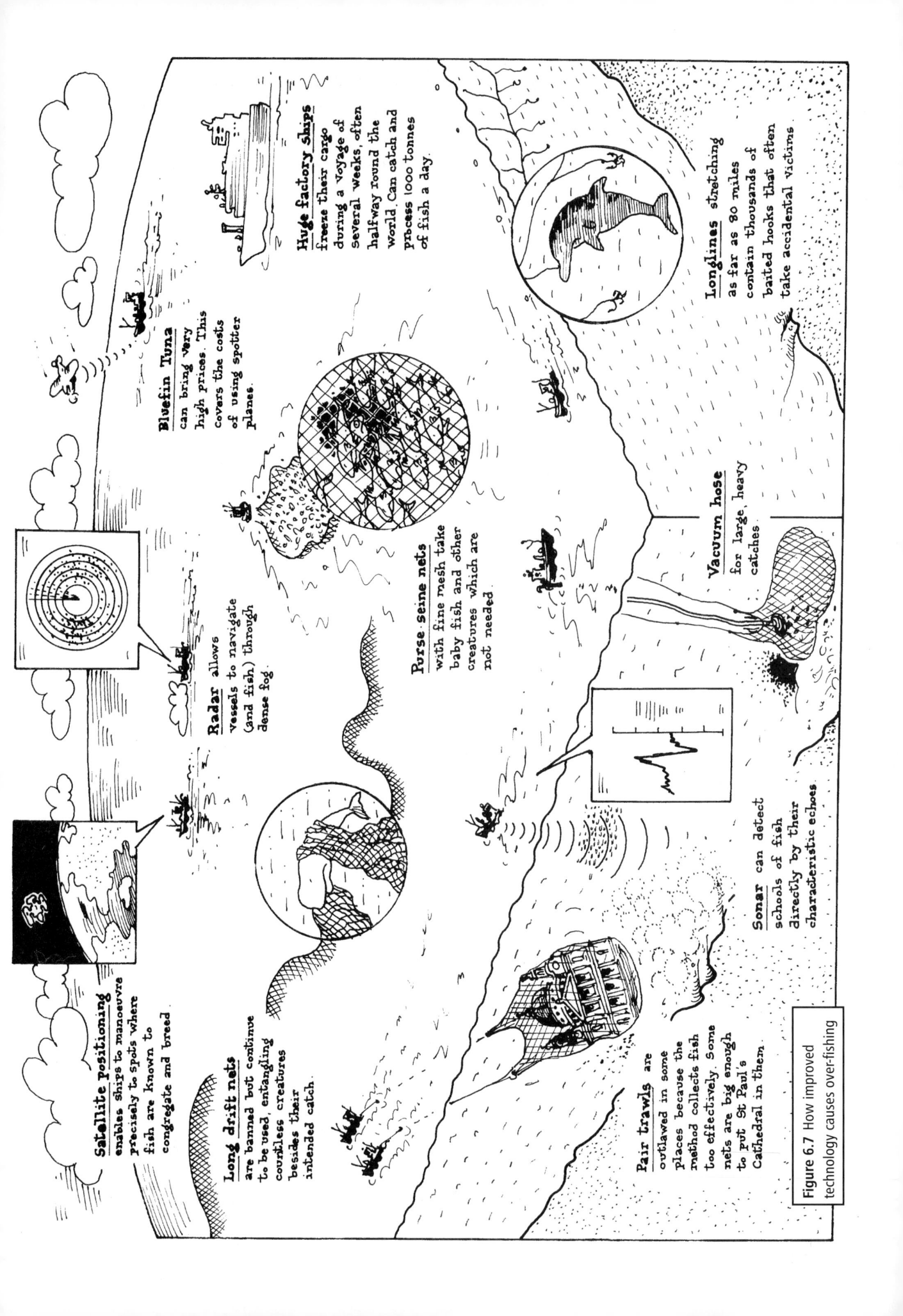

Figure 6.7 How improved technology causes over-fishing

> **Check this!...**
>
> 1. Describe how and why the demand for natural resources is changing.
> 2. Give two examples of natural resources from another part of the world that have recently become popular in the UK.
> 3. Explain the meaning of the term 'over-fishing'.
> 4. Describe the changing fishing techniques that have led to the environmental effect of over-fishing.

What are the environmental effects of the development of the resource?

- The technology used in the fishing industry has meant the volume of fish caught on one fishing trip has dramatically increased.
- Fish stocks are dwindling rapidly because we are taking too many fish out and not leaving enough to breed and develop into mature adult-sized fish.
- When too many fish are taken from the sea it is called **over-fishing**. This is not sustainable.

Sustainable development of fishing

- The Food and Agricultural Organisation (FAO) states that 35 % of the world's fishing grounds are over-fished and that 60 % of the world's fish resources, including cod, hake, shrimps, shark, etc. are in urgent need of sustainable management.
- Sustainable management involves the control of fishing activities so that humans reduce the numbers of fish caught and only take out of the oceans what nature can replace.

Case Study Extra

North Sea fishing

Growth and environmental effects of fishing in the North Sea

The environmental effect of over-fishing in the North Sea has seriously depleted fish stocks and endangered the fishing industry that depends on this region.

Several factors have increased the competition for fish:
- The North Sea is on the doorstep of several national fishing fleets, Norway, Denmark, Belgium, UK, France and Spain.
- North-west Europe is a densely populated region which increasingly consumes large quantities of fish.
- Huge factory ships owned by large companies have increased in number.
- Large purse-seine nets with fine mesh are used. They are unselective, taking baby fish and species which are not needed.
- Vessels from Japan, Poland and the Russian Federation increase the pressure on fish stocks.

Since 1960 the fishing industry has declined because fishing is more mechanised and less fish are available.

Strategies for the sustainable development of North Sea fish

The European Union Common Fisheries Policy is a fishing policy for all nations to follow in the North Sea. It provides measures to prevent over-fishing, including:

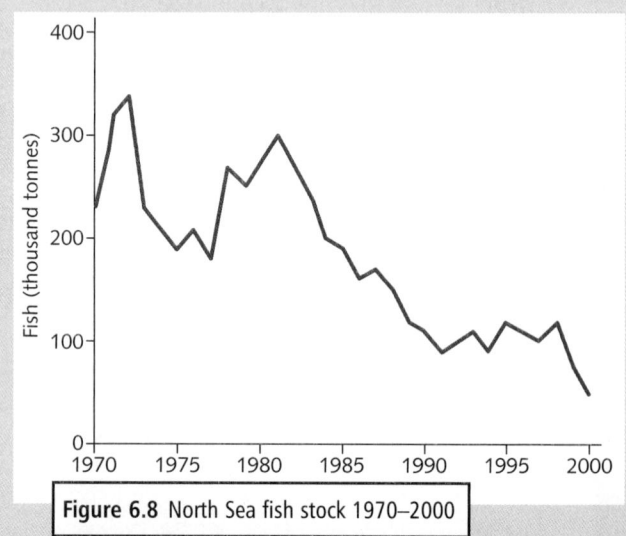

Figure 6.8 North Sea fish stock 1970–2000

- setting a 6 mile limit from a country's coastline – only fishermen from that country can fish within this area
- setting quotas (limiting the amount of fish taken) – these are being reduced since over-fishing is still occurring
- banning fishing at certain times of the year, e.g. breeding seasons, and only allowing boats out for a limited number of days each month. In 2004 this was 13 days per month
- setting up exclusion zones that are off limits for all nationalities of fishermen
- using satellite tracking systems to check boats – heavy fines and impounding of boats if rules are not obeyed
- reducing the size of the fishing fleet by limiting fishing licences

- adding taxes to the fish caught
- imposing the use of rigid and large mesh nets so only adult fish are caught and small fish can escape; drift nets being phased out
- involving local fishermen to look after fish stocks in community projects
- promising grants to help fishermen buy environmentally-friendly fishing gear, to decommission boats and to rejuvenate the old port areas.

Publicity surrounding the fishing industry is common. Cod fishing was banned from the North Sea in 2003 because cod had become an endangered species. In response, Birds Eye will no longer use cod to make its fish fingers, as it has for the last 50 years. Instead it will use other non-threatened white fish.

Using your case study

Use the information to answer questions on:
- the growth in demand for a resource (fish)
- the environmental effects of the development of the resource (commercial fishing)
- strategies for the sustainable development of the resource (fish).

Case study links

This case study links with Chapter 13 – population growth – as an increase in population in one part of the world creates demands for food which may only be found in another part of the world.

Learn it!

a) Explain the reasons for the growth in demand of the natural resource, fish.

b) Describe the environmental effects of over-fishing in the North Sea.

c) Describe the EU strategies for the sustainable development of the fishing industry.

Conservation

Conservation means the total protection of animals and their habitats, as in nature reserves. In other cases, conservation can include artificial environments. In fishing one method of conservation is through **fish farms** which can provide a sustainable supply of fish.

Key words to know

Conservation
Fish farm

Fish farms (aqua culture)

Approximately ¼ of the fish we eat comes from farmed sources. China produces ⅓ of this amount and is the only country where the production of farmed fish is greater than that of caught fish. In the USA ⅓ of the shrimps, ½ of the salmon and nearly all the trout are farmed. Farmed salmon in Scotland is a major business, supplying British supermarkets.

Aqua culture was seen by many, at first, as a solution to the reduction of fish stocks and the rising demand for fish. However, there are many drawbacks to this type of fish production.

For	Against
In 2003 35 million salmon were eaten, three times more than in 1993	One salmon is given the equivalent of a bath full of water in which to survive
Aqua culture provides 6500 jobs on a world scale	Fish food may contain dead fish (think about BSE). Antibiotics are fed to fish which may enter our food chain. A poor diet of pellets means salmon lose their colour so pink artificial colouring is added to the fish food.
The government recommends fish as part of a healthy balanced diet	
As wild salmon and sea trout are driven towards extinction this is an effective way of rearing salmon	Some farms are plagued by parasites (sea lice) and disease; there is a high death toll amongst young fish
Large profits made by fish farming companies	Fish excrement is pink (because of added colouring) and is polluting the shell fish (mussels) further down stream and on the seabed

Figure 6.9 The arguments for and against fish farming

Sustainable development of energy and other resources

Check this!...

1. Is fish farming the answer to the increased demand for fish from around the world?
2. Look at the arguments for and against fish farming. Give your opinion as to whether you think fish farming is sustainable. What can be done to improve this situation?

EXAM PRACTICE

Figure 6.10 Possible sites for a wind farm

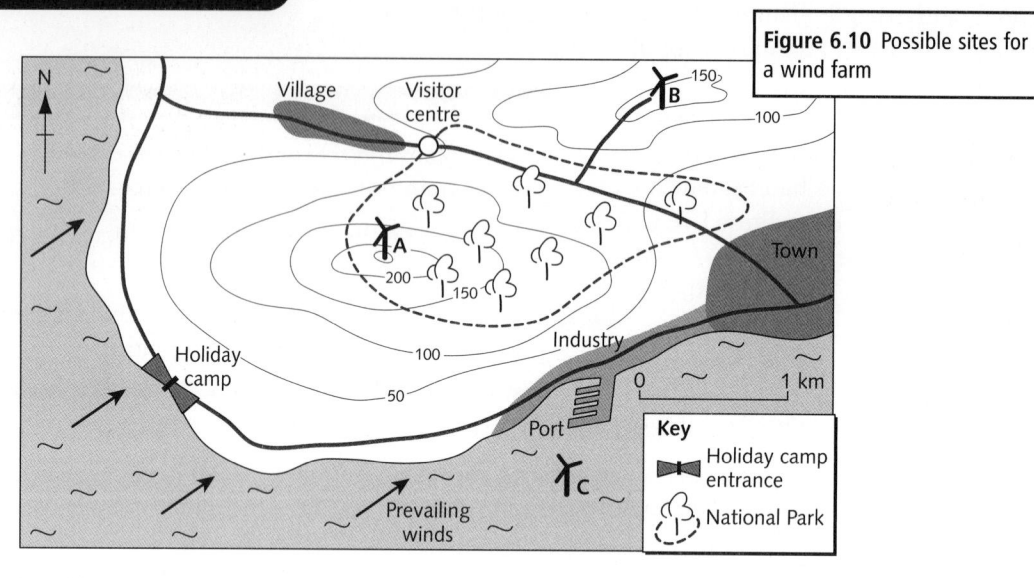

a Study Figure 6.10.
  i Give the height of the highest land. (1)
  ii Give the direction of the prevailing winds. (1)
  iii Give the shortest distance by road from the holiday camp entrance to the National Park Visitor Centre. (1)

b On Figure 6.10 **A**, **B**, and **C** are possible sites for three proposed wind farms.
  i Give **one** advantage and **one** disadvantage for site **A**. (2)
  ii Give **one** advantage and **one** disadvantage for site **B**. (2)
  iii Give **two** advantages and **two** disadvantages for site **C**. (4)
  iv State which you think is the best site. Explain what you think is the most important consideration when making your choice. (3)

c i Explain the term 'sustainable resources'. (2)
  ii Using a resource you have studied:
    1 describe **one** environmental effect caused by the development of the resource. (2)
    2 describe how future plans will ensure the sustainable development of the resource. (7)

Back to ...
The New Wider World website to check your answers to the Exam Practice question.

EXAM TIPS

Note the marks given in each question. This should reflect the time you spend on each answer. The number of lines on your exam paper below each question is another clue as to how much to write. Do not give one-word answers if there are 5 lines. On the other hand, do not overflow on to the extension pages unless you have made a mistake. Going on to these pages means you may be mistiming your answer and have difficulty finishing the exam.

The New Wider World, pp218–220; 256–268

7 Environmental change: Desertification and global warming

1 What are the physical and human causes of desertification in the Sahel?

Desertification means 'turning the land into desert'. Figure 7.1 shows the physical and human causes and effects of desertification.

Case Study

Desertification in the Sahel

Back to ...

The New Wider World pp256–258 for the case study of desertification in the Sahel.

Using your case study

Use the information in this case study and Figure 7.1 to answer questions on the physical and human causes and effects of desertification in the Sahel. Figure 15.38 on p256 of *The New Wider World* shows the extent of desertification in the Sahel. The outer limits extend and contract with periods of drought and rain. Figures 15.41 and 15.42 on p257 of *The New Wider World* show the results of overgrazing.

Case study links

This case study links with:
- Chapter 13 which explains population growth
- Chapter 12 which gives more detail about Kenya, a country on the edge of the Sahel.

Update

For more information on desertification in the Sahel use the link on *The New Wider World Coursemate* website.

Learn it!

a) Draw a map of the location of the Sahel giving the names of some of the countries involved and labelling the Sahara desert.

b) Explain how physical and human causes combine to create desertification.

c) Describe and explain the effects of desertification.

KEY QUESTIONS

1. What are the physical and human causes of desertification in the Sahel?

2. How effective are strategies in dealing with desertification?

3. What are the physical and human causes of global warming?

4. How effective are strategies in dealing with global warming?

Key words to know

Desertification
Overgrazing
Overcultivation
Deforestation

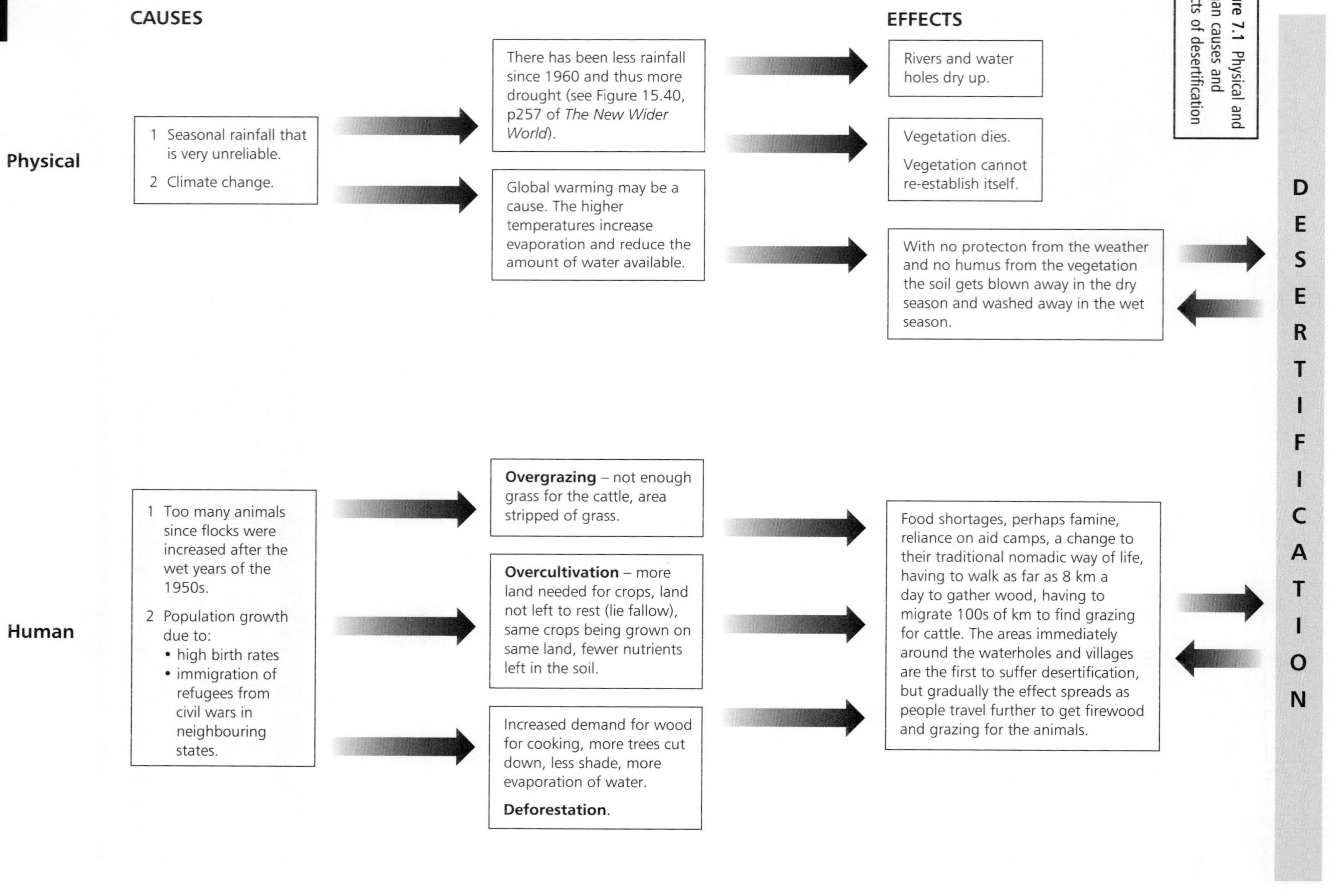

DESERTIFICATION

Figure 7.1 Physical and human causes and effects of desertification

EFFECTS

- Rivers and water holes dry up.
- Vegetation dies.
- Vegetation cannot re-establish itself.
- With no protection from the weather and no humus from the vegetation the soil gets blown away in the dry season and washed away in the wet season.
- Food shortages, perhaps famine, reliance on aid camps, a change to their traditional nomadic way of life, having to walk as far as 8 km a day to gather wood, having to migrate 100s of km to find grazing for cattle. The areas immediately around the waterholes and villages are the first to suffer desertification, but gradually the effect spreads as people travel further to get firewood and grazing for the animals.

CAUSES

Physical

- There has been less rainfall since 1960 and thus more drought (see Figure 15.40, p257 of *The New Wider World*).
- Global warming may be a cause. The higher temperatures increase evaporation and reduce the amount of water available.

1. Seasonal rainfall that is very unreliable.
2. Climate change.

Human

- **Overgrazing** – not enough grass for the cattle, area stripped of grass.
- **Overcultivation** – more land needed for crops, land not left to rest (lie fallow), same crops being grown on same land, fewer nutrients left in the soil.
- Increased demand for wood for cooking, more trees cut down, less shade, more evaporation of water. **Deforestation.**

1. Too many animals since flocks were increased after the wet years of the 1950s.
2. Population growth due to:
   - high birth rates
   - immigration of refugees from civil wars in neighbouring states.

2 How effective are strategies in dealing with desertification?

Case Study Extra

Strategies in the Sahel

Figure 7.2 Solutions to desertification

- Cloud seeding
- sand dune
- Rows of trees planted to prevent sand movement & act as wind break
- NO PASTORALISM
- Water trapped
- Magic stones trap water
- Lake could be extended by diverting River Zaire
- To L. Chad
- To El Salhiya
- CONSERVE WATER
- Nomadic Pastoralist
- Fence
- PROTECTED TREE providing shade for crops and animals.
- Woven basket, mud-lined, keeps out rodents and stores grain
- Settle down and the Government will show you how to look after the area.
- slow-burning stove
- Melons, tomatoes, maize, millet grown with extra water and fertiliser from animals.

SOLUTIONS TO DESERTIFICATION

Environmental change: Desertification and global warming

Strategies for reducing the effects of desertification in the Sahel

1 Make rainfall more reliable
- Cloud seeding. This would be a large-scale, high-tech solution which is not always successful. Some people consider that the atmosphere should not be tampered with.

2 Obtain more water
- Large-scale dam schemes to irrigate crops, e.g. areas of the Sudan from the Nile. This is successful initially but gradually, in this climate, crop growth becomes stunted. The high temperatures and dry conditions mean the soil moisture moves up to the surface carrying minerals in solution. The water evaporates leaving salt concentrations on the surface. This is called **salinisation**.
- Large scale water diversions, e.g. River Zaire to Lake Chad.
- Irrigation in Niger combined with better water management, increased mechanisation on farms, and education, resulted in increasing rice yields by threefold in the 1990s.
- Ditches dug in depressions between dunes to tap seasonal water have doubled wheat yields near Lake Chad.
- Drilling boreholes deep into rocks. This needs money and expertise from outside.
- Magic stones: piles of stones placed across the slope stops surface water from quickly running away and eroding the soil. The collected water has time to sink into the dry soil.

3 Regenerate vegetation
- Plant trees and shrubs across the southern fringe of the Sahel to create a green belt, e.g. Tree Aid, a British charity.
- Control grazing in enclosed areas, become less nomadic.
- Plant trees for fuel, fodder, shade and windbreaks, e.g. The Green Cross programme in Burkina Faso with education on plant growth, nurseries of young trees and fuel saving stoves.
- Re-seed areas with new varieties of drought resistant crops, use chemical fertilisers and pesticides, e.g. millet and cotton, Senegal, early maturing millet from south Mali planted now in north Mali.

4 Improve soils
- Use dung from animals as fertiliser, e.g. increased maize yields by threefold in Mali.
- Re-introduce crop rotation.

Opinions on the strategies
Some people think that the most effective solutions are large-scale, **high-tech** strategies provided as aid money and expertise from governments outside the region. Others think that many smaller self-help schemes that use **local technology** are more effective in reaching individuals. These are usually associated with **non-governmental organisations (NGOs)**, e.g. Oxfam.

Key words to know

The Sahel
Salinisation
High-tech
Local technology
Non-governmental organisation (NGO)

Using your case study
Use this case study to answer questions which ask you about plans/strategies to reduce the effects of desertification in the Sahel. The opinion section and Chapters 12 and 13 explain the significance and effects of values and attitudes in developing such strategies.

Case study links
This case study links with:
- Chapter 12 which discusses the level of success in tackling desertification in Kenya
- Chapter 13 which describes the different types of aid.

Update
For more information on desertification in specific countries use the link on *The New Wider World Coursemate* website.

Learn it!

a) Describe the strategies that are used to deal with desertification.

b) Different people have different opinions as to the best strategies to use; what do you consider to be the best way forward? Give your reasons.

3 What are the physical and human causes of global warming?

What is global warming?

The **greenhouse effect** may be causing world temperatures to rise – **global warming**.

The greenhouse effect is caused by human activity increasing **greenhouse gases** which trap heat below them.

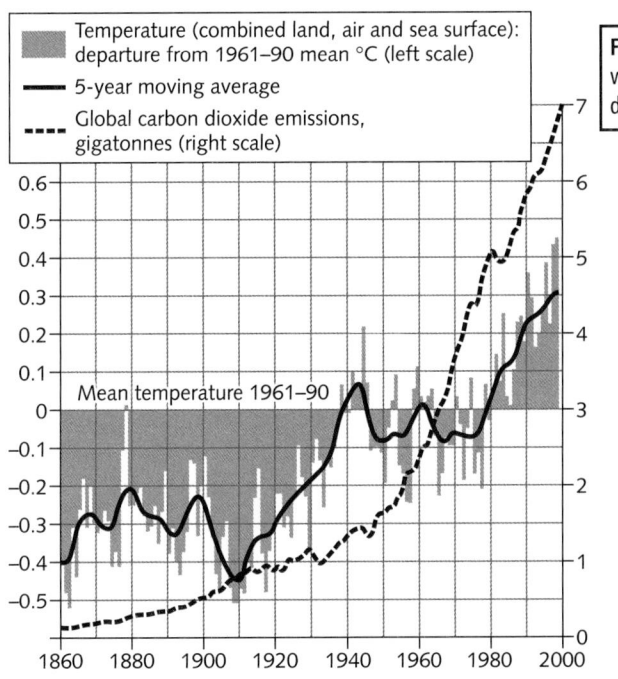

Figure 7.3 Global warming and carbon dioxide emissions

Temperature (combined land, air and sea surface): departure from 1961–90 mean °C (left scale)
— 5-year moving average
--- Global carbon dioxide emissions, gigatonnes (right scale)

Key words to know

Greenhouse effect
Global warming
Greenhouse gases

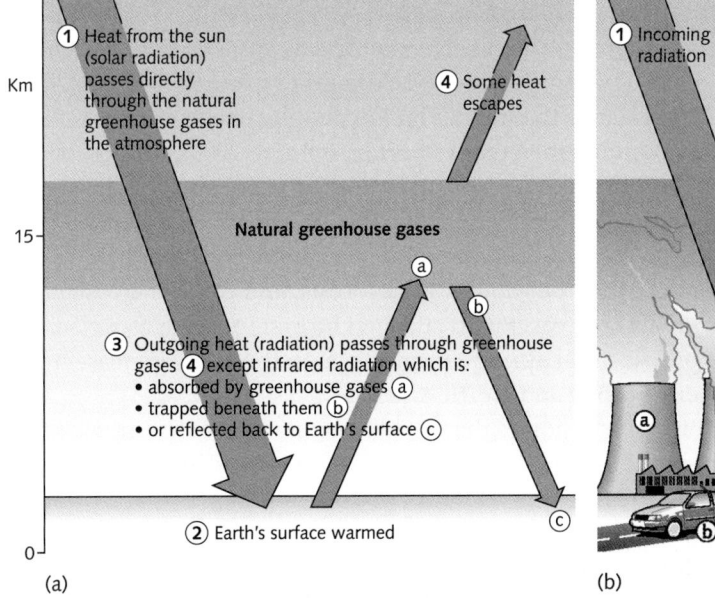

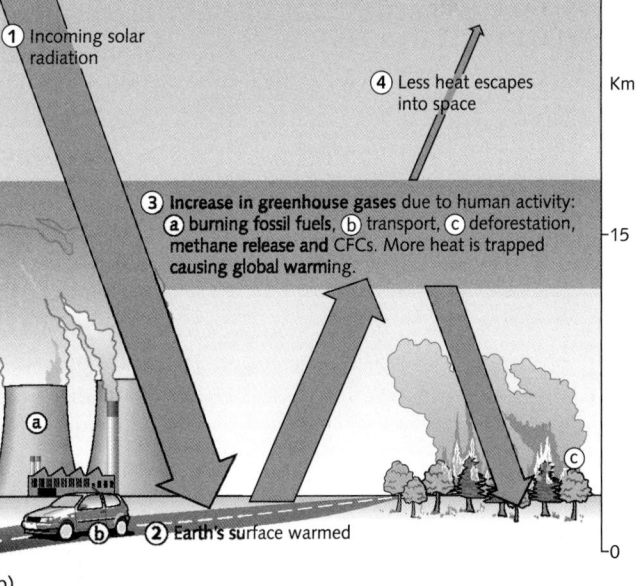

Figure 7.4 The greenhouse effect
(a) Balanced system keeping the Earth's temperature constant with little human activity
(b) Unbalanced system with increased CO_2 from human activity

(a)
1. Heat from the sun (solar radiation) passes directly through the natural greenhouse gases in the atmosphere
2. Earth's surface warmed
3. Outgoing heat (radiation) passes through greenhouse gases 4 except infrared radiation which is:
   • absorbed by greenhouse gases (a)
   • trapped beneath them (b)
   • or reflected back to Earth's surface (c)
4. Some heat escapes

Natural greenhouse gases

(b)
1. Incoming solar radiation
2. Earth's surface warmed
3. **Increase in greenhouse gases** due to human activity: (a) **burning fossil fuels**, (b) transport, (c) deforestation, methane release and CFCs. More heat is trapped **causing global warming**.
4. Less heat escapes into space

Environmental change: Desertification and global warming

Causes of global warming

The major contributors to global warming are 'greenhouse gases' released into the atmosphere. The proportions of greenhouse gases are:

• 72 % carbon dioxide produced by: – road vehicles – burning fossil fuels in power stations, in factories and in the home – deforestation and the burning of the tropical rainforests.	• 13 % CFCs (chlorofluorocarbons) from: – aerosols – air conditioners – foam packaging – refrigerators. These are the most damaging of the greenhouse gases.	• 10 % methane is released from decaying organic matter: – peat bogs – swamps – landfill sites – animal dung – farms.	• 5 % nitrous oxide is emitted from: – car exhausts – power stations – agricultural fertiliser.

Effects of global warming

1 Rise in sea-level caused by:
- icecaps and glaciers melting (since 1960, sea-ice in the Arctic has retreated by 15 per cent and is 40 per cent less thick). The release of water at present held in storage as ice and snow could raise the world's sea-level by a further 5 m.
- increasing sea temperatures. This causes water in the oceans to expand resulting in rising sea-levels (predicted rise of 0.4 metres). A rise of 1 m could flood 25 per cent of Bangladesh, 30 per cent of Egypt's arable land, and totally submerge several low-lying islands in the Indian and Pacific Oceans (Figure 7.5). At present, 40 per cent of the world's population live within 100 km of the coast – many people are vulnerable to rising sea-levels and storm surges (Chapter 3 p21).

2 The distribution of rainfall is predicted to change. Places with:
- sufficient rainfall are likely to get more, resulting in increased flooding (e.g. northern Europe)
- insufficient rainfall are likely to get less in terms of both amount and reliability, giving increased drought (e.g. much of Africa). One prediction claims that the 1.7 billion people (one-third of the world's population) already short of water in 2000 could become 5 billion by 2025.

3 Plants and wildlife may not have the time to adjust to rapid changes in climate, and die (coral reefs, mangrove swamps, wetlands, coniferous and tropical forests, and tropical grassland).

4 Crop yields are expected to fall even further in Africa as well as in parts of Asia and Latin America, although they may increase in northern Europe and North America.

5 A greater proportion of the world's population will be at risk from insect-borne (e.g. malaria and dengue fever) and water-borne (e.g. cholera) diseases.

The effects will be greatest in the LEDCs – in water and food shortages, diseases and natural disasters – places where people can least afford to adapt or are unable to migrate.

Figure 7.5 Predicted effects of global warming on the UK and the world

UK map labels:
- Cities likely to be subject to flooding
- Areas less than 5 metres above present-day mean sea-level, liable to flooding
- 0 — 200 km
- Arctic plants will face extinction
- Insufficient snow for winter sports in Aviemore to continue
- Area and yields of cereals will increase
- Higher yields of potatoes, sugarbeet and outdoor tomatoes
- Maize, vines, oranges and peaches will be grown in southern England
- More pests and diseases will exist due to mild winters
- Many coastal ports will be flooded
- Need for irrigation in summer
- Length of growing season will increase
- Trees such as Scots pine will grow higher up hillsides. More deciduous trees at lower levels
- Plants and shrubs will be able to grow further north
- Greater risk of forest fires
- Sea defences costing over £10 billion likely
- Valuable farmland in the Fens lost
- Loss of Norfolk Broads and salt marshes
- Houses of Parliament and Trafalgar Square flooded. The Thames Barrier will be ineffectual

World map labels:
- Flooding in The Netherlands
- Crops can be grown further north due to warmer weather
- Alpine ski resorts close down due to lack of snow
- Floods in Nile delta
- Floods in Bangladesh
- Drier conditions reduce grain harvest
- Too warm for coniferous forests
- Higher rainfall increases rice yields
- Drier conditions reduce grain harvest
- Arctic Ocean ice sheet could melt completely – already thinning by 40%
- Limit of permafrost will retreat northwards
- Longer growing season allows higher wheat yields
- Floods in Florida
- Increased tropical storm activity
- Pacific islands such as Tuvalu, Kiribati group and Marshall Islands likely to be submerged
- Tropical diseases in Africa likely to spread northwards
- Reduced rainfall in rainforests due to deforestation
- Drier conditions reduces cereal production and water supply
- Increased yields due to higher temperatures
- Icebergs from break-up of Antarctic ice shelf could endanger shipping
- Reduced rainfall in rainforests due to deforestation

Cities marked: London, Venice, Alexandria, Lagos, Tokyo, New York, Miami

Environmental change: Desertification and global warming

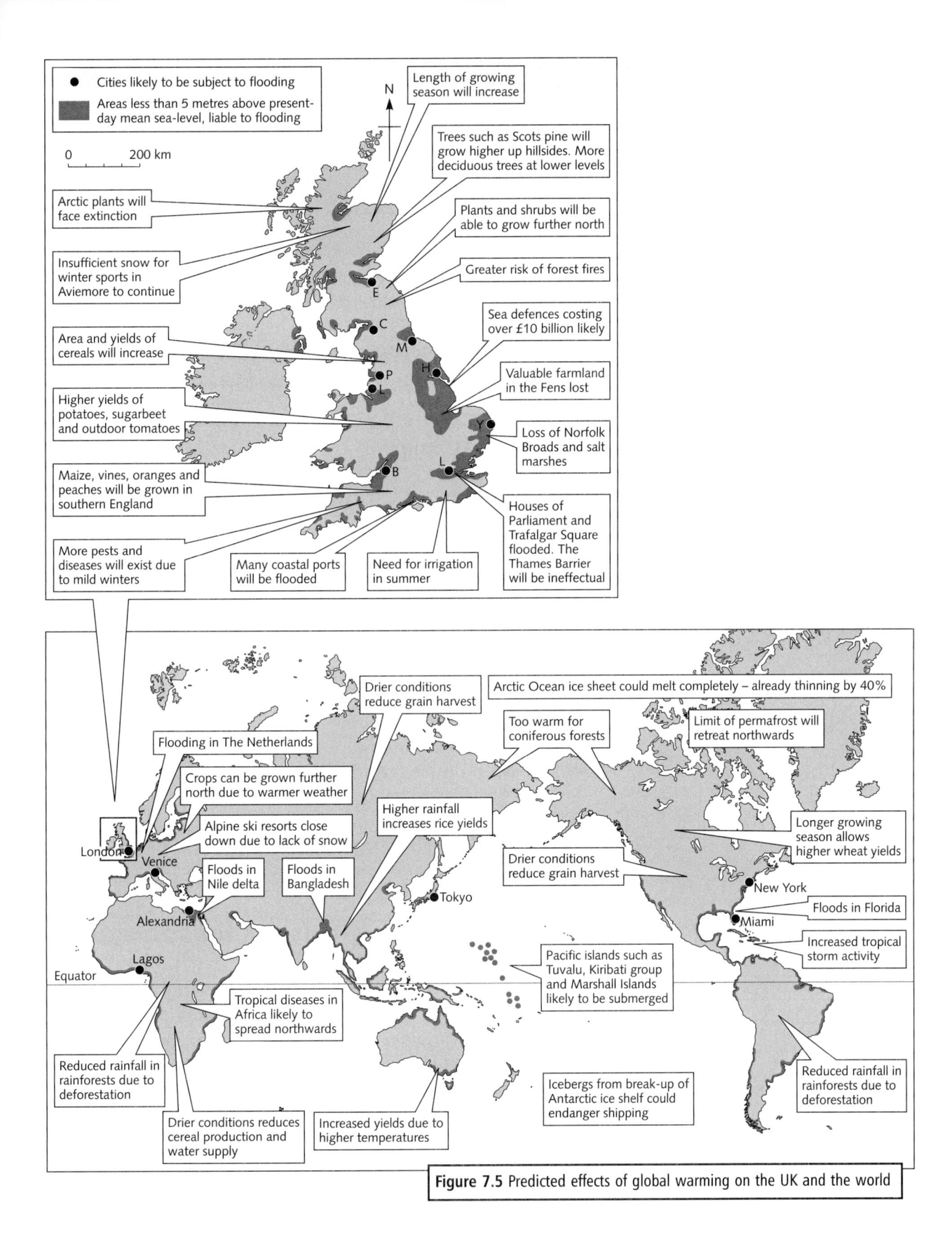

> *Check this!...*
>
> 1 Use Figure 7.3 to answer the following questions.
>   a) What happened to global temperatures from 1910 to 1945?
>   b) What has happened to temperatures since 1975?
>   c) Describe the global CO_2 emissions from 1860 to 2000.
> 2 Explain the greenhouse effect.
> 3 Design a poster to show the causes of global warming.
> 4 Draw up a table with two columns, one headed 'Benefits of global warming', the other, 'Problems of global warming'. Use Figure 7.5 to complete the table.

4 How effective are strategies in dealing with global warming?

What and who contributes most to global warming?

Since the MEDCs consume three-quarters of the world's energy, they are largely responsible for global warming.

Strategies to reduce global warming

1 Reduce CO_2 emissions.
- Change from fossil fuels to renewable energy.
- Invest in technology which uses less fuel.
- Cut down the number of cars:
  - develop public transport
  - tax fuel so people cannot afford to use the car as much
  - use alternative technology, e.g. electric cars, solar buses.

2 Plant more trees.
- Trees store CO_2 and reduce the amount of this greenhouse gas in the atmosphere. This is a contribution that can be made by non-industrialised and poorer tropical countries.

Effect of values and attitudes on the strategies for reducing global warming

In 1997 a World Summit was held in Kyoto to try to tackle this issue internationally. The agreement made was that all countries, including the poorer nations who are only just developing industrially, would cut greenhouse gas levels to 5 per cent below the 1990 level by 2010. This does not impress environmentalists who consider this is an inadequate target and wish to see emissions cut by 80 per cent.

In 2000 a follow-up conference was held in Holland at The Hague.

In 2001 under President Bush the USA pulled out of the agreement. The stated American policy was to use oil, one of the contributors to greenhouse gases, to increase the wealth of the country. The improved wealth would then be used to research into new technologies to reduce global warming.

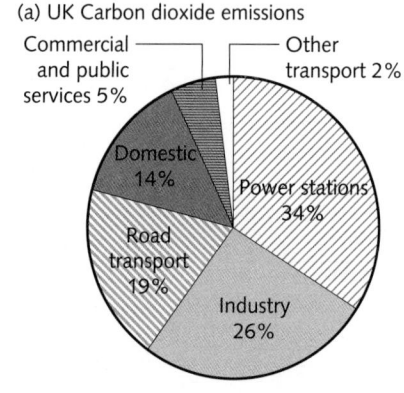

(a) UK Carbon dioxide emissions
- Commercial and public services 5%
- Other transport 2%
- Domestic 14%
- Power stations 34%
- Road transport 19%
- Industry 26%

(b) Main greenhouse gas emitters
- 1.7% Italy
- 1.9% Indonesia
- 2.4% UK
- 3.7% India
- 3.8% Germany
- 4.3% Brazil
- 5.1% Japan
- 9.9% China
- 13.6% Former USSR
- 19.1% USA

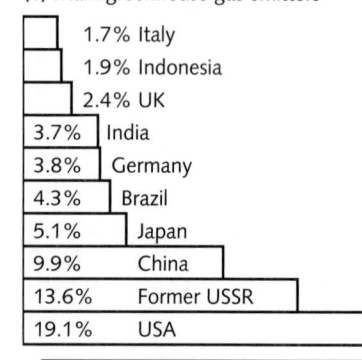

Figure 7.6 (a) Sources of UK carbon dioxide emissions (b) Countries that emit the most greenhouse gases

Check this!...

1. Which a) activities and b) countries contribute most to global warming?
2. Which strategy(ies) do you think will be the most effective to reduce global warming? In your argument include the strengths and weaknesses of each of the strategies mentioned on p58.
3. How do different values and attitudes affect the strategies adopted to reduce global warming?

EXAM PRACTICE

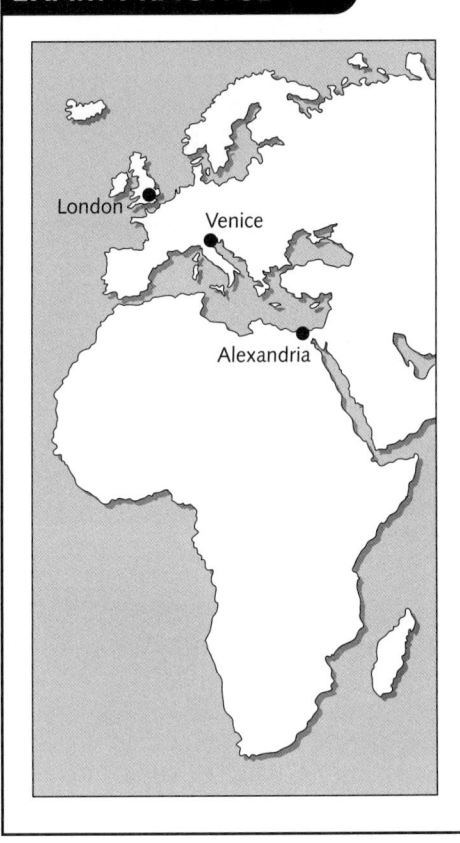

a Copy the map outline of Figure 7.7.
  i On the map, draw in the extent of the Sahel in North Africa. (2)
  ii Give **two** physical effects of desertification. (2)
  iii Give **two** human effects of desertification. (2)
  iv Explain how increasing use of firewood is causing desertification. (2)

b i On your copy of Figure 7.7, draw a labelled arrow to describe and show the location of:
   1 **one** positive effect of global warming
   2 **two** negative effects of global warming. (3)
  ii With the aid of a labelled diagram explain the term 'the greenhouse effect'. (5)

c i Describe strategies to reduce the effects of **either** desertification **or** global warming. (6)
  ii Which of the strategies you described in question ci do you think will be the most successful to reduce the effects of the environmental change? Explain why. (3)

Figure 7.7 A map of Africa and Europe

EXAM TIPS

The examiner has to mark the quality of your writing, especially in the extended answers. This includes the use of geographical terms. So use words such as deforestation or ozone layer in question ci.

Back to ...

The New Wider World website to check your answers to the Exam Practice question.

Environmental change: Desertification and global warming   59

8 The fragile world – decisions

Decision Making Excercise 1

The National Assembly of Wales wants to increase the proportion of electricity generated from renewable energy. Two proposals to generate electricity from renewable tidal energy in the Severn Estuary are under discussion. One involves a barrage to be built across the estuary and the other involves underwater turbines.

a Use Figures 8.1a and b to answer the following questions.

 i In which direction was the camera pointing when the photograph was taken? (1)

 ii Name the road on the bridge ① and the town ②. (2)

 iii Describe the change in the width of the estuary upstream. (1)

 iv This is a land area that is often flooded. Describe **two** physical features that might contribute to flooding in the area. (2)

 v Describe **two** effects of flooding south-west of Chepstow. (2)

Figure 8.1a Oblique aerial view of the Severn Estuary

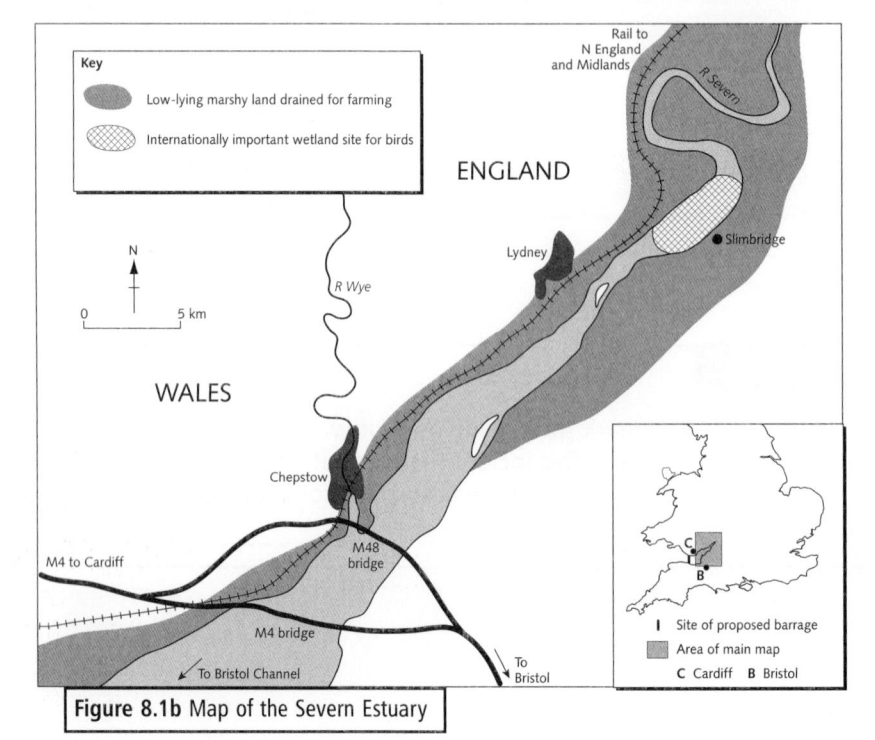

Figure 8.1b Map of the Severn Estuary

Key
- Low-lying marshy land drained for farming
- Internationally important wetland site for birds

I Site of proposed barrage
Area of main map
C Cardiff B Bristol

60

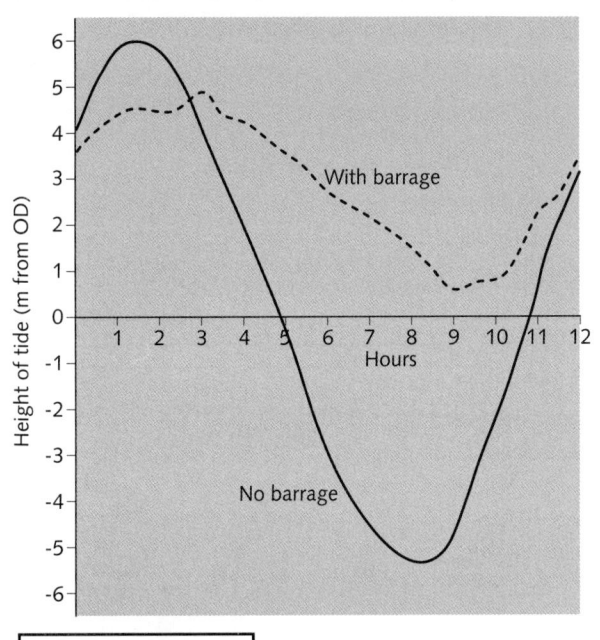

Figure 8.1c Tidal graph

b The water in the Severn Estuary near the bridges has the second highest tidal range in the world. Study Figure 8.1c.

  i Give the height at high tide with no barrage. (1)

  ii Give the height at low tide with no barrage. (1)

  iii Give the tidal range with no barrage. (1)

  iv Give the tidal range if the barrage was to be built. (1)

  v How would the change in tidal range caused by a barrage affect the speed of tidal currents flowing in and out of the estuary? (1)

The fragile world – decisions

c Mud flats created by tides are very important to wading birds. They provide food and resting grounds. The birds are a tourist attraction in the estuary. Slimbridge is a wildfowl and wetland centre where visitors go to watch the birds.

   i Give the type of graph you would choose to represent the values in Figure 8.2a. (1)
   ii Why is this the most suitable graph? (2)
   iii Describe the type of visitors to Slimbridge Wildfowl and Wetland Centre. (2)

(a)

Type of visitor to Slimbridge 2003	
Adults	48 000
Old Age Pensioners	29 000
Families, including children	25 000
Education	12 000
Total	114 000

Figure 8.2 (a) Slimbridge data
(b) Diagram of underwater tidal turbines

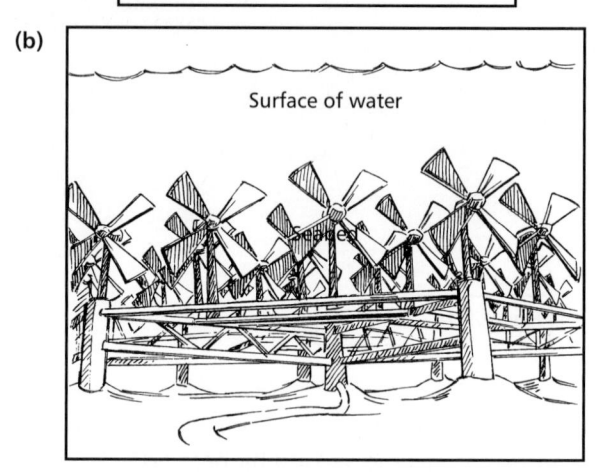

(b) Surface of water

A The Severn barrage
The original proposal to use the tidal energy of the Severn was to build a barrage (Figure 8.1b) of large concrete blocks with sluices and turbines in them. There was to be a road across the top and locks for ships to pass through. This plan was reconsidered in 2002 with the need to meet Government targets for increased use of renewable energy. The cost would be over £10 billion but the barrage would supply over 5 per cent of the current UK electricity consumption.

B New plan for electricity from tidal flow. BBC, 9 February 2003
The Government has given a grant of £1.6 million to develop underwater electrical generators (Figure 8.2b). The turbines will be dropped on the seabed between the two Severn bridges. Five turbines are proposed which will produce enough electricity to power hundreds of homes.

d Read schemes **A** and **B** above. Decide which **one** of the schemes you would support.

Use all the information provided in Figures 8.1 and 8.2 to make arguments for and against each proposal. (7)

Back to ...

The New Wider World website to check your answers to Decision-making Exercise 1.

EXAM TIPS

When describing an area from a map you are able to identify and measure the size, distance and direction of features. Photographs are better for describing what features look like.

To work out direction on a photo: find one easily recognisable feature on both the photo and map; find a second feature on both; then using the north point on the map work out the direction you are looking towards in the photo.

Decision Making Excercise 2

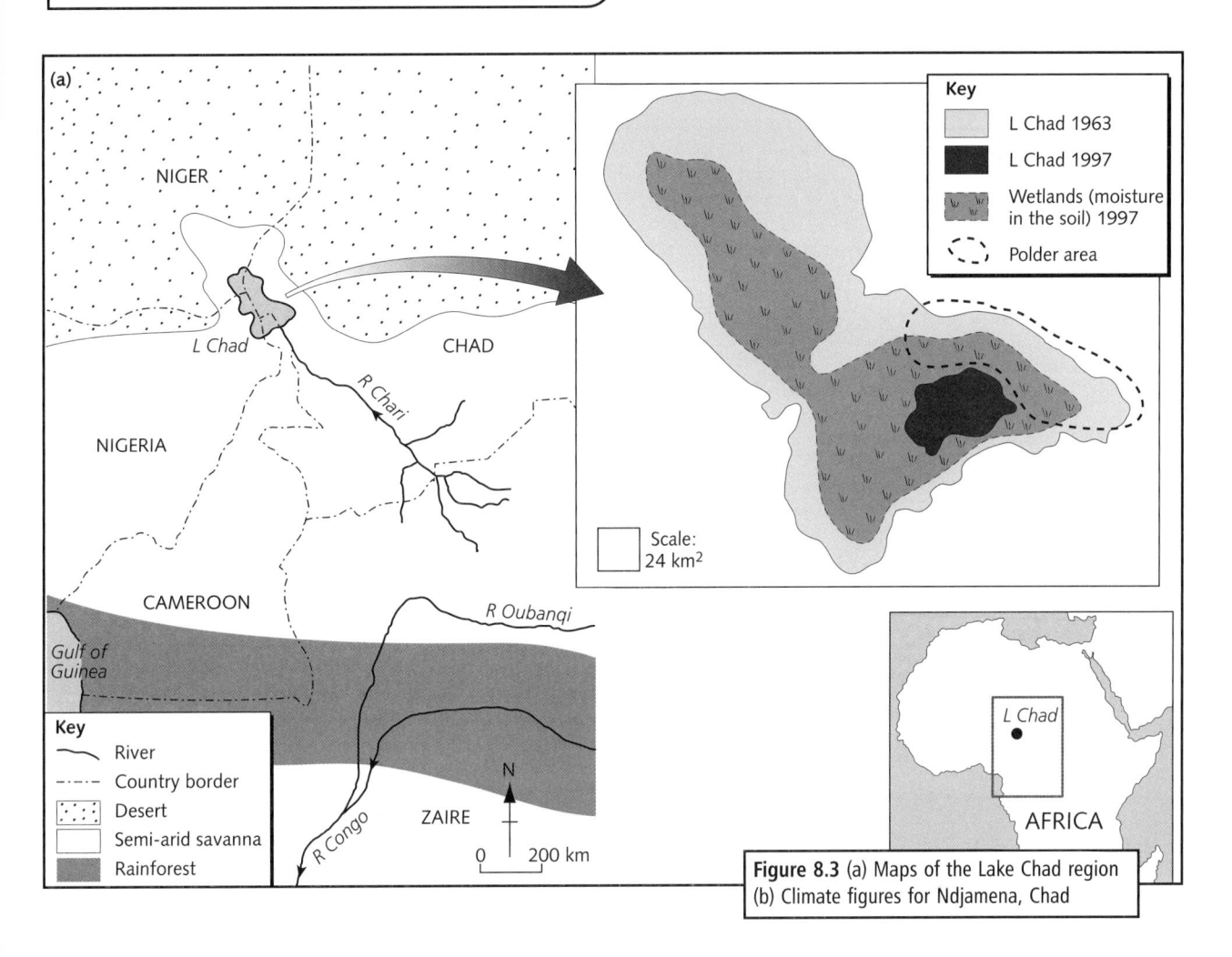

Figure 8.3 (a) Maps of the Lake Chad region (b) Climate figures for Ndjamena, Chad

(b)	Climate figures											
	J	F	M	A	M	J	J	A	S	O	N	D
Rainfall (mm)	0	0	0	10	20	50	140	175	85	20	0	0
Max temp (°C)	32	35	39	41	40	37	34	32	34	37	36	34
Min temp (°C)	14	17	21	25	26	25	23	22	23	22	18	15

a Study Figure 8.3a.
  i How many countries share Lake Chad? (1)
  ii What is the only source of water for Lake Chad (other than direct rainfall)? (1)
  iii Describe **two** changes in shape to Lake Chad from 1963 to 1997. (2)

b Study Figure 8.3b.
  i Give the temperature range in January. (1)
  ii Give the combined rainfall in July, August and September. (1)
  iii What percentage of the total rainfall occurs in these three months?
  5 %   50 %   80 %   90 %   (1)
  iv During the course of a year describe the effects of rainfall on lake levels. (1)

The fragile world – decisions

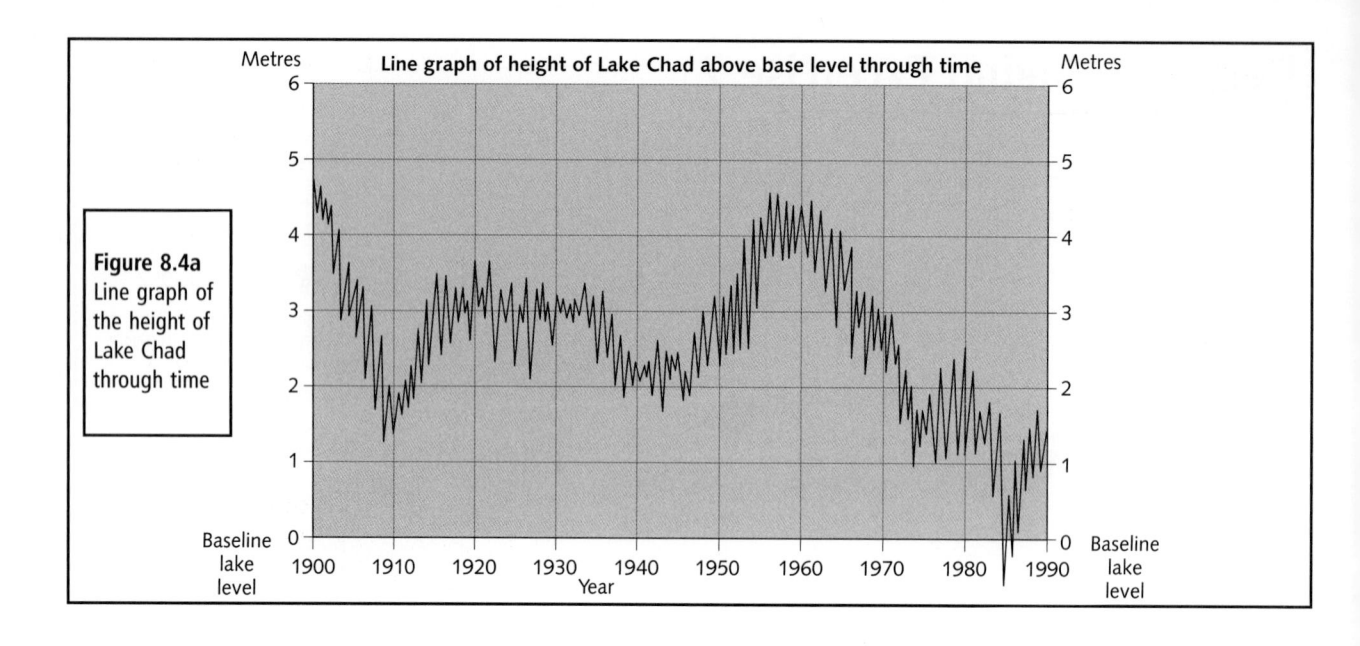

Figure 8.4a Line graph of the height of Lake Chad through time

Line graph of height of Lake Chad above base level through time (y-axis: Metres 0–6, from Baseline lake level; x-axis: Year, 1900–1990)

Lake Chad
30 % decrease in lake size 1966–1975
- 95 % due to climate change
- 5 % due to irrigation.

Further decrease in lake size 1983–1994
- 50 % due to climate change
- 50 % due to irrigation.

South Chad Irrigation Scheme
55 000 farming families were resettled with the number of villages rising from 40 to 100. The irrigation scheme has been inefficient with unlined canals, high water loss through seepage, undisciplined farmers who breach the canals to get more water and waterlog their fields.

Chad
1987 – the country had a debt of US$330 million, with a debt to GDP ratio of 28 %.
1997 – the country had a debt of US$1 billion, with a debt to GDP ratio of 55 %.
There is a history of local warfare in the region.

Figure 8.4b Some facts about the area of Lake Chad

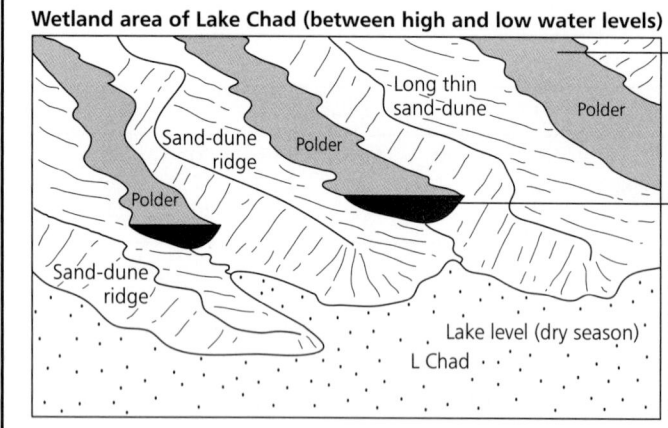

Wetland area of Lake Chad (between high and low water levels)

Labels: Long thin sand-dune, Polder, Sand-dune ridge, Polder, Sand-dune ridge, Lake level (dry season) L Chad

Polders – flat fertile areas between sand-dunes

Small earth dam stops water overflowing on to polder in wet season so crops can be grown. Small pumps bring in water from the lake in dry season. Crops can be grown all year.

Figure 8.4c Polder farming on the north east shores of Lake Chad

c Study Figure 8.4a.

  i Describe the changes in height of the lake shown by the graph. (4)

  ii An irrigation scheme, South Chad Irrigation Project, was developed in the mid 1960s to the south-west of Lake Chad in Nigeria. This depended on lake levels being 2 metres above base level. When did the lake stop being able to supply the irrigation system? (1)

  iii Use Figures 8.4a and b to give **three** reasons why this scheme has not brought sustainable development to the region. (3)

d Two new projects are proposed for the Lake Chad area:

- Connect the constantly flowing Congo Rivers, from the Central African Republic by canal to the Upper Chari and Oubangui rivers to Lake Chad to raise its water levels again (Figure 8.3a).
- Develop polder farming as shown in Figures 8.3a and 8.4c.

Using Figure 8.3a:

  i Give the distance from the nearest point of the River Oubangi to Lake Chad. (1)

  ii On what shore of 1997 Lake Chad is the polder area? (1)

  iii Which project do you consider to be better for the region? Give your arguments. (7)

EXAM TIPS

Some questions ask for your opinion. However, marks are not given for your opinion but for the argument, and evidence you give, which lead to your opinion. The best opinions are developed by arguing the pros/advantages and then the cons/disadvantages of each of the options you have been asked to consider. Arrive at your opinion/decision/conclusion by stating which arguments are the strongest.

Back to ...

The New Wider World website to check your answers to Decision-making Exercise 2.

Unit 2: The interdependent world

9 Farming and industry

➪ *The New Wider World*, pp96; 98; 100; 106–109; 136–142

1 What factors affect the location and characteristics of one major farming type?

The farming system

Farming is a **system** with **inputs** into the farm, **processes** which take place on the farm and **outputs** from the farm. You need to study one major type of farming. Hill sheep farming in Snowdonia is the one covered in this book.

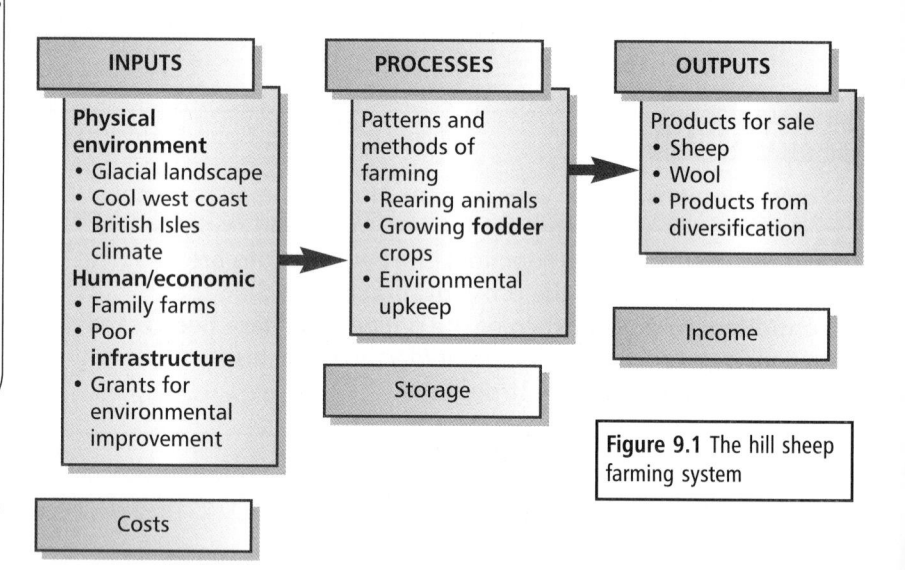

KEY QUESTIONS

1. What factors affect the location and characteristics of one major farming type?
2. What are the recent changes in this type of farming, and their social consequences?
3. Why have urban/industrial regions seen a decline in their traditional primary and secondary industries?
4. How successful are these regions in regeneration through modern secondary, tertiary or quaternary industry?

INPUTS

Physical environment
- Glacial landscape
- Cool west coast
- British Isles climate

Human/economic
- Family farms
- Poor **infrastructure**
- Grants for environmental improvement

Costs

PROCESSES

Patterns and methods of farming
- Rearing animals
- Growing **fodder** crops
- Environmental upkeep

Storage

OUTPUTS

Products for sale
- Sheep
- Wool
- Products from diversification

Income

Figure 9.1 The hill sheep farming system

Key words to know

System
Input
Process
Output
Infrastructure
Fodder

Case Study Extra

Hill sheep farming in Snowdonia

Using your case study
The information in Figure 9.2 can be used to answer questions on the factors affecting the location of one major farming type in one area within the UK.

Case study links
This case study has links with:
- Chapter 1 which describes the glaciated landscape of the area
- Chapter 4 which describes the climate.

Update
For more information on hill sheep farming in Snowdonia use the link on *The New Wider World Coursemate* website.

Learn it!

a) Draw a map of the location of Snowdonia National Park.

b) Explain the physical and economic factors that result in hill sheep being the main type of farming in the area.

66

1 A glaciated mountainous area, rising to over 800 m in Snowdonia, Berwyn and Cader Idris range, Plynlimon. Deep, steep-sided glaciated valleys with marshy, flat floors. Steep relief means low levels of mechanisation on valley sides (tractors cannot work on slopes over 15°). Quad bikes are used on mountain tops for collecting the sheep.

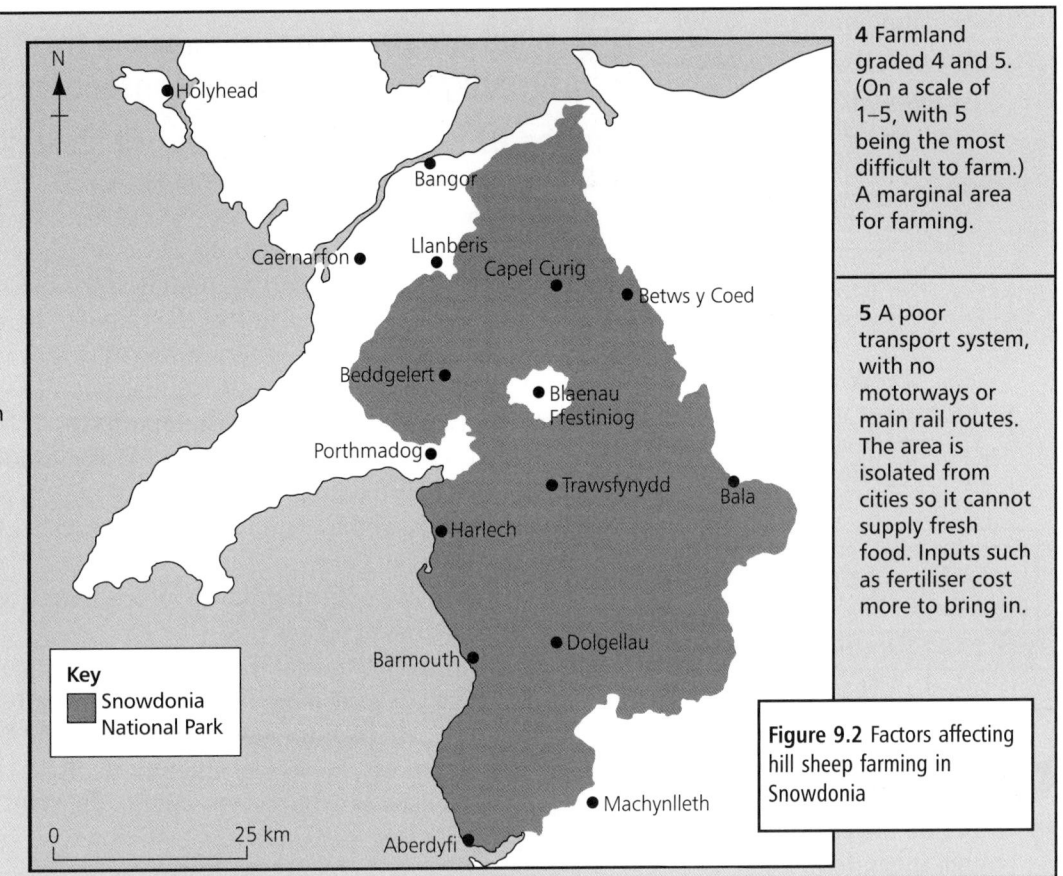

4 Farmland graded 4 and 5. (On a scale of 1–5, with 5 being the most difficult to farm.) A marginal area for farming.

5 A poor transport system, with no motorways or main rail routes. The area is isolated from cities so it cannot supply fresh food. Inputs such as fertiliser cost more to bring in.

Figure 9.2 Factors affecting hill sheep farming in Snowdonia

2 Over 2000 mm of rain, often in the form of downpours, with some heavy snow in winter. A problem of fertiliser or lime, used to improve pasture on the valley sides, being washed away. Temperatures 4–5°C in January, 15–16°C in July, with the deep valleys often shaded from the sun. The area has a short growing season. Lambing is late so there is no access to the higher prices of 'early spring lamb'.

3 Very thin soils on the steep mountain sides with thick, clayey, waterlogged soils in the valley floor and peaty, acid soils on the mountaintops.

6 Family run farms. The grazing areas are commonland.

What are the characteristics of hill sheep farming?

Figure 9.3 Land use on a hill sheep farm, mid Wales

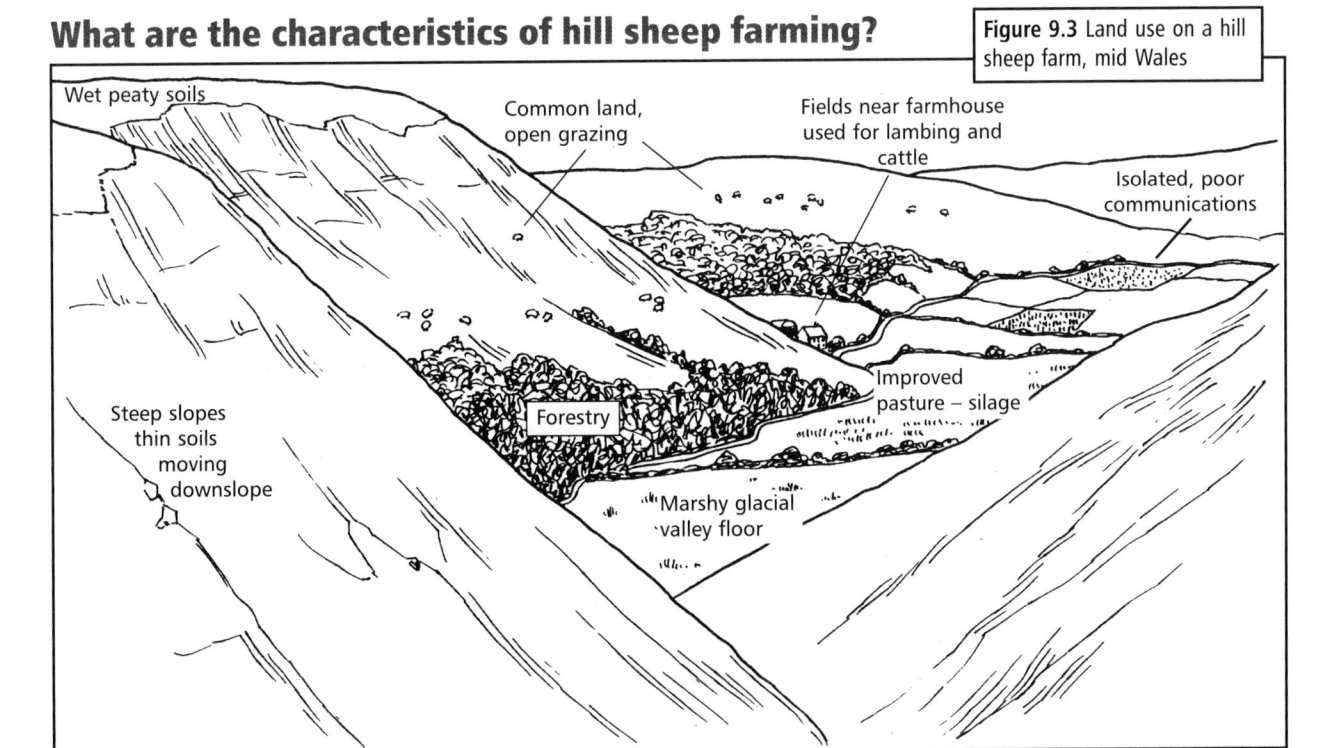

Farming and industry 67

Key words to know
Subsidies
Common Agricultural Policy (CAP)
Tariffs
Set-aside

Back to ...
The New Wider World **p107** for further information on the EU and its policies affecting farming.

Figure 9.4 Annual income from hill sheep farms (DEFRA – Department for Rural Affairs)

1995–1998	2001–2002	2002–2003
£11,700	£4,800	£9,500

Check this!...

1. Describe the characteristics of hill sheep farming in Snowdonia. Use the sketch in Figure 9.3.
2. Explain the causes of change in hill sheep farming.

2 What are the recent changes in this type of farming, and their social consequences?

Causes of recent changes in hill sheep farming

a) Decrease in European Union (EU) **subsidies**.
   The **Common Agricultural Policy (CAP)** 1962:
   - created a single market across the EU in which agricultural products could move freely without **tariffs** (see Chapter 14)
   - gave subsidies which meant that the EU would buy any farm produce for a fixed price. This resulted in overproduction and food mountains.
   - encouraged an increase in field and farm size
   - provided **set-aside** grants to leave fields as meadowland.

b) Other reasons for the decline in hill sheep farmers' income:
   - The high value of the pound means less lamb has been exported to Europe.
   - A fall in the price of farm produce means it now costs more to produce lamb than people pay to buy it.
   - Hard wearing Welsh wool was used for carpets but synthetic fibres are now used. It costs more to employ a shearer than the Wool Marketing Board pays for a fleece.
   - The loss of exports due to foot and mouth disease in 2001. Local abattoirs have been shut down so animals have to be moved a long way to a larger abattoir. An abattoir in Gaerwen, Anglesey received infected animals from Yorkshire. Many farms in Powys were involved in the policy of slaughtering all the livestock within a given distance of infected animals.

c) Supermarkets now control 84 per cent of the food sold in the UK. As the main market they control where they buy lamb, and the quality and type of meat they require, e.g. less fat, organic production. Some farmers now have contracts with the main supermarket chains.

Case Study Extra

Recent changes in hill sheep farming in Snowdonia

What are the changes?

Farms in the area have had to change to earn extra money in order to survive. They have changed in a number of ways:

a) Increased the size of the farms. 800 hectares is typical in Snowdonia.
b) Through **diversification**. This includes:
   - tourism, e.g. a stay at Snowdonia Farm Cottages includes taking part in the traditional way of life of sheep farmers
   - caravan/camping parks, e.g. in the Tal-y Llyn valley
   - developing wood products, e.g. wood flooring
   - wind farm rents, e.g. near Caemaes
   - pony trekking
   - rearing special breeds, e.g. Jacob sheep, deer
   - educational visits, e.g. to Merthyr Farm, Gwynedd
   - outdoor activities on the farm, e.g. quad biking, paintball, archery.
c) Environmental developments. New grants to maintain the traditional rural landscape.
   Tir Gofel 1999 took the best features of the previous **agri-environment schemes** – the 'Tir cymen' and 'environmentally sensitive areas scheme', already in existence in the Lleyn Peninsula and the Cambrian Mountains. Farmers apply for a five year agreement to receive payments for: *'farming in a way which conserves the landscape, wildlife and archaeological and historic interest of an area'*.

Figure 9.5 The Tir Gofel scheme

- Wildlife – provide streamside and pond environments
- Field boundaries – keep slate walls and hedges
- Organic farming – pay farmers not to use herbicides, pesticides, fertilisers
- Old farm buildings – to be restored and no new buildings built
- Increase public access – within Snowdonia by maintaining footpaths across farmland.

Back to …

The New Wider World p108 Figure 7.31 for a photograph showing the advantages of hedgerows and p109 for further information on organic farming.

2000	£4 million
2001	£7.5 million
2002	£10.9 million
2003	£12.4 million

Figure 9.6 Money given in Tir Gofel grants across Wales

d) **'Farming Connect'**. The Snowdonia National Park advises on grants provided by the Welsh Assembly. More money is available to 'young farmers' (18–39 years) in an attempt to stop young people leaving the farms. Grants available in 2004 include:

- enterprise – developing alternative crops/animals, processing of non-food farm products, providing rural services to the community
- tourism
- food processing – changing to 'added-value' farm products, e.g. selling lamb burgers
- timber processing.

What are the social consequences of these changes?

If farms did not change they would go out of business. Fewer farms would mean:

1 Economic decline.
- The National Farmer's Union estimate that for every £1000 earned by a hill farmer, £2500 is earned by *supporting industries*, e.g. in transporting inputs to the farm.
- *Rural tourism* relies on the landscape the farmers preserve.
- *Lowland farms* buy sheep for breeding and fattening from hill farms.

2 Farmers would become people who look after the countryside for tourists.

3 **Rural depopulation** especially of younger (16–30) people. 64 per cent of hill farmers are over 50. In half of hill farming families the children do not want to take over the farm. This means a change in population structure with the growth of an **ageing population**.

Figure 9.7 The effects of a decline in hill farming in Snowdonia

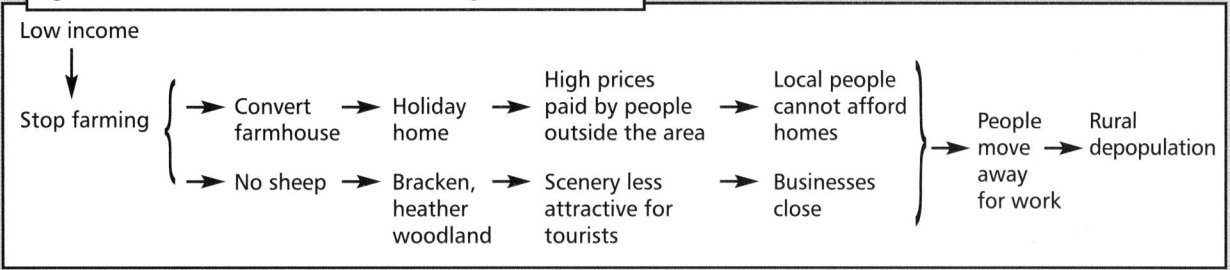

Low income → Stop farming →
- Convert farmhouse → Holiday home → High prices paid by people outside the area → Local people cannot afford homes
- No sheep → Bracken, heather woodland → Scenery less attractive for tourists → Businesses close

→ People move away for work → Rural depopulation

Using your case study

The information in this case study can be used to answer questions on the nature of changes and their consequences in one major farming type in one area within the UK.

Case study links

This case study links with:
- Chapter 6 which describes wind farms in the area
- Chapter 5 which describes tourism in a similar area in England
- Chapter 11 which describes change in rural areas affected by urban growth
- Chapter 13 which describes the social effects of population structure.

Key words to know

Diversification
Tir Gorfel
Agri-environment schemes
Farming Connect
Rural depopulation
Ageing population

Update

For more information on hill sheep farming in Snowdonia use the link on *The New Wider World Coursemate* website.

Learn it!

a) Describe the nature of recent changes, and social consequences, in hill sheep farming in Snowdonia.

3 Why have urban/industrial regions seen a decline in their traditional primary and secondary industries?

Industry as a system

Industry, like farming, can be regarded as a system. There are inputs into the industry, processes that take place and outputs. For an industry to be profitable the value of its outputs must be greater than the cost of its inputs and processes.

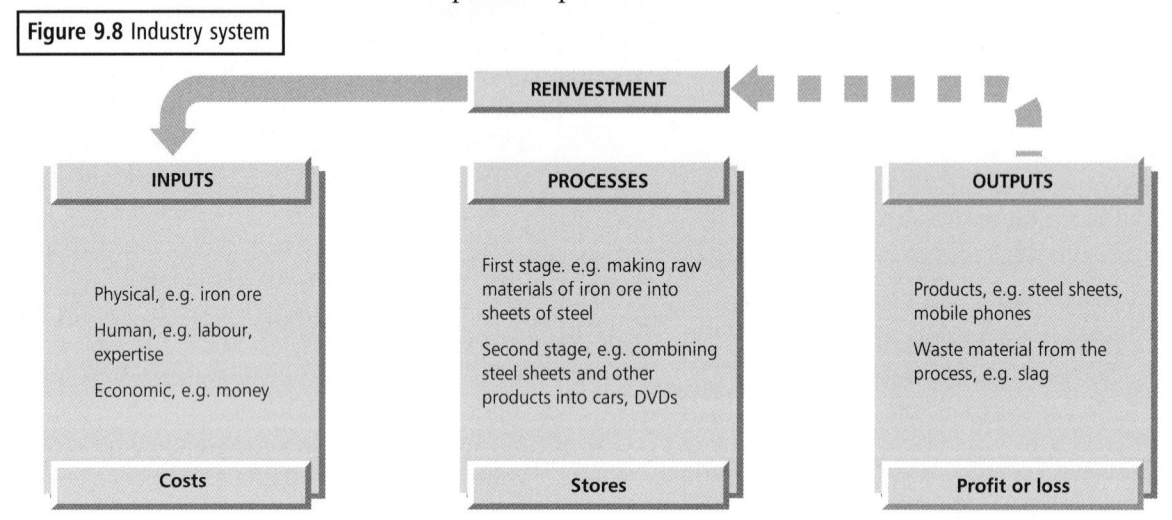

Figure 9.8 Industry system

```
                    REINVESTMENT ◀━━━━━━━━━
                         ▲                 ┃
                         │                 ┃
    INPUTS           PROCESSES           OUTPUTS

 Physical, e.g.    First stage. e.g.    Products, e.g. steel sheets,
 iron ore          making raw           mobile phones
                   materials of iron
 Human, e.g.       ore into sheets      Waste material from the
 labour,           of steel             process, e.g. slag
 expertise
                   Second stage, e.g.
 Economic, e.g.    combining steel
 money             sheets and other
                   products into cars,
                   DVDs

    Costs             Stores            Profit or loss
```

Traditional industries are those that first developed in the Industrial Revolution and often required heavy **raw materials** with high transport costs, much power and high levels of labour. They were:
- **primary industries** – extracting raw materials, e.g. coal mining, forestry
- **secondary industries** – processing or **manufacturing**, e.g. steel.

Case Study

South Wales, traditional iron and steel industry

Back to ...

The New Wider World pp138–139 for the case study of iron and steel in South Wales, and information on the iron and steel industry.

Using your case study

Use the information in the case study to answer questions on:

a) **The characteristics of the South Wales iron and steel industry**
  - Describe the raw materials, processes, the labour force and settlements involved in the manufacture of iron.
  - Describe the changes which led to steel manufacture.

b) **Original location factors**
  - Explain the original location factors for the iron industry and the pattern of iron works in the Valleys.
  - Explain the different location factors of integrated iron and steelworks on the coast. See Figure 9.8 on p139 of *The New Wider World* which gives reasons for the changes in the location of the industry.

c) **The decline of iron and steel in South Wales**
  This was due to:
  - exhaustion of the coal (only one private deep mine is now open at Hirwaun)
  - exhaustion of iron ore – needed to be imported from Brazil, North Africa and

70

North America
- overseas competition, e.g. steel tariffs US, cheaper production in China
- global overproduction, less steel required with newer metals on the market. Also more steel can be produced with higher levels of efficiency. This means lower prices followed by production running at a low profit or loss.
- UK Government policy not to give financial assistance to help companies.

Case study links

This case study links with:
- Chapter 11 – for the location and type of inner city industry
- Chapter 12 – for the time and growth of an MEDC city associated with traditional industry, Cardiff.

Update

For more information on traditional industry in South Wales use the link on *The New Wider World Coursemate* website.

Learn it!

a) What are the characteristics of the iron and steel industry in South Wales?

b) Look at Figures 9.7 and 9.9 on pp138–139 of *The New Wider World*. Draw annotated maps based on these to show the original location factors of i) the iron industry and ii) the present-day traditional steel industry in South Wales.

c) What factors led to the decline of the iron and steel industry in South Wales?

4 How successful are these regions in regeneration through modern secondary, tertiary or quaternary industry?

Key words to know

Traditional industry
Raw materials
Primary industry
Secondary industry
Manufacturing
Modern industry
Tertiary industry
Quaternary industry
Hi-tech
Footloose

What are modern industries and what are their location factors?

Modern industries are those that developed after the traditional industries declined and are associated with the regeneration of regions since the 1980s.
- Secondary industries manufacture modern products, e.g. cars, game boys.
- **Tertiary industries** provide a service, e.g. finance, law, education, health, office work, retailing, transport and entertainment.
- **Quaternary industries** provide information and expertise. They include the high-technology (**high-tech**) industry and information technology industries involving computers, telecommunications and micro-electronics.

Location of modern industry

Factors affecting the location of modern industry

Modern industry is called **footloose** because access to raw materials is relatively unimportant so they have a free choice of location. However, a highly skilled and qualified workforce is essential. As a result, the industry is found in areas which the workers find attractive.

Other location factors are mentioned in the web extract, Figure 9.9.

Farming and industry

> **'Why bring your business to Wales?'**
> - Wales has a **tariff-free** access to the market of Europe, which is as big as the US and Japanese markets combined.
> - There are incentive packages provided by the regional government and the EU which include rent-reduced, purpose-built accommodation.
> - There is a world class skilled workforce which adjusts to rapid technological change (and which is paid less than other parts of the UK).
> - There is a good **infrastructure** with the M4 and A55, Cardiff airport, free broadband network.
> - It offers mountains, National Parks, coastal scenery, the entertainment of a thriving capital city, many sports facilities including many new golf courses.
> - Universities with international links and expertise.

Figure 9.9 Advert to attract modern industry to Wales (Welsh Development Agency website)

Key words to know
Tariff-free
Infrastructure
Business park
Greenfield site
Science park

Sites
Modern industries are found on:
- **business parks** which have grown up on edge-of-town **greenfield sites** where there:
  - is low cost land
  - is a pleasant working environment – modern buildings, landscaped – grass, trees, ornamental gardens and lakes
  - are eating areas, hypermarkets and leisure complexes
  - are many high-tech firms located near to each other, having the advantages of being able to exchange ideas and information with neighbouring companies, sharing maintenance and support services, sharing basic amenities such as connecting roads, and building up a pool of highly skilled, often female labour.
- **science parks** which have direct links with universities
- redeveloped urban areas (see Chapter 11).

Check this!...

1 The following industries came to South Wales in 2003. For each, state the type of industry – secondary, tertiary, quaternary.
   a) Sogeti Filtration, making air filters for cars, invested £4m on Tredegar's Crown Business Park
   b) the Swedish company, Creditsafe financial services
   c) Hills Industries from Australia, invested £2.2 m in their rotary clothes driers plant at Pontgwindy
   d) an American firm producing moulded wood pulp at Blackwood
   e) Zurich financial services contact centre in Cardiff doubled in size
   f) £9.7 m visual media development at Gelli Aur mansion, near Llandeilo.

2 Explain the factors affecting modern industry. How do they differ from the factors for traditional industry?

3 Investigate a local industrial/business park. Draw a map of the location of an industrial/business park near to your school. Who cleared/built the site? Was any local government, Welsh Assembly, EU money used to develop the site or build new infrastructure, e.g. roads? Why was this particular site chosen? List and classify the industries on the site. What are the characteristics of the workers – age, male or female, type of jobs? Are there any other amenities on the site, e.g. conference centres, pubs? Would you like to work in the Park? What do you like about the environment? What do you dislike about it?

Case Study Extra

Growth and location of modern industries in South Wales

a) Growth of modern industries in the region
- The Welsh Development Agency (WDA) was set up in 1976 to attract industry into Wales and to encourage local people to set up businesses. The WDA has the money to build factories, reclaim land and invest in new industries by giving loans and grants.
- **Urban development corporations (UDCs)** were set up, e.g. Cardiff Bay.
- Government decentralised some of its national industries, e.g. the Mint, Llantrisant; Income Tax, Llanishen, Cardiff; Patents Office, Newport.
- The region became a development area and qualified for EU and British government assistance. The Valleys had extra grants.
- New town of Cwmbran was developed.

b) Patterns of location of modern industries in the region

Modern industry is located in four main groupings in South Wales:
- the M4 corridor, e.g. Ford, Bridgend
- the outskirts of towns in the 'Valleys' where tips were reclaimed and business parks developed, e.g. Aberdare
- redeveloped old industrial sites within urban areas, e.g. Swansea Enterprise Park and Waterfront development
- existing industrial estates, e.g. Treforest.

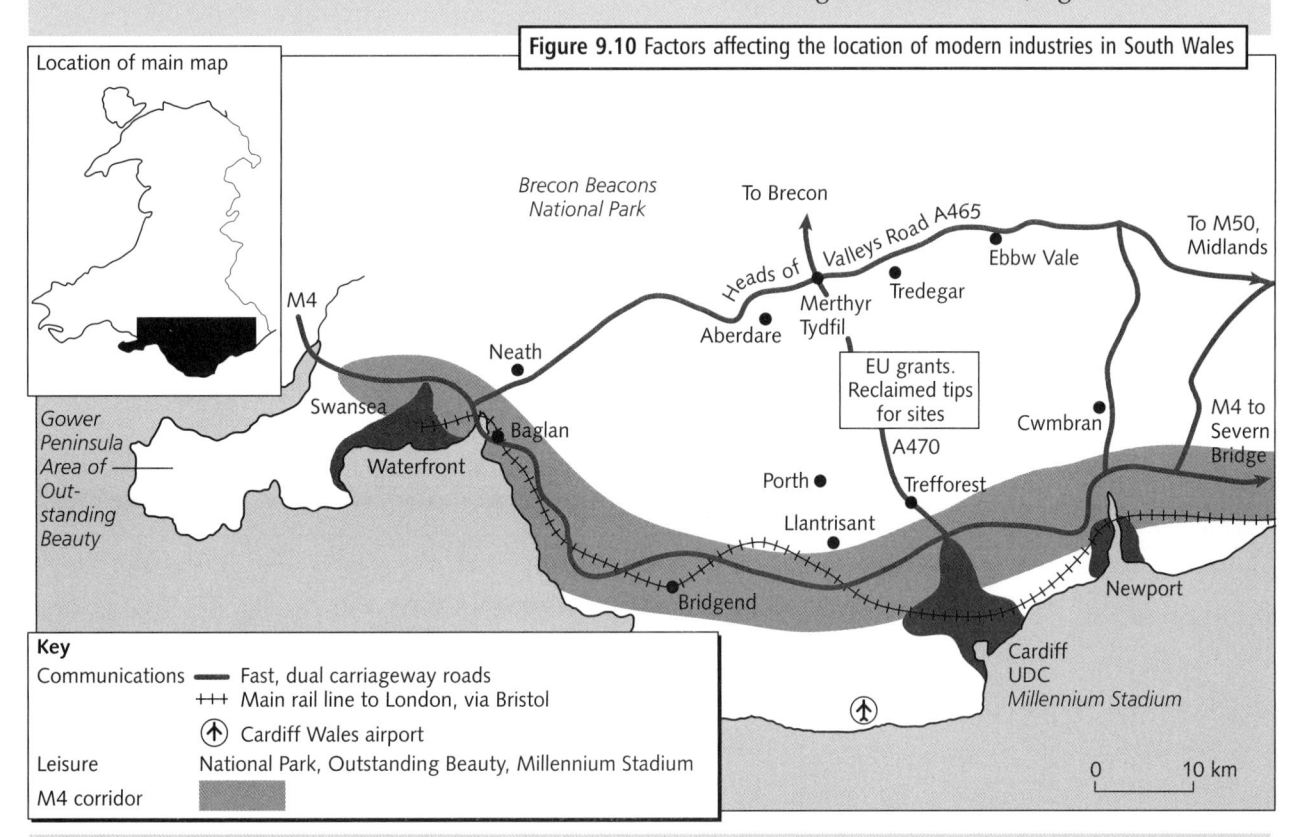

Figure 9.10 Factors affecting the location of modern industries in South Wales

c) Example of location and growth of modern industry, South Wales – SA1 Swansea Waterfront
- Swansea Waterfront is advertised as 'not just another dockland makeover' but an area that has a 24 hour life with places to both live and work.
- Grade II listed buildings, e.g. the J Shed, are being redesigned to have restaurants, bars, arts arcade with New York style 'live and work' duplex lofts above.
- The aim is to attract creative, technological and knowledge-based businesses, e-commerce sector industries, of the small medium sized enterprises (SMEs).
- The area houses a new development, Technium, where companies can: have offices; meet with other companies; have access to the research expertise of the Universities of Wales via broadband; link with international companies who are looking to invest in new products. This

Farming and industry 73

was so successful for the 12 firms in Technium 1 that Technium 2 was started in 2004.

d) **What is the level of success of regeneration in South Wales?**
- In the 1980s over 400 projects were brought into South Wales: 130 American companies came; 130 European companies were attracted to Wales. The Japanese had more factories in Wales (over 20) than in any other European country.
- The self-employed sector increased by 27 %.
- Modern industry was attracted to South Wales: biotechnology; optics; information technology; electronics (23 % rise compared with 1% rise in the UK); financial services.
- Manufacturing grew to be 30 % Gross Domestic Product (GDP) of Wales in 2003.
- Large multinational companies continue to have their European bases here, e.g. Airbus, Ford, Sony, Bosch, Toyota, Agilent Technologies.
- Most urban areas in South Wales now have modern business parks.
- New parks continue to spread westward along the M4 corridor.
- South Wales used only for assembly, components manufactured elsewhere.
- Lucky Gold Star investment north of Newport collapsed with Korean recession.
- Jobs are heavily subsidised by WDA.

Key words to know

Urban development corporation (UDC)

Using your case study
Use the information in this case study to answer questions on:
- the location and growth of modern industries in South Wales
- the levels of success of regeneration in South Wales.

Case study links
This case study has links with Chapter 11 – the growth of out-of-town modern industrial sites and Cardiff Bay, UDC.

Update
For more information on new industrial developments in South Wales use the link on *The New Wider World Coursemate* website.

Learn it!

a) Describe the characteristics and growth of modern industry in South Wales.

b) Draw a map to show the pattern of location, and factors affecting the location of modern industry in South Wales.

c) Describe examples of modern industrial development in the region.

d) Evaluate the levels of success in the regeneration of South Wales.

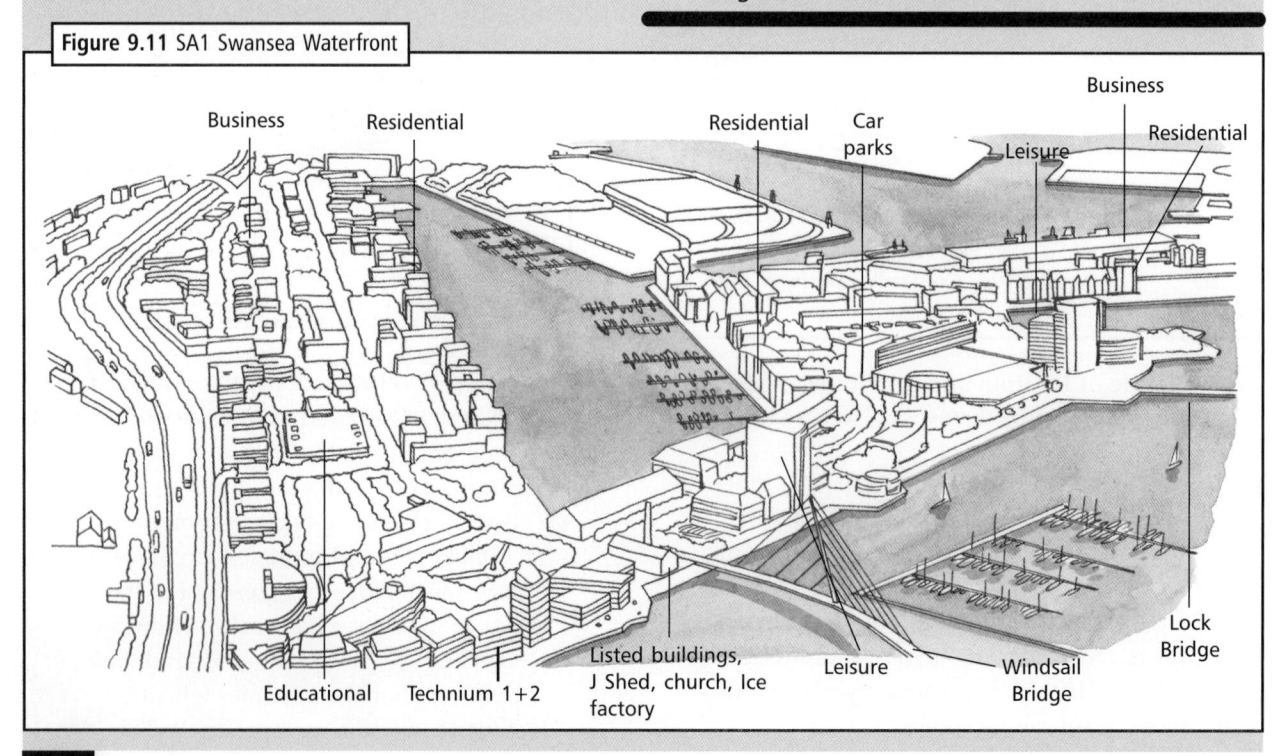

Figure 9.11 SA1 Swansea Waterfront

EXAM PRACTICE

In 2002 the building of Baglan Energy Park (BEP) in Swansea was started on the old industrial site of BP Chemicals. The park is 'an energy intensive manufacturing industrial park delivering quality jobs to the local community'. The area qualifies for EU grants for skills training and infrastructure and the highest level of UK Government assistance.

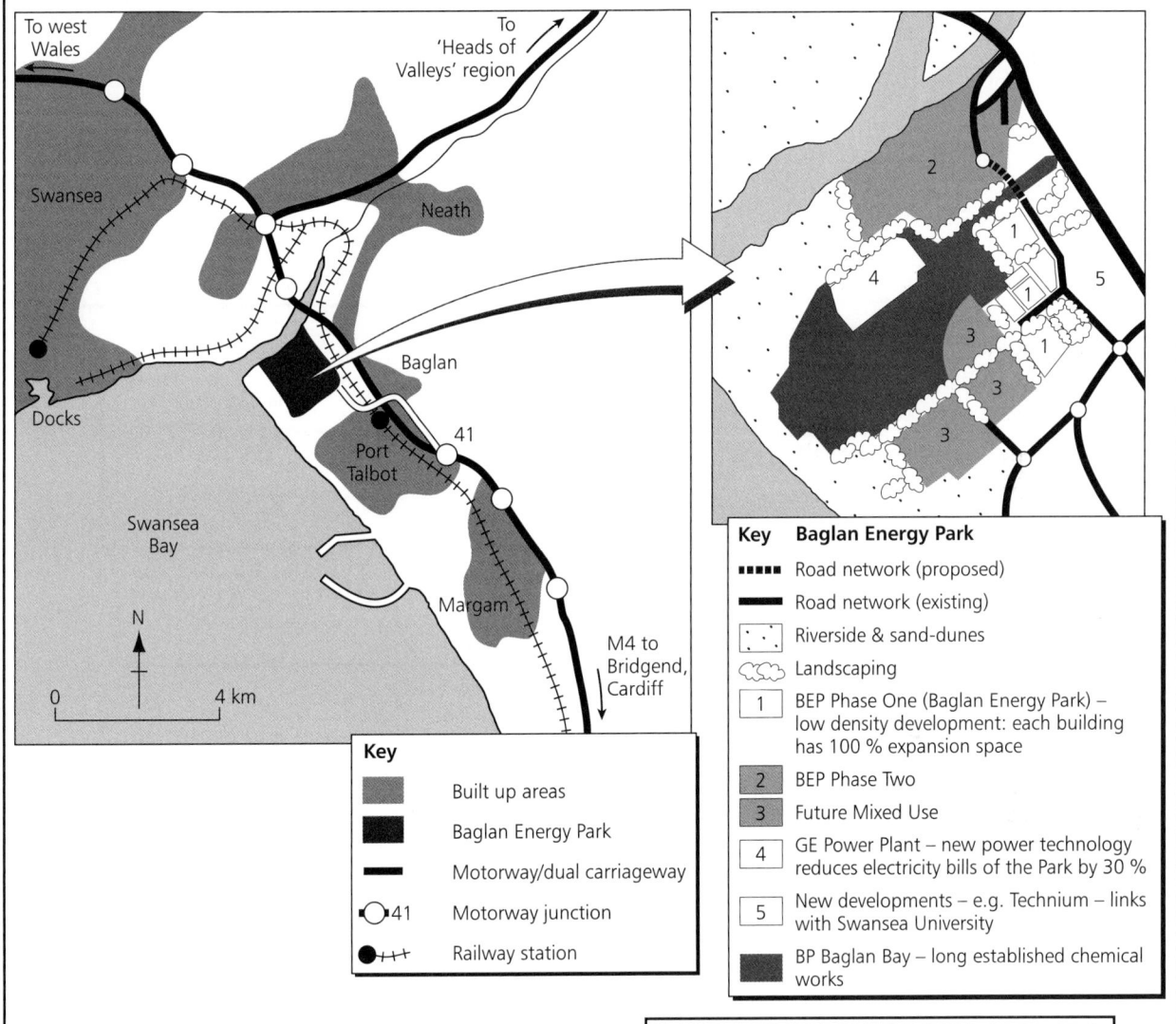

Key
- Built up areas
- Baglan Energy Park
- Motorway/dual carriageway
- ○41 Motorway junction
- ●+++ Railway station

Key Baglan Energy Park
- ▪▪▪▪▪ Road network (proposed)
- ▬▬▬ Road network (existing)
- Riverside & sand-dunes
- Landscaping
- 1 BEP Phase One (Baglan Energy Park) – low density development: each building has 100 % expansion space
- 2 BEP Phase Two
- 3 Future Mixed Use
- 4 GE Power Plant – new power technology reduces electricity bills of the Park by 30 %
- 5 New developments – e.g. Technium – links with Swansea University
- BP Baglan Bay – long established chemical works

Figure 9.12 Location and site of Baglan Energy Park

> A new paper making plant which will create 300 jobs is set to come to Baglan Energy Park after beating off stiff competition from Europe. Intertissue also converts paper into paper products, e.g. toilet paper, kitchen rolls.
>
> **April 2003 Press statement**

a
- **i** What type of industry is Intertissue? Use the following list: Primary Secondary Tertiary Quaternary (1)
- **ii** Give **two** transport advantages of the location of Baglan Energy Park (BEP). (2)
- **iii** Explain the special feature of the BEP site that makes it attractive to firms requiring a high level of power. (1)
- **iv** Describe the grants available for firms coming to BEP. (2)
- **v** Describe other features of the site of BEP. (4)

Farming and industry 75

Figure 9.13 The workforce in the region

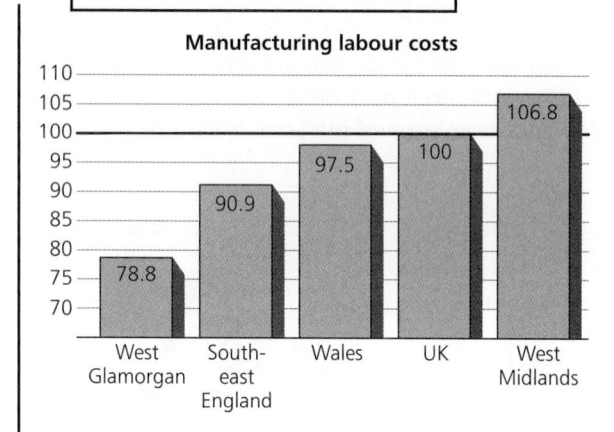

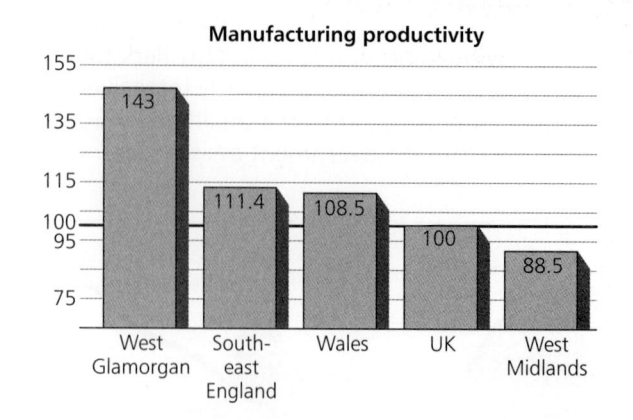

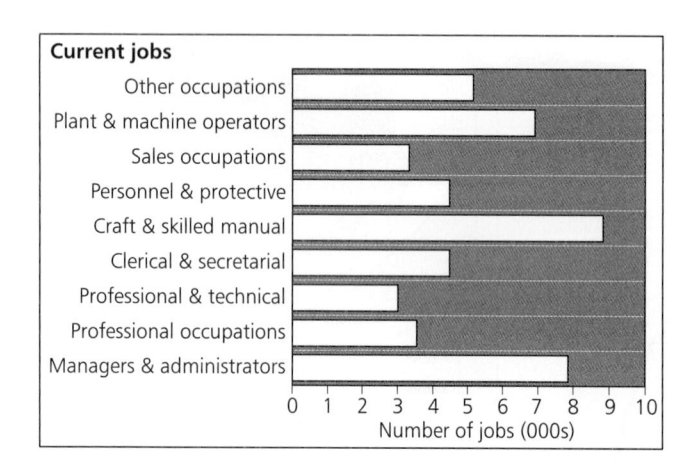

Manufacturing labour costs
- West Glamorgan: 78.8
- South-east England: 90.9
- Wales: 97.5
- UK: 100
- West Midlands: 106.8

Manufacturing productivity
- West Glamorgan: 143
- South-east England: 111.4
- Wales: 108.5
- UK: 100
- West Midlands: 88.5

Current jobs (Number of jobs (000s))
- Other occupations
- Plant & machine operators
- Sales occupations
- Personnel & protective
- Craft & skilled manual
- Clerical & secretarial
- Professional & technical
- Professional occupations
- Managers & administrators

490 000 working population } within 45 minutes of
31 000 available workforce } Baglan Energy Park

	Neath Port Talbot	Great Britain
Employment in Manufacturing	31.7%	15.1%
Employment in Service Sectors	58.5%	78.8%

Average days lost per 1000 employees
▶ Wales 2
▶ UK 12

b Use the data in Figure 9.13 to explain why the nature of the local workforce makes this area attractive for new manufacturing industry. (4)

c i Describe the recent changes to the workforce in a major **farming** type of your choice. (3)

ii Describe the nature and causes of other changes that have taken place in this farming type in recent years. (8)

Back to ...

The New Wider World website to check your answers to the Exam Practice question.

EXAM TIPS

Many questions will ask for knowledge of case studies which you must learn. Make sure you know which of your case studies to use since questions needing case study material will be general and not specify the case study you have learned, e.g. one farming type may be hill sheep farming. Go through your case studies and the WJEC GSCE specification and make sure you know which case study to use for each topic. Use accurate facts and detailed information you have learned to answer case study questions. You will not get high marks if you only make general comments.

➡ *The New Wider World, pp44–47; 58–59; 62–63*

10 Shopping

Throughout this chapter most stated examples refer to Cardiff. However, you are encouraged to investigate shopping near you and use local examples in any answer you give to an exam question that asks about UK shopping.

KEY QUESTION

1 How do changing shopping habits affect the distribution and nature of retailing?

1 How do changing shopping habits affect the distribution and nature of retailing?

Shopping hierarchy within the urban area

Shops are where we go to buy goods.
- **Low order goods** are low cost and bought often, e.g. bread, newspapers.
- **High order goods** are expensive but bought only occasionally, e.g. DVD players, beds.
- The **sphere of influence** is the area from which people travel to visit a shop.

When something is organised in order of importance it is called a **hierarchy**. The shops in the table below are organised into a hierarchy with the most important at the top.

	Location	Shops	Shoppers' visits	Trade area
CBD	A large area in the city centre	High order goods	Once a month or less	People travel a long distance, e.g. from Gwynedd to Liverpool
Suburban centre	A group of shops in a housing estate	Low order goods	Once or twice a week	Travel within the estate, e.g. up to 2 km
Corner shops	Single shops	Low order convenience goods	Most days of the week	Less than 1 km walking distance

Figure 10.1 Original patterns of shopping in urban areas

Changing shopping habits

As towns and cities grew, urban zones developed. Each of these zones had distinctive types of shops and most people went into the urban area for their shopping. Modern urban growth has meant a change to this traditional pattern since access and car parking is now easier for shops on the edge of urban areas.

Traditional shopping patterns
- The **central business district (CBD)** (see Chapter 11) contained shops, offices and commercial buildings. The shops included:
  - large department stores and superstores
  - those selling **comparison goods**, e.g. clothes and shoes
  - **specialist shops**, those which had a high turnover, a high profit margin or a large **threshold population** (a large number of people), e.g. jewellery and electrical goods

Key words to know

Low order goods
High order goods
Sphere of influence
Hierarchy
Central business district (CBD)
Comparison goods
Specialist shop
Threshold population

Shopping

> **Key words to know**
> *Suburban*
> *Old inner city*
> *Out-of town*
> *Supermarkets*

Check this!...

1. What order of goods are: CDs; mobile phones; designer jeans; pop magazines; ice cream?
2. Carry out a survey of your friends' families. Where do they go, and how often, to visit shops for: furniture; milk; vegetables; PCs; a hair cut?
3. Name the locations of the hierarchy of shops in your urban area.

← **Back to ...**
The New Wider World **pp62–63** for more information on the move to out-of-town shopping and a case study of the MetroCentre in Gateshead (an out-of-town shopping centre).

– small scale food shops (bakers, grocers, butchers and fishmongers).
- The **suburban** shopping parades included:
  – a sub-post office and newsagent
  – a small chain store (providing mainly low-order convenience goods)
  – several specialist shops (butcher and chemist)
  – one or two supplying non-essential services (hairdresser).

  As each new housing estate was built, its distance from the shops of the CBD increased. The small shopping parades within the estate saved people time in travelling and reduced transport costs. Most shopping parades had space for limited car parking and green spaces.
- The **old inner city** areas included:
  – numerous corner shops each serving a few streets.

  The shops opened for long, irregular hours and provided a social meeting place for local residents.

Move to out-of-town shopping

- The traditional shopping in CBDs declined because:
  – many of the older properties were in need of improvement and modernisation
  – the narrow streets were often congested
  – the large volume of traffic caused air pollution and was a danger to the health and safety of shoppers and other pedestrians
  – there was insufficient space for car parks
  – buses found it difficult to keep to time
  – smaller shops (butchers and grocers) were forced to close as the area became increasingly expensive.
- Corner shops closed in the inner city areas as they became redeveloped (see Chapter 11, p84).
- There was a move to **out-of-town** shopping initially for **supermarkets** and then for other specialists stores and departmental stores.

Figure 11.1b on p83 shows the location of Culverhouse Cross, an out-of-town shopping area to the west of Cardiff. Figure 10.2 shows the typical site, type of shops and advantages of an out-of-town location.

Consequences for traditional shopping

The CBDs became 'run down' with boarded up shops, charity shops, shops to let and high crime. Major changes were needed to provide modern, carefully planned city centres that considered social, economic and environmental demands to regenerate CBDs by:
- reducing traffic congestion and pollution
- creating a safer and a more pleasant environment
- satisfying the demand for more leisure amenities, especially during the evening
- segregating shoppers and traffic.

Ways of making shopping more attractive include:
- sitting areas, erecting hanging baskets, planting flower beds and shrubs and adding small areas of grass
- cafés with outside tables, small restaurants and theme bars
- more staff to remove litter and prevent vandalism
- escalators and lifts for the disabled

Figure 10.2 Advantages of out-of-town shopping areas, Culverhouse Cross

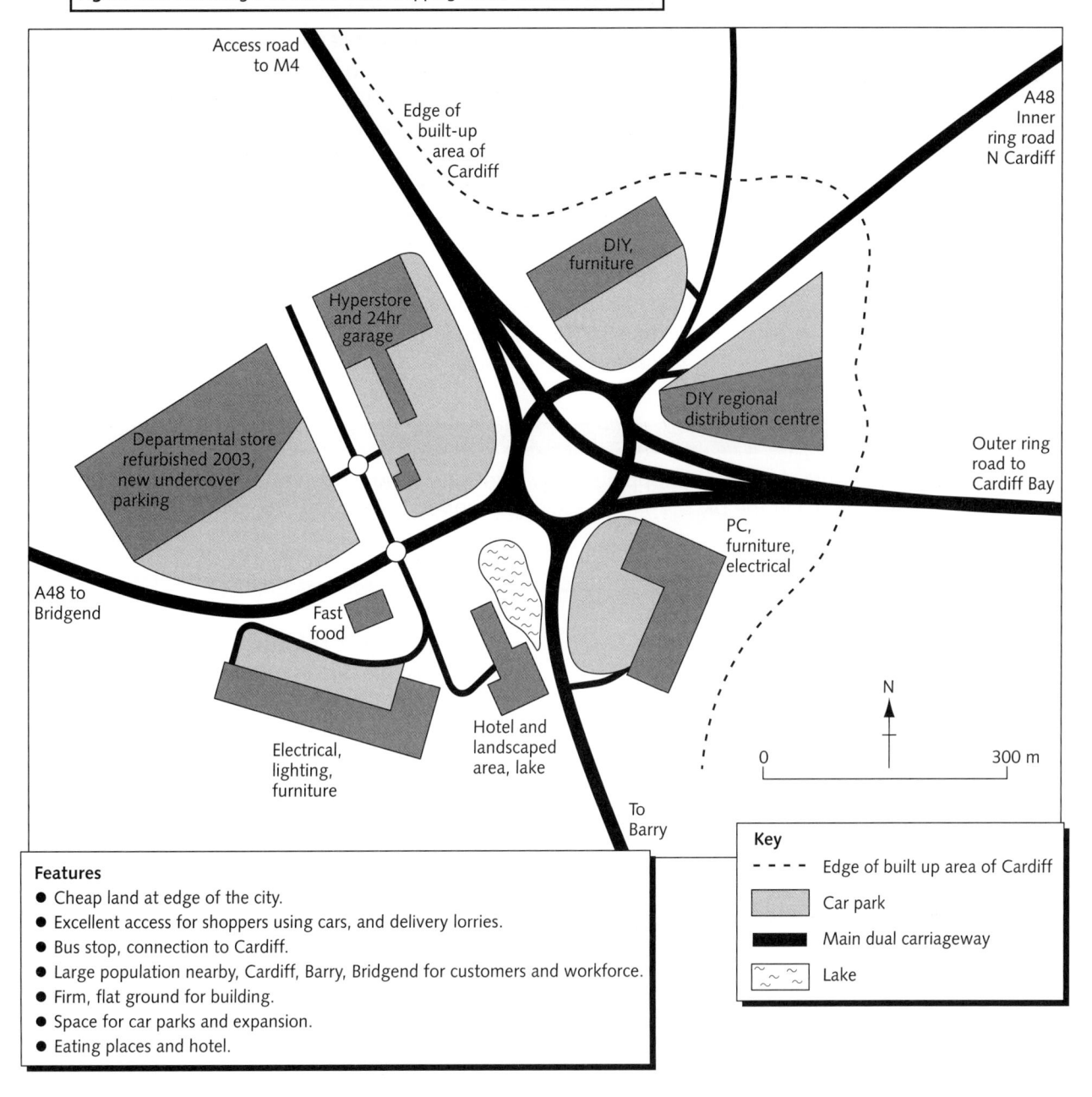

Features
- Cheap land at edge of the city.
- Excellent access for shoppers using cars, and delivery lorries.
- Bus stop, connection to Cardiff.
- Large population nearby, Cardiff, Barry, Bridgend for customers and workforce.
- Firm, flat ground for building.
- Space for car parks and expansion.
- Eating places and hotel.

- market-style effect with small street barrows
- cinema
- crèche and play areas for children
- **shopping malls** which are also **pedestrianised** and built under cover so that shoppers are protected from the weather and have shorter distances to travel between shops to compare styles and prices.

Redeveloped areas in Cardiff CBD include the pedestrianisation of Queen Street, the malls of St David's Centre and Capitol Centre.

Changing types of shops
- Shopping malls located in big out-of-town sites, e.g. Cribbs Causeway, Bristol.

Key words to know

Shopping malls
Pedestrianised

Shopping 79

- Factory shops, or 'designer outlets' developed on out-of-town sites either as a change of use, e.g. Ebbw Vale on the former Garden Festival site (see redevelopment of declining industry, Chapter 9 p73), or new sites, e.g. the M4 Bridgend junction, S Wales.
- Increase in travel agents and estate agents as well as in specialist shops selling clothes and mobile phones, and in opticians in CBDs.
- Supermarkets are moving back into CBD areas as 'Metro' shopping, sited by main railway or bus stations or on garage forecourts. They concentrate on convenience foods, e.g. sandwiches, ready-made meals, everyday food.
- Since the millennium there has been a major increase in Internet home shopping. Christmas 2003 saw 7 per cent of UK shopping through the Internet, the biggest proportion of any country in Europe.

Check this!...

1. Describe and explain the changes in shopping in the CBD in an urban area in the UK.

2. Suggest what impact on-line shopping has on:
   a) shops and shopping centres
   b) employment
   c) the environment.

3. Fieldwork investigation. Investigate an out-of-town shopping centre near you.
   a) Planning: First, decide on a general question about the shopping centre to which you would like to find the answer. Make a plan of the information you need to gather to answer the main question. One part of the investigation may be about the people who use the shopping centre. If so, before you visit the centre, design a questionnaire. Make sure your individual questions are focused on your overall aim. Try to make most of your questions closed, i.e. have a one-word answer. You could include a more open question at the end to ask shoppers' opinion. Think about how you are going to sample the shoppers. Make a map of the shopping centre. You need to prepare any forms, e.g. Environmental impact, before you go.
   b) Fieldwork: Complete the map, questionnaire and forms.
   c) Write up your investigation. Explain how you designed your plan to get answers to your main question. Explain how you designed the questionnaire. Choose and draw appropriate graphs/maps to show your results. Explain what the results show. Draw your conclusions and make sure you relate them back to the original question.
   d) Evaluation: Was the investigation successful? What would you improve if you had to do a similar task again? What further questions or lines of enquiry occurred to you during the investigation?

Back to ...

The New Wider World website to check your answers to the Exam Practice question.

EXAM TIPS

The answer to some questions come from the data given, whereas you will need to use your revision for other questions. Look out for commands such as 'study the data' or 'use the information in Figure X'. These indicate the answer is in the data. Don't look for answers in the data for questions that start with 'Use your own knowledge'.

EXAM PRACTICE

Figure 10.3 The Bristol region

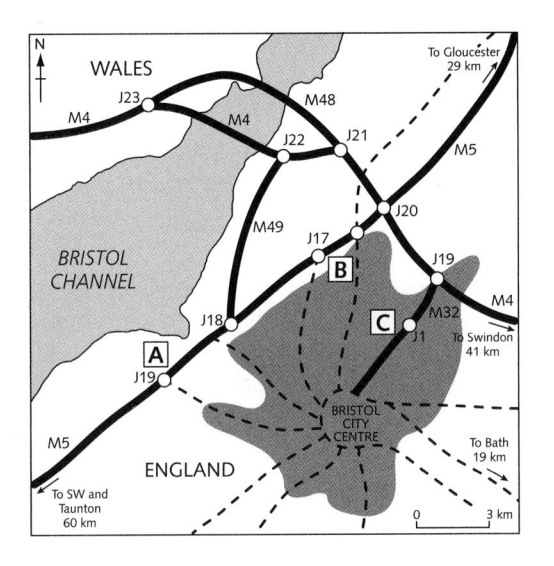

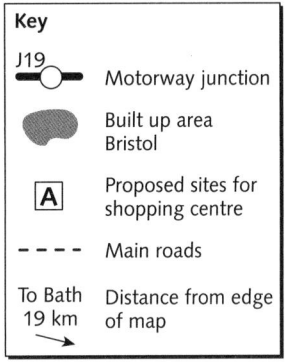

a i The Bristol region has been selected for a large out-of-town shopping centre. Using Figure 10.3 calculate the distance customers would have to travel from:
1. Bristol city centre to A
2. Bath to C. (2)

ii Explain how the development of a new shopping centre in this region has advantages for:
1. customers (3)
2. the workforce (1)
3. the delivery of goods. (3)

b Describe the shops found in out-of-town shopping centres. Illustrate your answer with examples. (5)

c The developers for the region have an option of three possible sites:

Site A A derelict industrial area prone to flooding at high tide. Mud banks attract birds.

Site B Low-grade farmland with derelict barns. It is well drained.

Site C Close to an existing industrial estate.

i State which site would be opposed by the wildlife organisations. (1)

ii What argument might local residents put forward to try to stop the development at site B? (1)

iii Give a problem that might occur if site C is chosen. (1)

iv Use your own knowledge to describe the physical conditions needed to build a large shopping centre. (2)

d Which of the three sites in question **c** would you recommend to the planning committee? Write a report giving the arguments for and against the development at the three possible sites. (6)

Shopping   81

11 The consequences of urban development in the UK

⇨ *The New Wider World*, pp42–49; 58–67

Throughout this chapter case studies refer to Cardiff and its fringes. However, you are encouraged to investigate an urban area near you and use local examples in any answer you give to an exam question that asks about UK urban areas.

1 What urban land use patterns can be identified?

Urbanisation is an increase in the proportion of people living in towns and cities.

Urban land use patterns

A model is a theoretical framework which may not actually exist, but which helps to explain the reality. Towns do not grow in a haphazard way, but develop with recognisable shapes and patterns. Although each urban area is unique, with its own distinctive pattern, it shares generalised characteristics with other settlements.

There are three different zones in urban areas, CBD, inner city and suburbia. Each has distinctive land use. Figure 11.1 shows a land use model compared to the actual pattern of land use in Cardiff.

Explanation of urban land use patterns

The four main functions within each land use zone are shops (see chapter 10, p77) and offices, industry, housing, and open space.

The location of land use zones and functions are related to several factors:

- *Land values and space*   Land values are highest and available sites more limited in the urban centre where competition for land is greatest. As land values decrease towards the outskirts of the urban area the amount of space and the number of available sites increase.
- *Age*   As towns developed outwards, the oldest buildings were near to the city centre and the newest ones in the outskirts.
- *Accessibility*   The urban centre where the main road and rail routes from the suburbs and surrounding towns meet, was the easiest place to reach from all parts of the city.
- *Wealth of the inhabitants*   Poorer people lived in cheaper housing near to the centre and inner city. They could not afford the higher transport and housing costs of the outskirts.
- *Changes in demand*   Land use and functions change with time. Traditional industry was found in the centre whereas modern industry prefers edge-of-city sites. There is a current demand for housing in central redeveloped areas.

Figure 11.2 shows a typical view across a modern city.

KEY QUESTIONS

1. What urban land use patterns can be identified?
2. What are the consequences of urban change and what attempts are being made to respond to these consequences?

Key words to know

Urbanisation
Accessibility

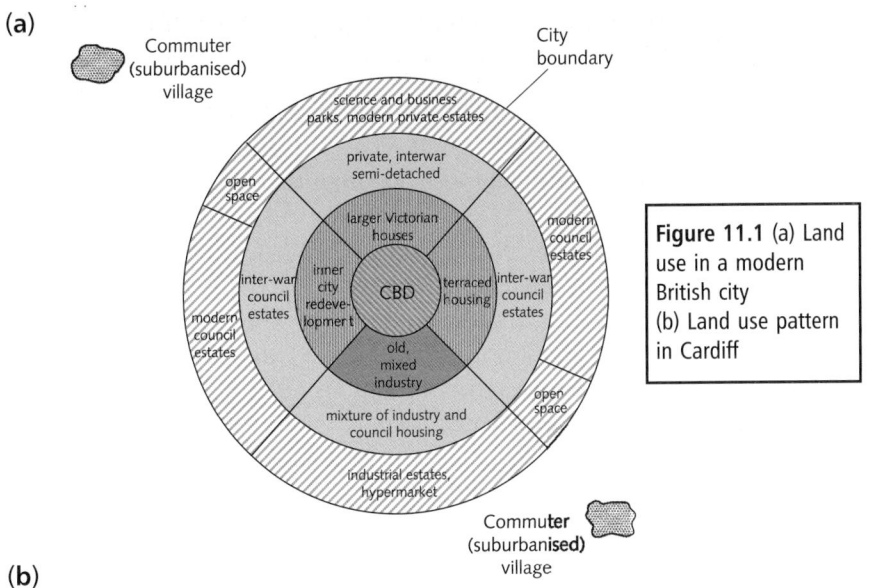

Figure 11.1 (a) Land use in a modern British city (b) Land use pattern in Cardiff

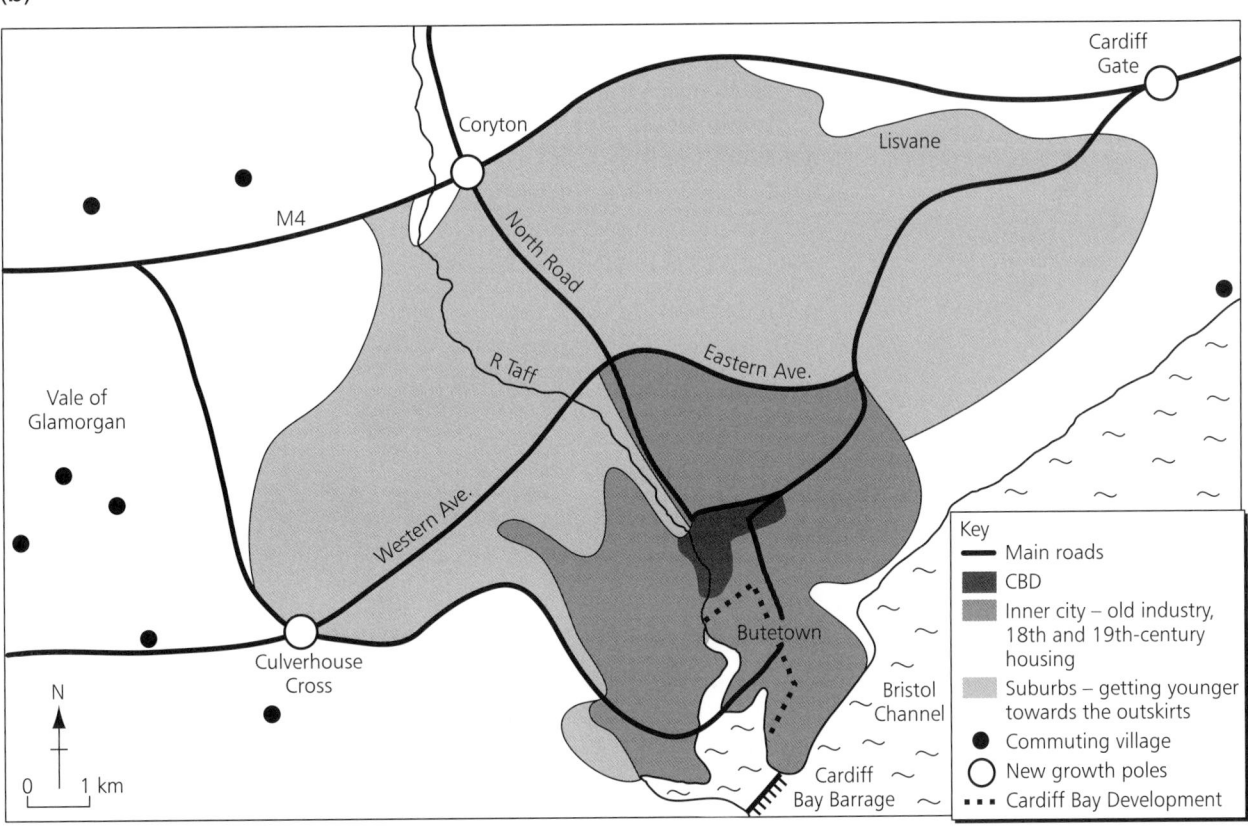

Figure 11.2 Transect across a typical British city

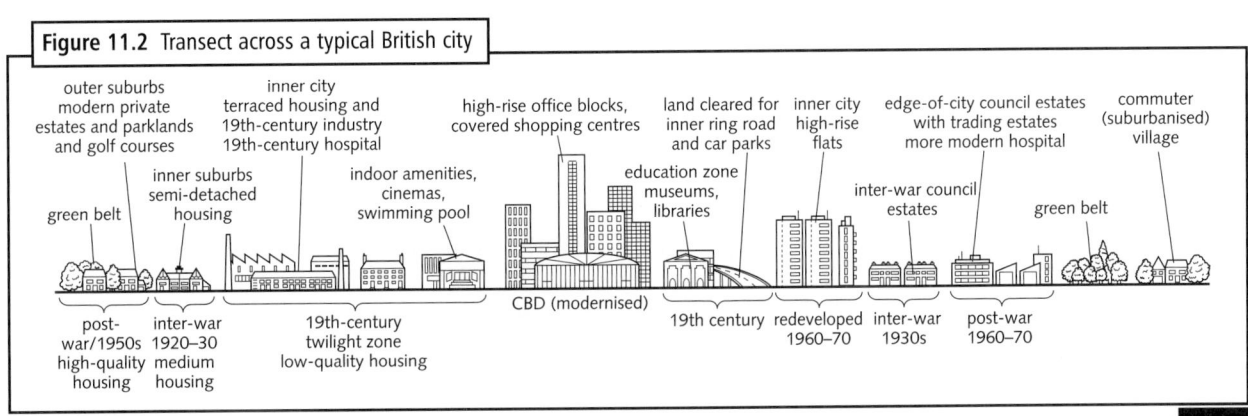

The consequences of urban development in the UK

Characteristics of the different urban zones

CBD

The major land users are shops, banks and offices who need to be accessible to a large number of people. They can afford the high cost of land. Many offices locate in high-rise buildings to offset high rates and rent.

Figure 11.1b shows the location of the CBD in Cardiff and Chapter 10, p77 describes its shopping characteristics.

Other land uses in Cardiff, the capital city, include the National Museum and University of Cardiff in Cathays Park. The Millennium stadium, theatres, cinemas, a thriving restaurant and club scene, leisure attractions, e.g. The Big Weekend, open air winter ice skating rink, all combine to make it a centre for leisure. Many new hotels have been built and brownfield sites are developing as mixed residential/shopping/café areas, e.g. Brains Brewery site became Hard Rock Café complex in 2004.

Inner city

Figure 11.3 shows the pattern and type of housing, and the types of people living in the inner city.

People moved from rural areas to the towns for work in the nineteenth century. They wanted low-cost houses in which to live. They needed to live close to their work since they did not have transport. Despite the cramped conditions there was a strong community spirit amongst local inhabitants.

(a) The layout of a typical **old** inner city area

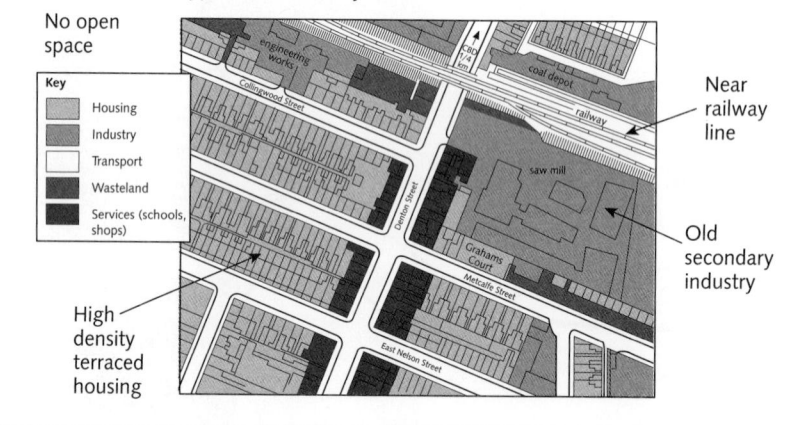

(b) Bar graphs to show the housing types, employment and socio-economic characteristics of **Butetown**, the **redeveloped** inner city area of **Cardiff Bay**, 2001. For location see Figures 11.1b and 11.5.

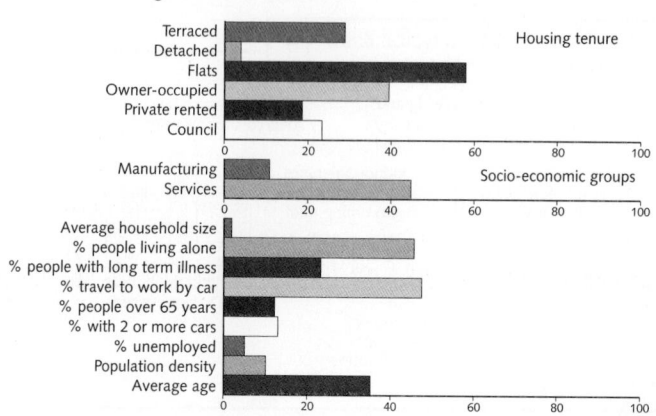

Figure 11.3 Characteristics of inner city areas

The factories in the zone, built near canals, railways, rivers or the coast (e.g. Cardiff docklands) have now closed either due to a lack of space for expansion and modernisation, or due to narrow, congested roads.

Suburbia

Figure 11.4 shows the pattern and type of housing, and the types of people living in suburbia.

Figure 11.4 Characteristics of suburbia

(a) The layout of a typical suburban area

(b) Bar graphs to show the housing types, employment and socio-economic characteristics of **Lisvane**, a suburb of Cardiff, 2001. For location see Figure 11.1b.

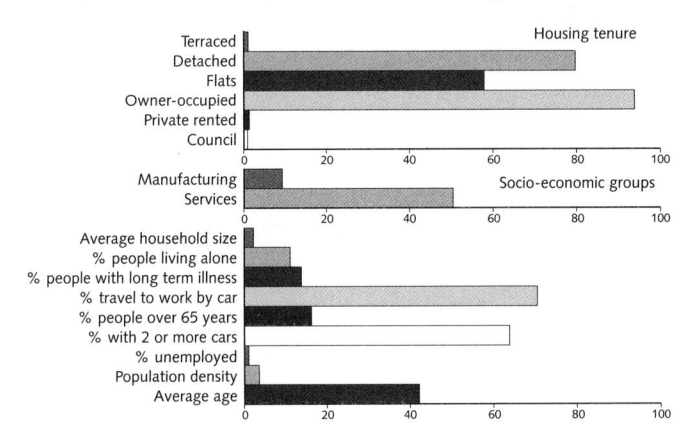

During the 1920s and 1930s (the inter-war period) urban areas grew rapidly due to:
- the introduction of public transport
- the increase in popularity of the private car
- in London, the extension of the Underground.

The outward growth is known as **urban sprawl**.

Inter-war estates have their own small park or play area due to the:
- decrease in land values away from the CBD
- increase in land available towards the edge of the urban area
- gradual introduction of town planning.

The inter-war estates rarely had industry nearby so residents had to **commute** to work.

Key words to know

Urban sprawl
Commute
Rural–urban fringe

The consequences of urban development in the UK

After the 1960s, urban sprawl continued with land on the **rural–urban fringe** being used for:
- private estates or outer-city council housing
- new industrial and/or trading estates.

New private estates have low-density, high-quality large detached housing built either in a cul-de-sac or along winding rural roads.

Outer city council estates have a higher density than on the private estates.

Check this!...

1 Either walk around a town near you or use a local OS map and map the different land use zones. Compare your map with the model shown in Figure 11.1a.

2 Explain why urban areas all have a similar general pattern.

3 Look at Figure 3.18 on p41 of *The New Wider World*. Match the following grid references with the correct urban land use zone listed alongside:

160330	Inner city housing
137302	Suburbia
145322	Inner city industry
150294	Rural–urban fringe

4 Compare the characteristics of Cardiff's CBD with the CBD in your home town.

2 What are the consequences of urban change and what attempts are being made to respond to these consequences?

Key words to know

Urban decay
Slum clearance
Urban redevelopment
Brownfield site
Urban development corporation (UDC)

Issues and strategies associated with inner city changes

Inner city areas have suffered **urban decay** because of the loss of traditional industry.

Strategies for regeneration
- **Slum clearance** – bulldozing large areas in the 1960s.
- **Urban redevelopment** – building high-rise flats in the 1960s. Despite having modern amenities of a bathroom, running water, etc. high-rise flats created social problems, e.g. broken down lifts, vandalism. Many have since been pulled down.
- Urban renewal – improving existing properties in the 1980s.
- Many factories have been demolished to leave large areas of derelict land (**brownfield sites**).
- 13 **urban development corporations (UDCs)** were set up in the 1980s by the government to regenerate those inner city areas that had large amounts of derelict and unused land and buildings. With public and private-sector investment UDCs were able to promote industrial, housing and community developments.

Case Study Extra

Cardiff Bay urban development corporation – strategy for regeneration

Figures 11.5 and 11.6 summarise the redevelopment of Cardiff Bay and evaluate the level of its success. The location of the area is shown in Figure 11.1b on p83.

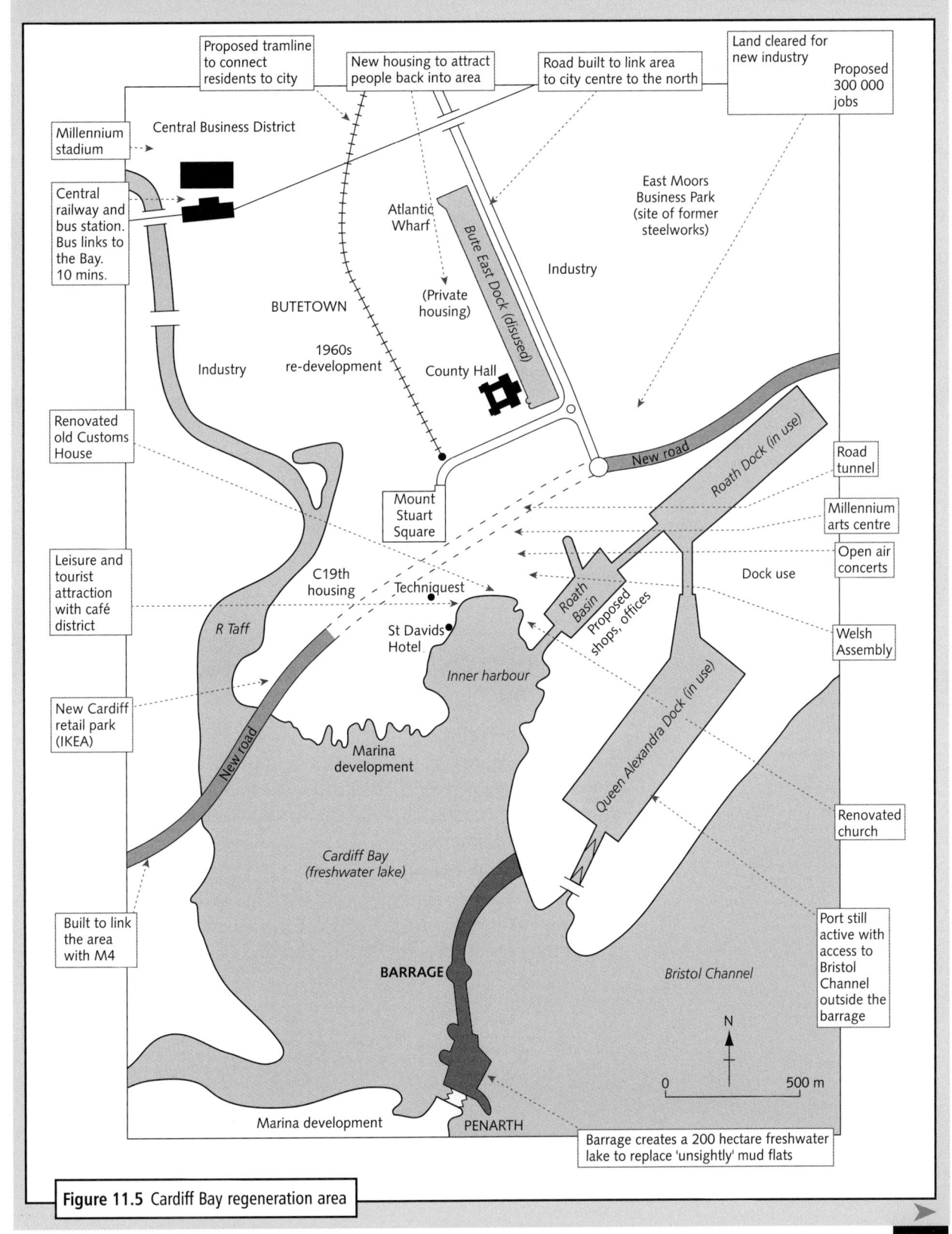

Figure 11.5 Cardiff Bay regeneration area

Labels on map:
- Proposed tramline to connect residents to city
- New housing to attract people back into area
- Road built to link area to city centre to the north
- Land cleared for new industry
- Proposed 300 000 jobs
- Millennium stadium
- Central Business District
- Central railway and bus station. Bus links to the Bay. 10 mins.
- Atlantic Wharf
- Bute East Dock (disused)
- East Moors Business Park (site of former steelworks)
- BUTETOWN
- (Private housing)
- Industry
- 1960s re-development
- County Hall
- Industry
- Renovated old Customs House
- Mount Stuart Square
- New road
- Roath Dock (in use)
- Road tunnel
- Millennium arts centre
- Leisure and tourist attraction with café district
- C19th housing
- Techniquest
- Roath Basin
- Open air concerts
- R Taff
- St Davids Hotel
- Proposed shops, offices
- Dock use
- Welsh Assembly
- New Cardiff retail park (IKEA)
- Inner harbour
- Marina development
- Queen Alexandra Dock (in use)
- Renovated church
- Built to link the area with M4
- Cardiff Bay (freshwater lake)
- Port still active with access to Bristol Channel outside the barrage
- BARRAGE
- Bristol Channel
- Marina development
- PENARTH
- Barrage creates a 200 hectare freshwater lake to replace 'unsightly' mud flats
- 0 — 500 m

The consequences of urban development in the UK

Figure 11.6 Level of success of Cardiff Bay UDC

Problems	Successes
Housing in the bay is too expensive for local people. New housing is next to old docklands and poor quality housing. High crime rate. Home owners are single or young married couples who are at work all day – little community spirit. Lack of schools, shops. Some business units empty. Shops not successful on the waterfront, the CBD has a greater choice.	Reunites the city to the waterfront. Improved access into Cardiff with new roads. New industries. Improved landscaping of the area with an attractive waterfront. Restored historical buildings. Cleared waste from derelict land. Provided many new homes. Major tourist attraction.

Using your case study
Use the information in this case study to illustrate answers on strategies for regeneration of inner city areas.

Case study links
This case study provides links with:
- Chapter 9 – modern industrial growth
- Chapter 10 – site of new shopping area
- Chapter 11 – characteristics of the inner city
- Chapter 12 – speed of growth of MEDC city, Cardiff.

Update
For more information on Cardiff Bay use the link on *The New Wider World Coursemate* website.

Learn it!
a) Describe the strategies for inner city regeneration either in Cardiff or an urban area near you.

b) How successful has the regeneration been? What problems still exist?

Back to ...
The New Wider World pp60–61 for a different example of regeneration, London Docklands.

Issues and strategies associated with suburban expansion

1 Green belt strategy
Green belts are areas of land around most urban areas where the planning permission for houses and other buildings is restricted and where the open character of the countryside is to be preserved for farming and recreation.

2 Rural–urban issues
There is conflict between those who wish to see the economic development and extension of the urban area and those who wish to protect the rural environment that surrounds it.

Economic pressures from urban area	Competition for land at the rural–urban fringe	Environmental pressures from rural area
Business and science parks near to motorway interchanges (see Chapter 9). Regional shopping complex: hypermarket, hotel and office development (see Chapter 10). New suburban housing estates (see rural–urban fringe, p85). Suburbanised villages create more traffic (see below). Areas of sewage works, landfill waste sites. Land for urban by-passes, national motorways and service stations.	RURAL–URBAN FRINGE	Country park: near enough to city for use by urban dwellers for walking, riding, etc. Reduces cost of getting to, and pressures upon, National Parks (see Chapter 5, p37). Conservationists want to protect wildlife habitats, e.g. nature reserves. Farmers wish to use and protect their farmland. Residents in nearby villages.

Figure 11.7 Competition for land at the rural–urban fringe

3 Transport issues and strategies

Traffic in general, and the car in particular, create numerous problems in urban areas. Urban traffic problems are at their worst as commuters travel to and from work. Improvements in roads mean that commuters can live further from their place of work. This has led to large **commuter hinterlands** (the rural areas around large cities where commuters live).

A more recent trend is a 'reversed' flow of commuters. This group includes:
- the less skilled and poorly paid who live in inner city housing and who travel to work on edge-of-city industrial and retail parks
- some well-paid people who have moved into regenerated areas near to the city centre but who work on science and business parks on the rural–urban fringe.

Key words to know
Commuter hinterland

Strategies for the reduction of traffic congestion in Cardiff
- Pedestrianised areas, e.g. Queen Street.
- Improving the bus services from Queen Street train station.
- Subsidised buses from major commuter areas every 15 minutes.
- Improvements to Valley line trains to Cardiff.
- Cycle lanes from some suburban locations into the city.
- Bus priority lanes.
- During the morning rush hour there are three traffic lanes open going into Cardiff and one lane going out on North Road and then the lane system is reversed for the afternoon rush hour.
- Residents of the city have parking permits near their home. Commuters are not allowed to park in residential areas. They are clamped or fined by traffic wardens.
- Increasing use of the park and ride system which allows free out-of-town parking and subsidised buses every 15 minutes into Cardiff. This system is also used for international sports events and Christmas shoppers.
- Cardiff City Council is reducing the number of car parking places and is charging higher parking rates per hour.
- Companies are encouraged to work flexi-time to help stop congestion in the rush hours.
- A battery operated ultra taxi train is planned to run from Cardiff CBD to Cardiff Bay. This is three times quicker than car, train and bus and reduces pollution from exhausts.

Figure 11.8 Traffic strategies

Check this!...
1 Describe the strategies to manage transport issues in Cardiff and another urban area near you.

The consequences of urban development in the UK

Key words to know

Greenfield site
Counterurbanisation
Suburbanised village
Dormitory settlement

4 Should future development be in inner cities or in the rural–urban fringe?

Britain is short of houses. Estimates suggest that 4.1 million new homes could be needed by 2016. In 1998 the government announced that:

- 60 % would be built on brownfield sites
- 40 % would be built on **greenfield sites**, i.e. in the countryside, including places in green belts.

In the south east of England, where most houses are needed, the brownfield sites are limited. In industrial South Wales, Midlands and North England, brownfield sites are available but the demand for new housing is less.

Why build on brownfield sites?

Environmental groups argue that:

- one million unoccupied houses, old industrial and commercial sites in cities could be upgraded
- 1.3 million homes could be created by either subdividing large houses or using empty space above shops and offices
- 1.6 million homes could be built on vacant and derelict land
- urban living reduces car use and maintains shopping services in city centres.

The government assumes that 80 per cent of the demand for new houses will come from single-parent families who wish to live in cities.

Why build on greenfield sites?

Developers claim:

- British people want a rural home, (unlike continental people who prefer to rent an apartment)
- people have a better quality of life in rural areas
- the current trend shows that 160 000 people a year move into the city and 250 000 people a year move out into the countryside
- greenfield sites are cheaper to build on than brownfield sites since they have lower land values and are less likely to need clearing up after industrial use.

Figure 11.9 Arguments for brownfield and greenfield sites

Check this!...

1 Describe the conflicts in the rural–urban fringe.
2 Look at the map of Cardiff (Figure 11.1b on p83). Do you think there should be further development at the growth pole sites marked on the map?

Issues and strategies associated with change in rural areas

Suburbanised villages – effects on rural communities

There has been a reversal of the movement of people to large urban areas, with groups of people moving out into surrounding villages. This movement, **counterurbanisation**, has led to changes in the characteristics of these settlements. They are called **suburbanised villages** because they adopt some of the features of urban areas. They are also known as commuter or **dormitory settlements** as many of their residents travel to nearby towns and cities for work.

Characteristic	Original village	Suburbanised village
Population structure	An ageing population; mostly born in village; labouring/manual groups	Young/middle-aged married couples with children; very few born in village; wealthy professional/executive groups; some wealthy retired people
Community/social	Close-knit community (many people related) have lived here for several generations	There may be division between locals and newcomers; may be deserted during the day (commuters absent)
Housing	Detached, stone-built houses/cottages; old farms	New detached houses, renovated barns and cottages; expensive estates
Services	Village shop; small junior school; public house; village hall; church	Enlarged school; public houses/restaurants; garage
Transport	Bus service (limited); some cars; narrow, winding roads two cars;	Bus service (often reduced by constant use of private car); most families have one or
Employment	Farming and other primary activities (forestry, mining); low-paid local jobs	New industry; good salaries
Environment	Quiet, relatively pollution-free	Increase in traffic pollution; loss of farmland

Figure 11.10 Changes in a suburbanised village

Case Study Extra

Strategies to manage change in rural areas – Vale of Glamorgan

The Vale of Glamorgan is now one of the dormitory areas for Cardiff (see Figure 11.1b on p83). It is a lowland mixed farming region which still retains its agricultural character with a weekly market in Cowbridge. It is an area of old villages with views of rolling hills, valleys and a dramatic Heritage Coastline, yet is within 30 minutes of the capital city and its facilities. There is a demand for high quality housing.

Figure 11.11 graphs the changes in one small village in the Vale.

Using your case study
Use the information in this case study to illustrate answers describing the effects of urban growth on rural areas. It can also be used as a named example to show an understanding of issues and strategies to manage and respond to such change.

Case study links
This case study provides links with:
- Chapter 9 – farming and new industrial location (the M4 runs through the north of this region)
- Chapter 10 – relocation of shopping (Culverhouse Cross lies on the boundary of Cardiff and the Vale)
- Chapters 11 and 12 – urban development and growth.

Update
For more information on strategies to manage change in the Vale of Glamorgan use the link on *The New Wider World Coursemate* website.

Learn it!
a) Describe the effects of urban growth on rural communities in one area.

b) Describe the strategies to manage and respond to this change.

The consequences of urban development in the UK

Figure 11.11 Changes in a village in the Vale of Glamorgan, 1891–2000

Age structure in 1891 / *Age structure in 2000*

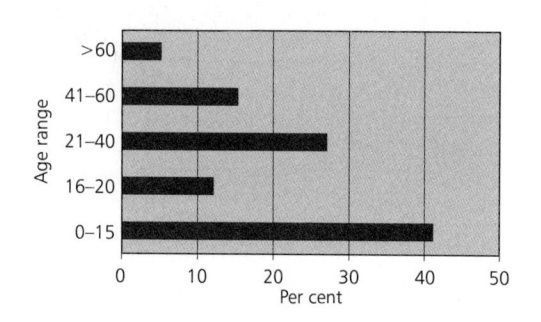

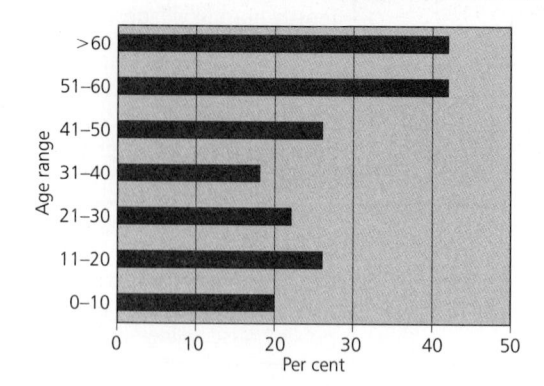

Employment in 1891 / *Employment in 2000*

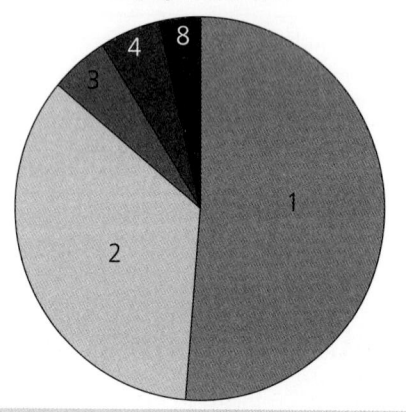

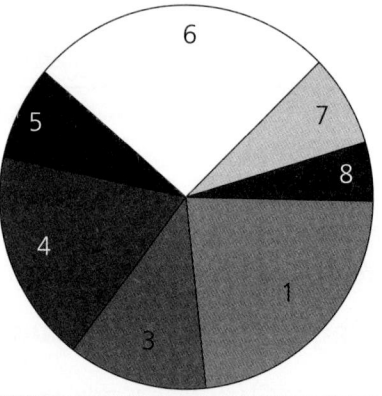

Key:
1. Farming & agriculture
2. Domestic service
3. Professions
4. Trades
5. Administration
6. Managerial
7. Banking/financial
8. Other

Census	1891	2000
No. of homes	38	73
No. of people	197	183
Born in village	23 %	16 %
Born outside UK	0 %	7 %
Work within village	98 %	20 % (farming, tourism, e-working)
Travel to work	Foot or by horse	74 % by car
Internet access		57 %
Shopping		10 km, Cowbridge 35 % 15 km, supermarket 50 % 30 km, Cardiff 10 % e-shopping 5 %
Village amenities	School Church Pub	School Church Pub Village Hall

- Increase the subsidy on public transport to reduce dependence on private car.
- Stem daily commuting and reduce travel distances by trying to attract more jobs into the region.
- Increase development on brownfield sites.
- Protect historic buildings and increase the recycling of older buildings.
- Prevent haphazard urban sprawl by maximising residential development along the coastal strip, Penarth to Rhoose, where there is already much housing.
- Put extra housing in the open spaces only within those villages which already have modern housing.
- Protect the character of the countryside by protecting those areas of fine landscape from any further development.
- Reinforce the attractiveness of local shopping centres.
- Encourage rural tourism on farms to ensure agriculture survives.

Figure 11.12 Strategies to manage rural change in the Vale of Glamorgan caused by urban growth (excerpts from The Vale of Glamorgan Community Strategy 2003–2013)

EXAM PRACTICE

Figure 11.13 Congestion charging in London

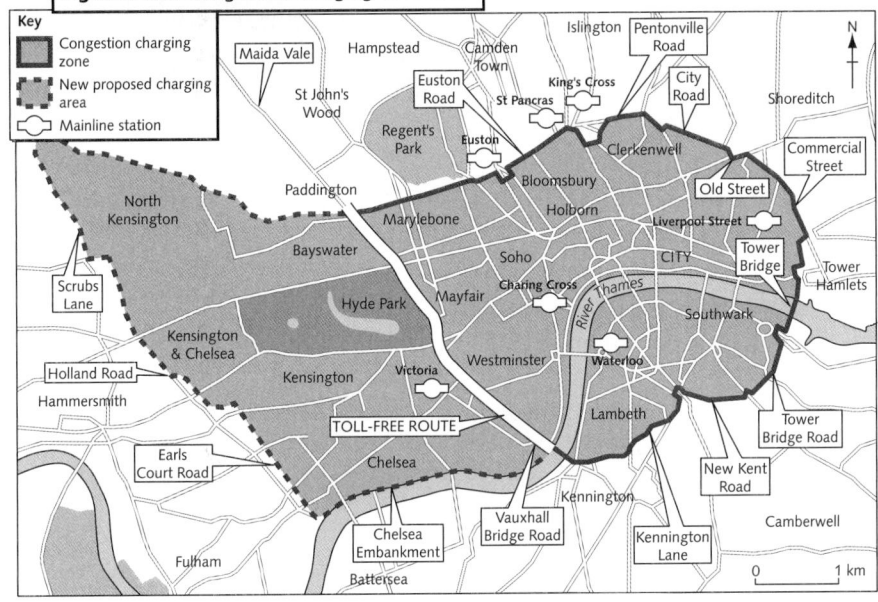

Congestion charging – first 6 months

- 40 000 vehicles drive through the zone everyday
- Motor vehicles entering zone down by 16 %
- Charge £5 per day
- 25 000 penalty charge notices issued a week
- Car journey times down 14 %
- Accidents in zone down 20 %
- Waiting time at bus stops down by a third. Cancelled services down 60 %.
- Taxi journeys up 20 %
- Cycling up 30 %
- 7am – 7pm Mon – Fri

a Congestion charging is one method used to reduce traffic in CBDs. It was introduced in London in 2003. Study Figure 11.13.

  i Select from the list below the area of the original charging area in London.
  6.5 km²
  30 km²
  65 km². (1)

  ii Give **three** advantages of congestion charging. (3)

  iii Suggest **two** disadvantages of congestion charging. (2)

b Figure 11.13 shows a plan to expand the congestion charging.

  i In which direction is the area to be expanded? (1)

  ii Give the length of the new toll-free route through the centre of the charging zone. (1)

  iii Explain why it is important to have a toll-free route through the larger area. (1)

c After one year, February 2004, there were 65 000 fewer commuters with 29 000 more travelling on buses.

  i Using the data and your knowledge of changes in urban areas make **three** suggestions to explain what has happened to the other 36 000 commuters. (3)

  ii Describe other changes that have been made to improve traffic flows in urban areas. (5)

d Do you think that future buildings should be built in the inner city on brownfield sites, or in more rural locations on greenfield sites? Give your reasons. (8)

EXAM TIPS

Using case studies to answer questions is not the only situation where you should give actual real-life details. An answer to question d would gain more marks if you included examples.

Back to ...

The New Wider World website to check your answers to the Exam Practice question.

The consequences of urban development in the UK

12 Global urban development

→ *The New Wider World*, pp78–81; 110; 121; 148; 150–151; 170–171; 193

KEY QUESTIONS

1. How and why do urban areas differ between MEDCs and LEDCs?
2. How does urban growth reflect internal inequalities within LEDCs?

1 How and why do urban areas differ between MEDCs and LEDCs?

The speed of urban growth in MEDCs and LEDCs

World **urbanisation** (the proportion of people living in towns and cities) is rising rapidly (Figure 12.1).

a) Numbers living in urban areas

The figures for urban growth can only be estimates. This is because there are:
- variations as to how an urban area is defined, e.g. is it Liverpool or Merseyside?
- inaccuracies in collecting population data or census details, e.g. street dwellers.

MEDCs have experienced urbanisation since the early 1800s. The main growth was in the nineteenth century associated with the Industrial Revolution. The growth rate in MEDC cities has now slowed down.

LEDCs have only seen rapid urbanisation since the 1950s. However, the speed of urbanisation in LEDCs is greater now than that of MEDCs in the nineteenth century. Many LEDC cities are expanding at a rate of over 25 per cent every decade.

Year	Percentage living in urban areas
1800	3 %
1950	29 %
2006	50 % (estimate)

Figure 12.1 Percentage of the world's population living in urban areas

Year	1840	1870	1900	1930	1960	1970	1980	1990	1995	2000
Cardiff	10	40	150	230	270	290	280	280	290	330
Nairobi	5	6	8	40	250	500	900	1400	1600	2200

Figure 12.2 Different rates of growth of a city in an MEDC (Cardiff) and in an LEDC (Nairobi). (Population figures in 1000s.)

Back to …

The New Wider World **p78** Figure 5.1 for a graph showing percentage of population living in urban areas.

The New Wider World **p79** Figure 5.3 showing a map of the location of the world's largest cities.

Key words to know

Urbanisation
Millionaire city
Megacity

b) The proportion of people living in urban areas in a country
- The MEDCs of North America, Western Europe and Australasia are usually those with the highest urban proportion.
- The LEDCs in Africa and south-east Asia often have the lowest proportion.
- South America has countries with an urban population exceeding 75 per cent.

c) Largest cities

In 1850 there were only two **millionaire cities** (cities with over 1 million people) – London and Paris. By 2002 there were 405.

Most of the millionaire cities:
- before 1950 were between 40° to 50°N in Europe and North America
- since 1950 are in tropical LEDCs.

Megacities are places with a population over 10 million.

Rank order	1970	1985	2000
1	New York 16.5	Tokyo 23.0	Tokyo 27.0
2	Tokyo 13.4	Mexico City 18.8	São Paulo 16.6
3	London 10.5	New York 18.2	New York 16.4
4	Shanghai 10.0	São Paulo 16.8	Mexico City 15.9
5	Mexico City 8.6	Shanghai 13.3	Mumbai (Bombay) 15.4
6	Los Angeles 8.4	Los Angeles 12.8	Shanghai 15.3
7	Buenos Aires 8.4	Buenos Aires 11.6	Beijing 12.7
8	Paris 8.4	Rio de Janeiro 11.1	Los Angeles 12.5
9	São Paulo 7.1	Kolkata (Calcutta) 9.2	Kolkata 11.8
10	Moscow 7.1	Mumbai 8.2	Seoul 11.7
			Jakarta 11.7

Figure 12.3 The world's largest cities (population in millions)

Key: ▓ = LEDC

The reasons for urban growth in MEDCs and LEDCs

The movement of people from country areas to towns and cities is called **rural–urban migration**.

In MEDCs primary and secondary industry developed in the nineteenth century (Chapters 9 and 11, South Wales and Cardiff). This needed much labour so people were attracted to towns and cities by jobs. They were often provided with housing near their work. Cities grew as industry and jobs expanded. Growth was due to urban pull.

In LEDCs movement to the city is due to both **rural push** and **urban pull factors**. The push of poor conditions in the countryside is as much the cause of migration as the pull of jobs and 'bright lights' in the city. However, there are few houses or jobs when migrants reach the cities. The rural push and urban pull factors found in Kenya and Nairobi (p100) illustrate rural–urban migration in an LEDC.

Key words to know
Rural–urban migration
Rural push factor
Urban pull factor

Check this!...

1. Draw a line graph of Figure 12.2 with two different coloured lines to show the rate of growth of an MEDC and LEDC city. Use a 10-year scale for the horizontal axis, keeping an equal space for each decade. Choose a suitable vertical axis.

2. Look at Figure 5.2 on p78 of *The New Wider World* showing the percentage of the total population of each country living in towns and cities in 2002. Describe the distribution of the most and least urbanised countries.

3. Use Figure 12.3 to:
   a) describe the difference in size of the largest cities 1970–2000
   b) compare the growth in MEDC and LEDC cities
   c) describe the changing location of MEDC and LEDC megacities 1970–2000.

4. Give the main differences in the cause of growth of cities in MEDCs and LEDCs.

Urban land use patterns and their recent changes

Chapter 11 describes the land use patterns and recent changes in cities in MEDCs. Cities in LEDCs also develop their own distinctive pattern although this differs from MEDCs in several ways:
- Most of the better-off housing is located near to the city centre.
- The quality of housing decreases rapidly towards the city boundary where many people are forced to live as squatters in shanty towns or informal settlements.
- Industry tends to locate along main roads and railways leading into the city centre.

Back to …
The New Wider World **p81**
Figure 5.9 for a diagram of an urban land use model for an LEDC.

Global urban development

Case Study Extra — **Nairobi, East Kenya, East Africa**

Figure 12.4 Nairobi, land use patterns and characteristics

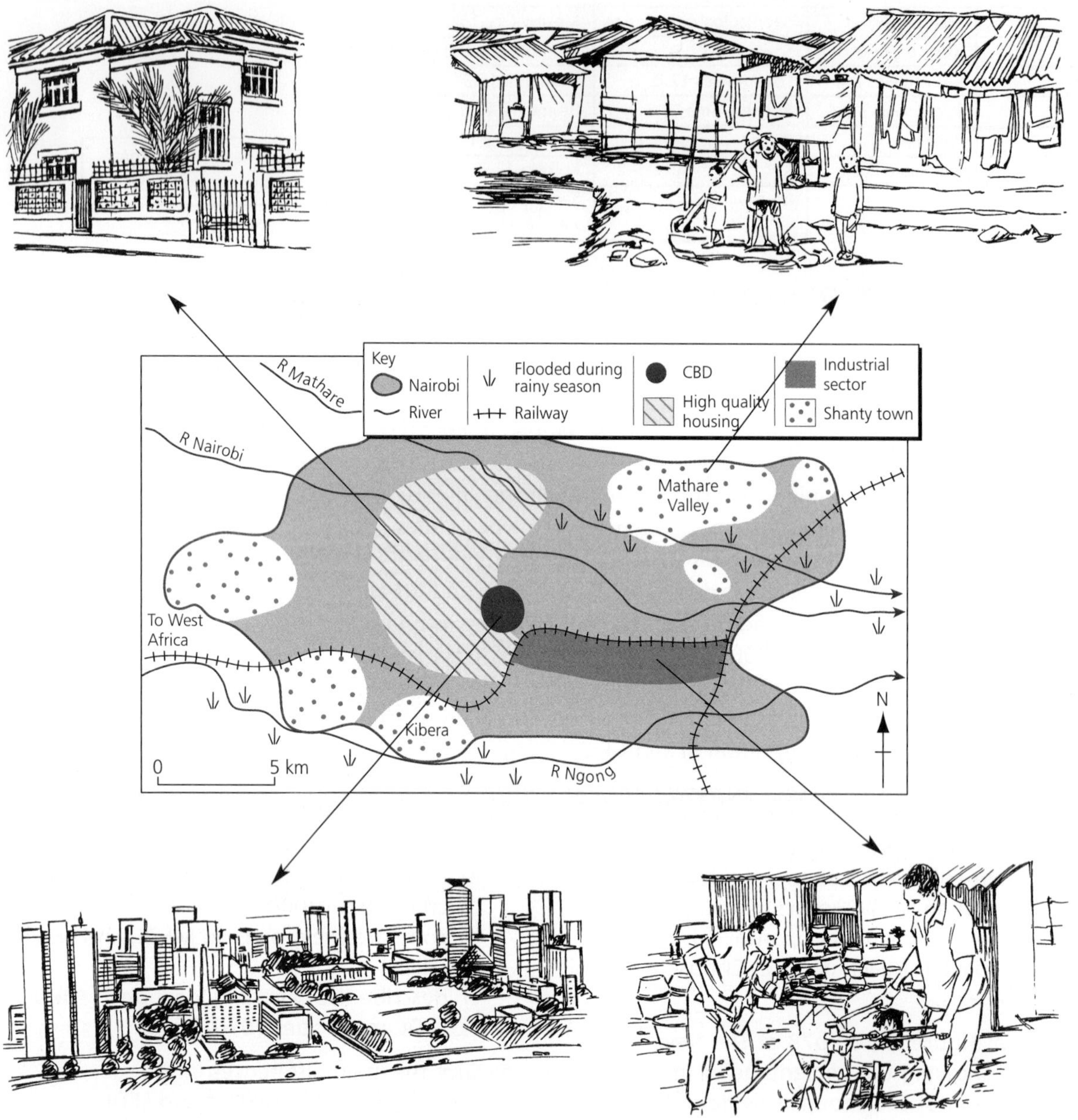

96

The growth of Nairobi as a rich, modern, commercial centre is due to its:
- position at the 'crossroads' of Africa. The main north–south Africa road crosses the main east–west Africa railway line here
- development as the centre of British colonial power in East Africa which also attracted many successful Asian immigrants.

The rapid growth in population is due to rural–urban migration (see section on Kenya, p100).

Characteristics of, and recent changes in, land use zones in Nairobi

Inner city (see Figure 12.4)
- The centre of the city comprises modern high-rise buildings including conference centres, government offices, hotels, banks, for international visitors. There are multinational names, some associated with the UK (Barclays, British Airways), world headquarters of United Nations Environmental Programme. Landscaped parks provide pleasant open spaces.

Inner city housing (see Figure 12.4)
- The high income houses near the city centre owned mainly by Europeans or Asians, are large, contain air conditioning, electricity and a bathroom with a shower.
- Each family has its own servant, car, TV and video and refrigerator. The houses are surrounded by high security fences often patrolled by guards. The children go to private school and university and there are modern hospitals for those who can pay.
- People work in higher paid jobs in the nearby CBD.

Shanty towns or informal settlements (see Figures 12.4 and 12.5)
- The rapid migration of the rural poor into the city has resulted in the development of shanty towns in areas not previously built on, because they are on the banks of polluted rivers which flood in the wet season. One-roomed shacks are made of any material that is available or cheap, e.g. cardboard.
- Families are larger in the shanty towns, (5–10 children) and parents cannot afford to send children to school.

Recent changes
- A women's self-help group organised daily cleaning of the toilets, reducing dysentery and diarrhoea by 30 per cent. In recognition of this the City Council has agreed to provide 15 water pumps to be operated by the women and land has been allocated for a community chemist.
- **Self-help schemes** are now in place. Houses can be built in the shanty towns using local products. Self-help groups manufacture low-cost roofing tiles from local clay and make 'bricks' from soil that has been compressed and heated.
- Loans are made to women to start small businesses. Any profit can then be used to buy for the family.
- Education and training in book-keeping, carpentry, plumbing is available.
- There is a good community spirit. One success story is the Mathare Youth Sports Association (MYSA) which has been nominated for the Nobel Peace Prize for its contribution to cleaning up Mathare.

Figure 12.5 Descriptions of shanty towns in Nairobi

Barefoot children line the narrow, wet tracks separating the hovels of 'the village'. Structures exist wherever there is space, with no thought of access for vehicles or even a breeze. Most of the time a visitor has to duck or walk sideways.
There are two public toilets whose systems collapsed long ago. The refuse everywhere, the excreta by the stream and the flies hovering over uncovered food items on sale give an indication of the problem at hand. There is no electricity, and the source of clean water is a tap owned by individuals who open it to those who have money. **Description of Mathare shanty town by Lydiah Kinyua, leader of the self-help group (WAB)**

Hundreds of ramshackle tin and timber houses in a Nairobi slum have been destroyed by fire, leaving 4500 families homeless. Officials were working to find shelter for the 30 000 people who lived in the slum who are now desperate, hopeless, sleeping in the cold.
George Maina, who was playing board games at his brother's single room house when the fire started, said: 'We could not put out the fire because it became very big very fast, because of the wind. The next thing I knew I was running for my life.'

The Guardian, Saturday 21 February, 2004

Industrial sector (Figure 12.4)
In the shanty towns many people are unemployed and try to earn a living any way they can. They work in **informal industry**. Jobs include cleaning car windscreens at traffic lights and shoe shining. They are badly paid.

Recent changes
In Nairobi there are several *jua kali* metal workshops. In one area the size of three football pitches, 1000 workers in small-scale enterprises hammer scrap metal into an assortment of products for the local people, e.g. stoves. Public and private aid supports these self-help projects.

Back to ...
The New Wider World p148 Figures 9.30, 9.31 and p150 Figure 9.33 for descriptions and photographs of the informal industrial sector in Nairobi.

Key words to know
Shanty town (informal settlement)
Self-help scheme
Informal industry

Using your case study
Use the information in this case study to answer questions on:
- growth
- land use patterns
- recent changes in a city in an LEDC.

Case study links
This case study provides links with:
- Chapter 12 which describes the speed and cause of growth of Nairobi
- Chapter 13 which describes types of aid.

Update
For more information on Nairobi use the link on *The New Wider World Coursemate* website.

Learn it!
a) Describe the rate of growth of Nairobi.

b) Explain the reasons for the growth of Nairobi.

c) Describe the characteristics and recent changes in the land use zones of Nairobi. Illustrate your answer with a sketch map based on Figure 12.4.

2 How does urban growth reflect internal inequalities within LEDCs?

Case Study

Kenya

Back to ...
The New Wider World p193 for the case study of Kenya's level of development.

Using your case study
The information on Kenya can be used to recognise the wealth, employment structure, population and social characteristics of an LEDC.

Case study links
This case study has links with Chapter 13 – population and development indices of an LEDC.

Update
For more information on Kenya use the link on *The New Wider World Coursemate* website.

Learn it!
a) Summarise the information that shows Kenya is an LEDC.

Case Study Extra

Inequalities in Kenya

Kenya is second only to Brazil in the levels of inequality found within the country.
- 50 % live on under US$1 per day
- 10 % earn 47 % of the country's income.

There is poverty in the rural areas whilst the centre of Nairobi continues to prosper commercially. Rural poverty and urban wealth cause the push-pull factors of rural–urban migration and the growth of shanty towns in the city, creating further inequalities in the urban areas. Recent priorities are to reduce inequalities and urban migration by improving rural areas.

Rural region 1 (Figure 12.6)
The pastoralist **Maasai** people live in this region. The northern area is within the Sahel and suffers from desertification.

Back to ...

The New Wider World p121 Figure 8.8 for a photograph of Kenyan women collecting wood for fuel, p171 Figure 10.33 for a photograph of Maasai people in front of their homes and p257 Figure 15.41 for a photograph of overgrazed land in Kenya, pp170–171 describe the development of tourism in the National Parks of Kenya.

Tourism has had an effect on the traditional way of life of the Maasai. The Maasai were moved from their traditional grazing grounds when these became National Parks, e.g. Maasai Mara National Reserve. Now they live near tourist honeypots and sell their craft products to, and perform traditional dances for, the tourists.

Rural region 2 (Figure 12.6)
Here the **Kikuyu** live in linear villages along roads. Houses are surrounded by gardens where **subsistence farming** supplies food of maize, bananas, beans, yams and millet for the family.

Figure 12.6 Physical causes of inequalities within rural Kenya

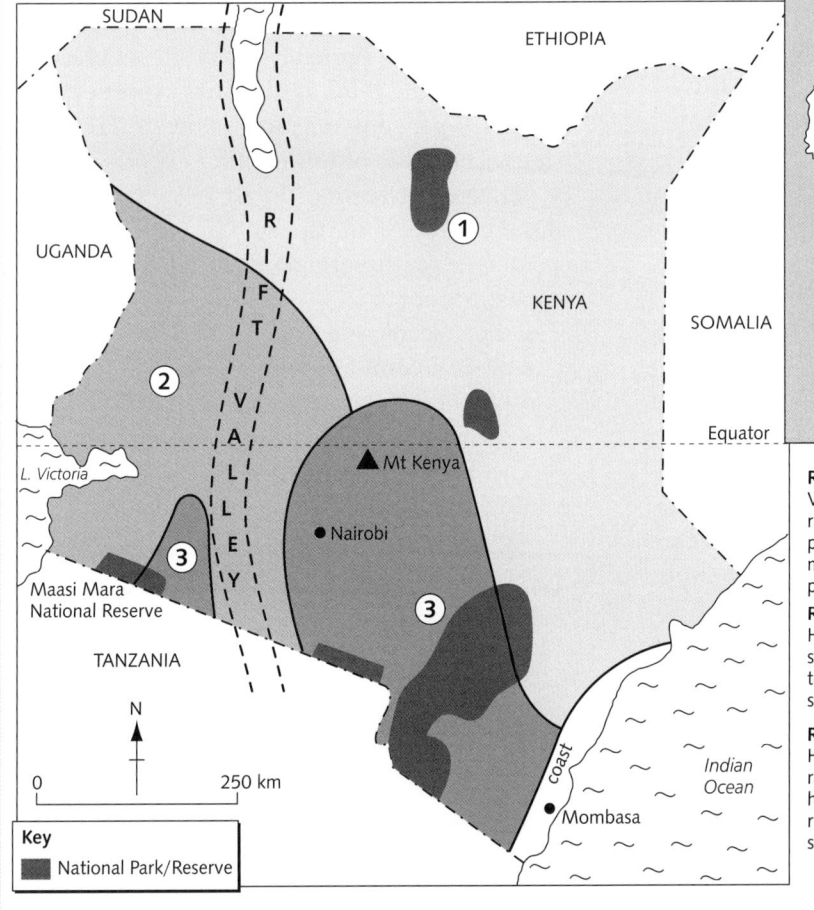

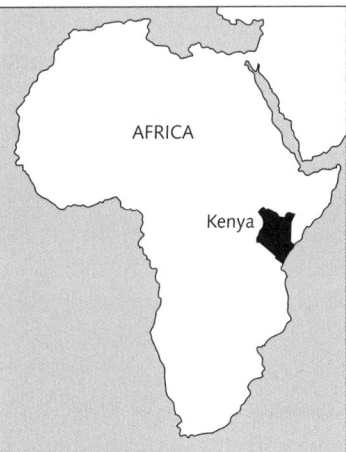

Rural region ①
Very little rain, frequent droughts, rivers often dry up, high temperatures, poor water supply, little vegetation, migrant pastoralists thus low population density.

Rural region ②
Highland, more rain than 1, but water supply still a problem, less high temperatures than 1 since high altitudes, some grass on the fertile volcanic soils.

Rural region ③
Highland over 1500 m, moderate rainfall, moderate temperatures in the high ground, water supply more reliable, deep rich volcanic soils, able to support higher density of population.

Global urban development

Originally large areas of land were cleared for British owned companies with a single **cash crop** grown across the whole **plantation**, e.g. Brooke Bond. In this region coffee is grown on the lower slopes, tea on the upper. Tea (19 per cent) and coffee (15 per cent) are the two main trade exports of Kenya.

Many plantations are now broken up into smaller units and farmed and owned by the Kikuyu.

	Small farmer	Multinationals
1963	2 %	98 %
1999	60 %	40 %

Figure 12.7 Ownership of land, Kikuyu region

Rural–urban migration, Kenya

Most of the rural–urban movement is from the Kikuyu areas to Nairobi.

Rural 'push' factors (why people leave the countryside):
- Lack of employment opportunities due to a change from the plantation system with many employed to ownership of smaller plots by some famililies.
- Overpopulation – Kenya has one of the highest birth rates in the world. The average family size is 7.6 people. As the population expands there is less land available for each family.
- Shortages of food, sometimes starvation, due to desertification in the Sahel region to the north and east of Kenya.
- Maasai forced to move because of the development of National Parks for tourism.
- The skills that are learned in the limited schooling cannot be used in the village.

Urban 'pull' factors (why people move to the city):
- People are looking for better-paid jobs. It is not far from Kikuyu territory to Nairobi so younger people can get home frequently to give money to their families.
- They expect to be housed more comfortably and to have a higher quality of life.
- Nairobi has big, modern buildings which include hospitals, shops, cinemas and a university.
- The Kikuyu have lived in villages and small towns for a long time. They think the change to city life should be easy.

Attempts to reduce inequalities in Kenya

To encourage the Maasai to stay in rural areas, the government has begun to share the wealth obtained from tourism to help improve their education, housing and water supply.

> **Back to ...**
> *The New Wider World* p151 which describes suitable, sustainable Intermediate Technology projects to reduce poverty in Maasai regions.

The **Intermediate Technology Development Group (ITDG)** is a charitable organisation which works with people in developing countries, especially in rural areas. ITDG projects have helped to reduce poverty in Maasai regions. For example, the Maasai Housing Project changed the construction of huts to improve health now the Maasai are more permanently settled. Other projects have trained local potters to produce a new type of stove (jiko) which is much more efficient and takes less wood.

The southern region is now an important exporter of fresh horticultural produce which has become the third agricultural export of Kenya (10 per cent), e.g. fresh flowers, French beans. The value of **horticulture** exports rose by 60 per cent between 1991 and 1996. 93 per cent of the produce is transported by air to its main customers, the supermarkets in the UK. The success is due to:
- the volcanic soils
- all year round growing season
- nearness to Nairobi airport
- giving business loans to women.

The 'Fairdeal' foundation is important in gaining a better deal for smaller growers.

> **Key words to know**
> *Maasai*
> *Kikuyu*
> *Subsistence farming*
> *Cash crop*
> *Plantation*
> *Intermediate Technology Development Group (ITDG)*
> *Horticulture*

Using your case study
The information in this case study will help you answer questions in the exam on the patterns and causes of internal inequalities in an LEDC and attempts to reduce the inequalities.

Case study links
This case study provides links with:
- Chapter 7 – desertification effects in north and east Kenya
- Chapter 13 – aid projects in Kenya
- Chapter 14 – trade characteristics of an LEDC.

Update
For more information on inequalities within Kenya use the link on *The New Wider World Coursemate* website.

Learn it!
a) Describe the patterns and causes of rural poverty within Kenya and urban wealth within Nairobi. Drawing an annotated map based on Figure 12.6 will help your answer.

b) Explain push/pull causes of migration between the rural and urban areas in Kenya.

c) Describe methods of reducing rural–urban inequalities in Kenya.

EXAM PRACTICE

% of people	UK (% of wealth)	Brazil (% of wealth)
100	100	100
80	60	33
60	35	16
40	18	7
20 poorest	7	2

Figure 12.8 Levels of inequality in the UK and Brazil

a Copy the sentences below and use Figure 12.8 to complete the gaps.

The poorest 20 % of people in Brazil only have ___ % of the wealth of the country. The poorest 60 % of people in the UK have ___ % of its wealth. The richest 20 % (100–80 %) of people in the UK have ___ % of the wealth of the country whereas the richest 20 % of Brazilians own ___ % of the country's wealth. _____ is the more unequal country as far as wealth of individuals is concerned. (5)

b Most of the wealthy people in LEDCs live in cities.

　i Give **three** pull factors attracting people to LEDC cities. (3)

　ii With reference to **one** LEDC city you have studied, describe and explain the location of shanty towns. (4)

　iii Describe **one** positive aspect of life in a shanty town. (2)

c i Describe and explain the conditions in the rural areas of an LEDC country of your choice that have led to many people migrating to the city. (8)

　ii How may inequalities within LEDC countries be reduced? (3)

EXAM TIPS
The wording of a question indicates how many examples you have to give. Some questions may ask you to state '**three** factors', others may not be specific. So look out for plurals, e.g. in question ci the word 'areas' means you have to describe and explain more than one rural situation.

Back to ...
The New Wider World website to check your answers to the Exam Practice question.

Global urban development

13 Patterns of world development and population change

➡️ *The New Wider World*, pp4–15; 180–183; 190–191

1 What contrasts in development are to be found in the world?

What are development indicators? How effective are they in showing us levels of development?

There are different levels of development within a country (see Kenya p99), or between countries of the world.

- **Gross national product (GNP) per capita** – the total value of goods and services produced by a country in a year, divided by the total number of people living in that country. GNP does not show differences in wealth.

Wealth

What can measure levels of development?

Social indicators
For example:
- population – **birth rates (BR)**, **death rates (DR)**, **natural increase**, **population structures**
- health – **infant mortality** rate, **life expectancy**, people per doctor.

Other indicators
For example:
- adult literacy
- diet
- employment structures
- energy consumption.

Figure 13.1 Indicators of development

KEY QUESTIONS

1. What contrasts in development are to be found in the world?
2. What are the global patterns of population change?

Key words to know

Gross national product (GNP)
Birth rate (BR)
Death rate (DR)
Natural increase
Population structure
Infant mortality
Life expectancy
Quality of life
Human Development Index (HDI)

Back to …

The New Wider World **p182** Figure 11.5 for a table showing the HDI of selected countries and **pp182–183** for more information on the HDI and inequality.

Many of the indicators are related to the wealth of a country. This suggests that a country has to increase its standard of living, i.e. its GNP if it is to improve the **quality of life**, i.e. cultural and social well-being of its inhabitants.

The **Human Development Index (HDI)** was designed by the UN in the 1990s to combine social and economic indicators.

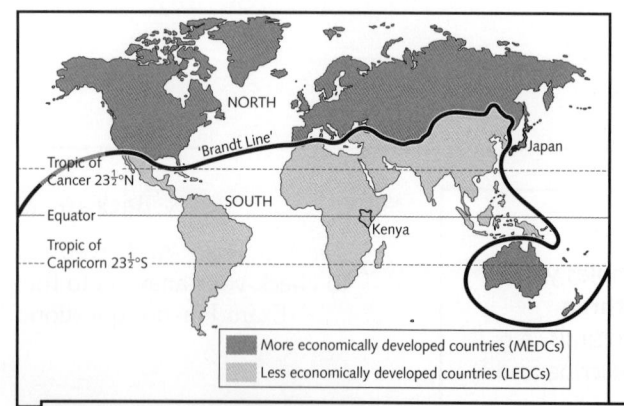

Figure 13.2 Global patterns of development. The 'Brandt' line separates MEDCs in the 'north' and LEDCs in the 'south'.

Global patterns of development

Patterns of development can be shown by:
- maps
- statistics.

The 'Brandt' line separates the countries of the 'north' (richer more industrialised countires) and 'south' (less industrialised countries) according to their level of development.

Development indicators can reveal information about levels of development in a country. The UK, Japan and Kenya are shown in Figure 13.3. The figures show contrasts between the countries but not within them.

102

Figure 13.3 Development indicators of selected countries

Economic wealth		Social indicators						Other indicators			
Country	GNP per capita (US$)	Birth rate (1000/year)	Death rate (1000/year)	Natural increase	Infant mortality (1000/year)	Life expectancy (years)	Population per doctor	% adult literacy	Calories per person per day	% in agriculture	Tonnes coal equivalent per year
UK (MEDC)	18 700	12	11	1	6	77	300	99	3276	2	5.40
Japan (MEDC)	39 640	9	8	1	4	81	600	99	2932	7	4.74
Kenya (LEDC)	280	34	14	20	76	48	10 000	80	1976	80	0.11

Check this!...

1 Copy Figure 13.1. Think of some more indicators of development. Add these in the appropriate place on the diagram.

2 Give the advantages and disadvantages of GNP as a development indicator. Give any advantages/disadvantages of other indicators.

3 Contrast the different characteristics of MEDCs and LEDCs. Use values to illustrate your answer.

How do aid agencies reduce global inequalities? Do they encourage sustainable development?

Aid is the giving of resources by one country, or by an organisation, (**donor**) to another country (**receiver**). The aid may be in the form of:
- money, although this may be given as a grant or a loan that has to be repaid
- goods, food, machinery or technology aimed at short-term relief or long-term benefit
- people who have skills and knowledge, e.g. teachers, nurses and engineers.

Aid donors
- Government (**bilateral aid**) – given directly by a richer country to a poorer country. It is often 'tied' (see Figure 13.5). UN agreed that 0.7 per cent of GNP of MEDCs was to be given to LEDCs.
- International organisations (**multilateral aid**) – e.g. World Bank, IMF (International Monetary Fund). These do not give to 'unstable' countries and money tends to be given for large projects that encourage trade rather than production for internal LEDC use.
- Voluntary – **NGOs (non-governmental organisations)**. There are 25 000 NGOs, e.g. Comic Relief has sent £130 million to Africa since it started.

In reality, the giving of aid is often complex and controversial as it does not always benefit the country to which it is given.

Types of aid
All three donors give two types of aid.

Key words to know

Donor
Receiver
Bilateral aid
Multilateral aid
Non-governmental organisation (NGO)

Patterns of world development and population change

Type of aid	How the aid is used
Short-term/emergency – for hazards, e.g. earthquakes and drought	• Immediate help – provides food, clothes, medical supplies and shelter • Goes direct to places and people in need • Helps refugees
Long-term/sustainable – helps people in LEDCs to support themselves, e.g. Intermediate Technology Development Group	• Encourages development of local skills and use of local raw materials • Trains local people to be teachers, nurses, health workers • Helps equip schools and development of local agriculture and small-scale industry • Prevents LEDCs from falling into debt

Figure 13.4 Types of aid

Figure 13.5 Some problems of long-term aid

1. TIED AID — "Here, have this but in return you must buy products from us and you must only use it for the projects we choose." "Thanks."

2. AID MAY NOT REACH THE NEEDY — "We need to transform the airports, build a dam, buy guns..." "Help!"

3. FOOD GROWN WITH AID MAY NOT GO TO FEED LOCAL PEOPLE

4. AID CAN LEAD TO CORRUPTION — "We need the money for food!"

5. PROBLEMS WITH AID DISTRIBUTION — WAR ZONE

6. UNSUITABLE AID — "Here, have these trucks." "Thanks, but I can't drive and how can I afford petrol? What happens if they break down?"

7. AID CAN CREATE DEBT — "How will I repay this?" INTEREST RATES / LOAN SHARK

8. EXPORT EARNINGS NEEDED TO PAY OFF AID DEBTS — "I'd like £££££ for interest payments." "We need clean water... industry... irrigation"

9. PROBLEMS WITH USE OF AID PRODUCT — Instructions: Mix contents with clean drinking water. SKIMMED MILK POWDER

10. AID CAN CREATE DEPENDENCE — "Why should I bother working?" FOOD AID

11. AID MAY UNDERMINE LOCAL PRODUCERS — MARKET / LOCAL PRODUCE £ / FOOD AID Free

NGOs are now receiving more money as grants from MEDC governments. This was 1.5 per cent of NGO's money in 1970 rising to 40 per cent in 2000. This is because NGOs:
- have established teams of experts in many countries
- have a good record of successful results
- concentrate on smaller low-tech projects, working with local people on long-term sustainable projects
- concentrate on very poor countries
- are independent and do not require anything in return.

Figure 13.6 Characteristics of sustainable development encouraged by NGOs

	Sustainable development
Socio economic	Family planning and HIV/AIDS health education
	Development of skills to produce better but still low-tech building materials
	Educating women in small business techniques to develop local trade
	Labour intensive projects since many people are unemployed and so any wealth is spread amongst more people
	Schemes that cost little to run so they can continue after the aid programme has finished
People and resources	Development of more efficient energy use, e.g. stoves for cooking
	Reafforestation to provide more renewable energy sources and reduce distance people have to travel to find fuel
	Soil conservation using handmade tools that can be mended locally
	Education to keep the water supply clean to avoid disease
	Development of local water supply to avoid long journeys for basic needs
	Simple machinery for making tools from recycled metal products

Examples of sustainable and non-sustainable aid in Kenya
- SIDA, Swedish International Development Authority has been promoting sustainable soil conservation since 1974, using local skills and resources, e.g. building a 15 metre dam for an individual farm with ox plough, spade and wheelbarrow. By 1995 over 30 per cent of Kenyan smallholder farmers had some form of soil conservation method on their land.
- Kenya's Green Belt Movement, sponsored by Comic Relief, involving 50 000 women has set up over 3000 nurseries and produced 20 million trees. Trees provide fruit, shade and sustainable firewood.
- Following the 1984 drought, Oxfam gave goats to the population in the north east of Kenya. Families received 30 goats which, 10 years later, had increased to over 250. Some goats were sold for different food and clothing. The increased wealth meant that the region was able to survive the 1992 drought.
- An unsuccessful project was to sink wells and a borehole for a reliable water supply near the village of Korr in north east Kenya. The pastoralist villagers stopped migrating to look for water and lived permanently in the village using the new water supply. The result was overgrazing with all the land within 60 km of the village desertified.
- The Fairtrade Foundation lobbies the big coffee sellers to ensure local farmers get a fairer price for their coffee beans.

Check this!...

1 Are the following types of aid short-term emergency or long-term sustainable?
   - Wateraid – providing clean water supplies to shanty towns in Mali's capital.
   - Sending doctors to Bangladesh following flooding.
   - Combined relief – sending tents to Bam, Iran after the earthquake in 2003.
   - USA sending genetically modified grain to sub-Saharan Africa following droughts of 2002.
   - Christian Aid educating women after the war in Afghanistan 2002.

2 You are a marketing consultant for an NGO and you have to provide a 30-second TV commercial asking for money for a sustainable aid project. Decide on a project you would like to promote. Write the story line for the commercial.

3 Use the Internet to research some of the current aid projects around the world. Do you think they are successful in reducing inequalities and promoting sustainable development?

2 What are the global patterns of population change?

Interpretation of the world population distribution

Distribution describes the way in which people are spread out across the Earth's surface. This distribution is uneven and changes over periods of time.

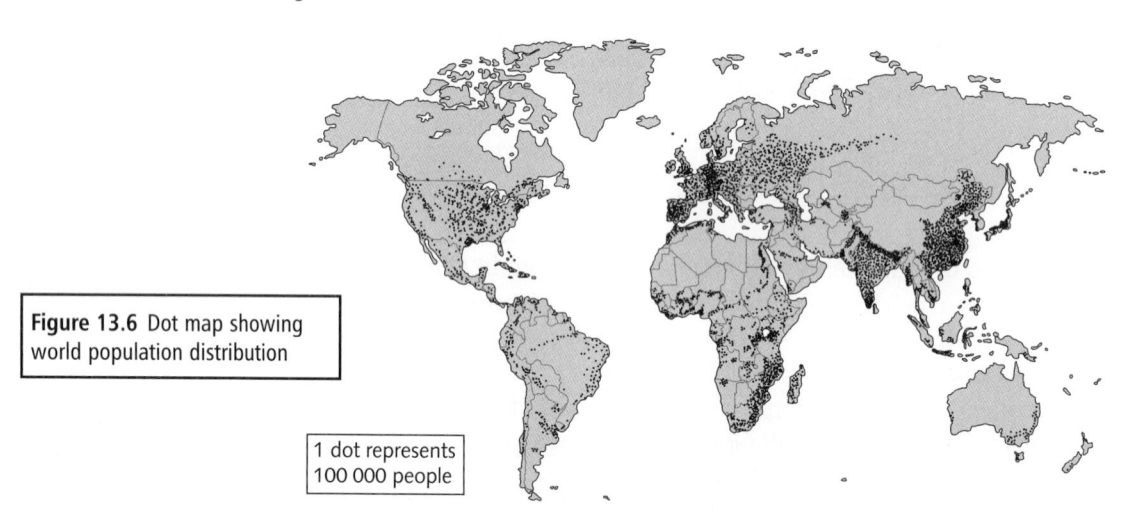

Figure 13.6 Dot map showing world population distribution

1 dot represents 100 000 people

People are concentrated into certain parts of the world – **densely populated** areas. Other areas have few people living there – **sparsely populated** areas.

You do not have to know the world population distribution but you do need to be able to explain why an area has a dense or sparse population once you are given information about the area.

Key words to know

Distribution
Densely populated
Sparsely populated

Check this!...

1 Find China in your atlas. Using Figure 13.6, describe the population density of China. Look up the physical and human characteristics of China in your atlas.

2 Using Figure 1.3 on pp4–5 of *The New Wider World* interpret (explain) the population distribution of China.

3 Repeat the exercise in question 2 for Kenya.

The demographic transition model

Population change depends mainly upon the balance between the:
- **birth rate (BR)** – the average number of live births in a year for every 1000 people in the total population
- and the **death rate (DR)** – average number of deaths per 1000 people in the population.

It is also, but to a lesser extent, affected by **migration**.

The **natural increase** of population (where the BR is higher) or the **natural decrease** (where the DR is higher) is the difference between the birth rate and the death rate.

The **demographic transition model (DTM)** describes the change in population growth rates over time.

Key words to know

Birth rate (BR)
Death rate (DR)
Migration
Natural increase
Natural decrease
Demographic transition model (DTM)
Child mortality

Figure 13.7 Demographic transition model

	STAGE 1 HIGH FLUCTUATING	STAGE 2 EARLY EXPANDING	STAGE 3 LATE EXPANDING	STAGE 4 LOW FLUCTUATING	POSSIBLE STAGE 5 LOW FLUCTUATING
	High BR due to: • no birth control or family planning • high **child mortality**, having many children increases chances some may live • many children needed to work on the land • religious beliefs (e.g. Roman Catholic, Muslims) encourage large families. *High DR, especially among children, due to:* • disease and plague (bubonic, cholera) • famine, uncertain food supplies, poor diet • poor hygiene - no piped, clean water and no sewage disposal • little medical science - few doctors, hospitals, drugs.	*Fall in DR due to:* • improved care - vaccinations, hospitals, doctors, new drugs • improved sanitation and water supply • improvements in food production • a decrease in child mortality.	*Fall in BR due to:* • family planning - contraceptives, sterilisation, government incentives • a lower infant mortality rate, less need to have so many children • increased mechanisation means less people required • increased material possessions (cars, holidays) less money for large families • more career women	Both BR and DR remain low.	The BR falls below the DR resulting in a decrease of population. Occurs in some MEDCs since 1990s.
Present world examples	Rainforest tribes	Kenya, Zimbabwe, Bangladesh	Brazil, Mexico, Egypt, India	China, Japan, USA, France	Germany, Italy, Spain
(UK sequence)	(Pre-1760)	(1760–1880)	(1880–1940)	(Post-1940)	?

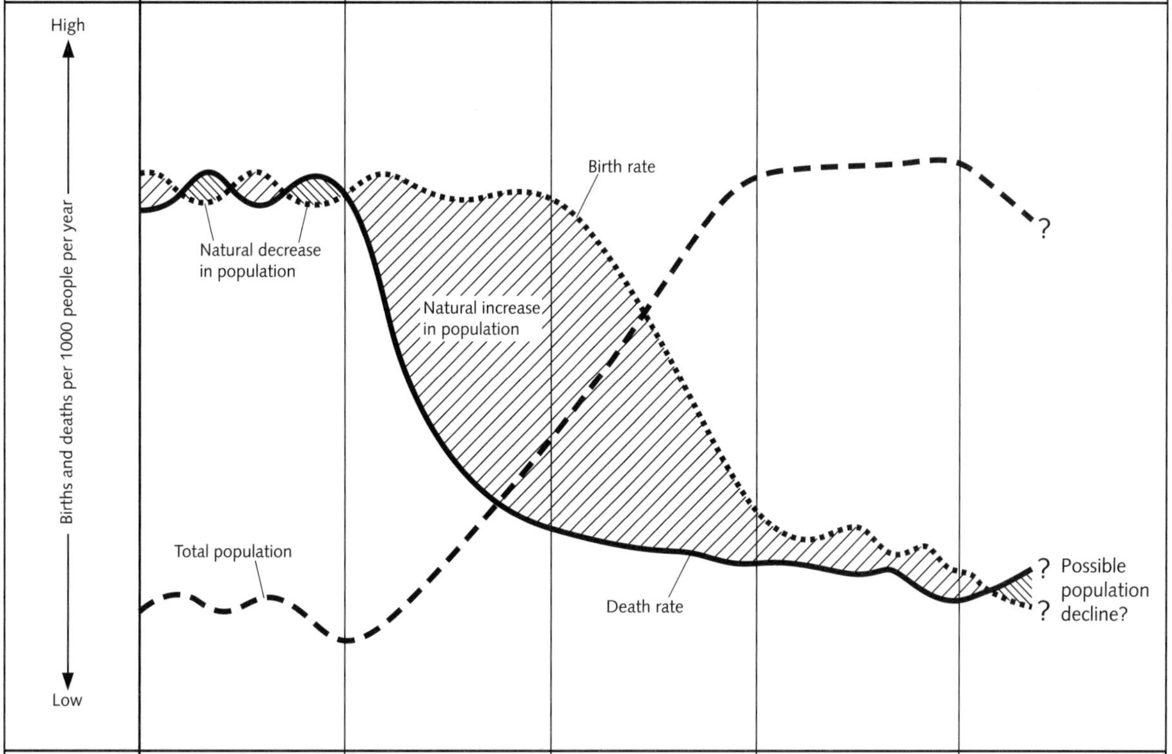

Key words to know

Population explosion

World population growth (See Figure 15.3 on p123)

There was a slow steady rise until 1900. The rise in population increased so fast after the 1970s that there was a **population explosion**. Since 2000 rates have slowed down or even declined in MEDCs; however, they continue to rise, but less quickly, in LEDCs.

Why, although people are living longer, is the annual growth rate slowing down?

This is due to:
- education, e.g. family planning, female literacy, have led to a faster decline in BRs than predicted
- the one-child policy in China, a country with over 20 per cent of the world's population
- disease, e.g. AIDS reduces life expectancies, especially in sub-Saharan countries that have the world's highest BRs.

Check this!...

1. Define the terms 'birth rate', 'death rate', 'child mortality' and 'natural increase'. What else may affect population numbers?

2. At which stage in the DTM are the following countries?

	BR	DR	Natural increase/decrease
Mexico	24	5	19
Italy	9	10	−1
Ethiopia	44	15	29
USA	15	9	6

3. Look at Figure 13.7. Why does the DR fall in Stage 2 of the DTM? Why does the BR fall in Stage 3? Why is education for women important in LEDCs?

4. Use Figure 15.3a on p123 in this book to describe the world population growth.

Key words to know

Population pyramid
Dependency ratio

Economic and social implications of population structure

The rate of natural increase, the BR, the DR and life expectancy (the average number of years that a person in the country can expect to live) all affect the population structure of a country.

Population pyramids show the population structure of a country. Unlike the DTM they include immigrants.

Population pyramids show:
- the total population divided into age groups, e.g. 15–19 years
- the percentage of the total population, subdivided into males and females, in each of those groups.

The shape of the population pyramid varies between MEDC and LEDC because the proportions of people of different ages differ.

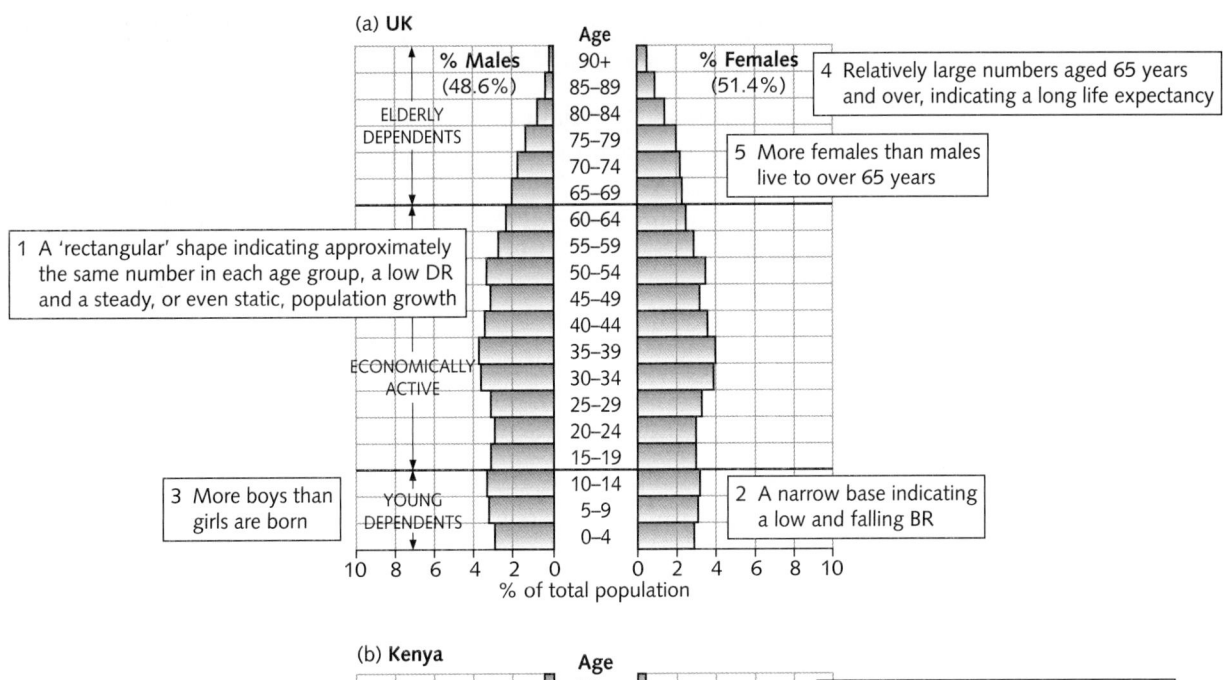

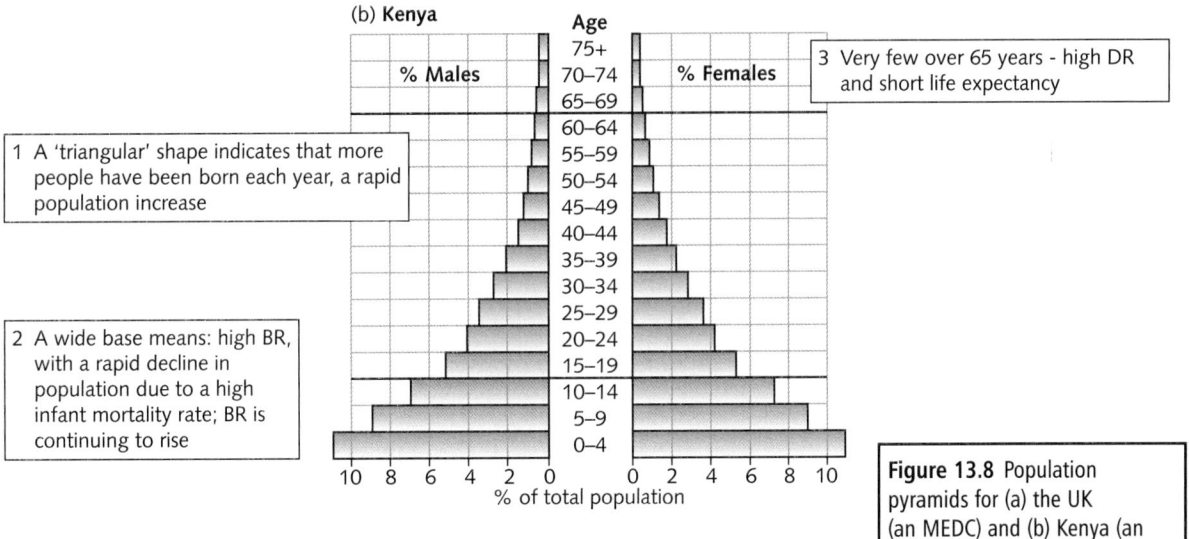

(a) UK

Population pyramid showing % Males (48.6%) and % Females (51.4%) by age group from 0–4 to 90+.

Annotations:
1. A 'rectangular' shape indicating approximately the same number in each age group, a low DR and a steady, or even static, population growth
2. A narrow base indicating a low and falling BR
3. More boys than girls are born
4. Relatively large numbers aged 65 years and over, indicating a long life expectancy
5. More females than males live to over 65 years

Categories: ELDERLY DEPENDENTS, ECONOMICALLY ACTIVE, YOUNG DEPENDENTS

x-axis: % of total population (10 8 6 4 2 0 0 2 4 6 8 10)

(b) Kenya

Population pyramid showing % Males and % Females by age group from 0–4 to 75+.

Annotations:
1. A 'triangular' shape indicates that more people have been born each year, a rapid population increase
2. A wide base means: high BR, with a rapid decline in population due to a high infant mortality rate; BR is continuing to rise
3. Very few over 65 years - high DR and short life expectancy

Figure 13.8 Population pyramids for (a) the UK (an MEDC) and (b) Kenya (an LEDC)

Dependency ratio

The **dependency ratio** is a ratio of the non-economically active to the economically active in the population.

Non-economically active are children (0–14) and elderly (65+).

Economically active are those of working age (15–64).

The dependency ratio does not take into account those of working age who are unemployed.

Most developed countries have a dependency ratio of between 50 and 70, whereas in developing countries the ratio is often over 100 due to the large numbers of children.

Patterns of world development and population change

Economic and social implications of population structure of MEDCs

An ageing population

By 2000, several MEDCs had more people aged over 65 than children aged under 15.

The proportion of over 65s is predicted to rise to over 20 per cent by 2020 and, in some countries such as Japan and Italy, to reach 35 per cent by 2050.

Figure 13.9 Implications of an ageing population

Problems created in a country...	Problems facing the elderly...
More money is needed for: residential homes and sheltered accommodation; health care (e.g. doctors, hospital operations, home visits and free prescriptions); social services (e.g. home help and providing meals), subsidies (e.g. free TV licences and bus passes).	Loneliness, many live alone
	Financial worries, most cannot afford the cost of a residential home
	Fear of crime and traffic
Higher dependence upon a smaller group of economically active people to provide consumer goods and services as well as money through taxation.	Increasing reliance on public transport which is reducing, especially in rural areas
	Age prejudice, few jobs for the elderly
Less money is available for younger age groups, e.g. for education, improvements in transport or the provision of leisure and social amenities.	

Too few under 15s

In future these countries may:
- have too few consumers and skilled workers to keep their economy going
- see a reduction in their competitive advantage in science and technology
- have closures of schools and shops, especially in smaller towns and villages
- experience problems in providing pensions and social care for an **ageing population**.

Key words to know

Ageing population

Economic and social implications of population structures of LEDCs

Too many under 15s

- at present the large youthful population needs child health care and education. LEDCs cannot afford these services.
- in the future there will be more people reaching child-bearing age, which could cause a further population explosion.

Check this!...

1. Draw the simplified shape of population pyramids that show:
   a) high birth rates and high death rates
   b) low birth rates and low death rates
   c) a sudden recent decline in the birth rate
   d) shanty town populations which have a high death rate, a high birth rate, more men than women and large numbers of men in the age range 20–40.

2. Look at Figure 13.8. Estimate the dependency ratio in Kenya. Is this dependency from an ageing population or young population?

3. Contrast the issues of high dependency ratios in MEDCs with those in LEDCs. Which do you think is the greater problem? Why?

The causes and consequences of migration

Migration is a change of home. It can be applied to temporary, seasonal and daily movements as well as to permanent changes both between countries and within a country. Permanent international migration is the movement of people between countries. **Emigrants** are people who leave a country; **immigrants** are those who arrive in a country.

International migration can be divided into two categories:
- **Voluntary migration** is the free movement of migrants looking for an improved quality of life, e.g. employment – to find a job, to earn a higher salary. These people are classed as economic migrants.
- **Forced migration** is when the migrant has to move due to natural disaster or to social situations, e.g. religious and/or political persecution; wars. These people are classed as **refugees**.

Key words to know
Emigrant
Immigrant
Voluntary migration
Economic migrant
Forced migration
Refugee

Check this!...

1 What type of migrants are the following?
- UK doctors moving to USA.
- People once living in Iraq who opposed Saddam Hussain.
- People who live in north-east Wales who work in Liverpool.
- East European students picking fruit in the UK.
- UK people retiring to South Africa.
- Sudanese people moving into north-east Kenya following drought.

Case Study

Migration of Turks into Germany

Back to ...

The New Wider World pp28–29 for the case study of migrant Turkish workers in West Germany.

Using your case study

Use the information in this case study to describe the:
- push factors resulting in emigration from Turkey, and the pull factors resulting in immigration into Germany
- consequences for both the losing country of Turkey and the receiving country of Germany, using only German examples (not British ones) in Figure 2.19 on p29 of *The New Wider World*. Refer to the consequences of the dismantling of the Berlin Wall on Turkish migrants.

Use the information to answer questions on **one** major population migration.

Learn it!

a) Explain the push factors causing Turks to leave Turkey.

b) Explain the pull factors attracting Turks to Germany.

c) Give the consequences of this migration for:
   i) Germany
   ii) Turkey.

d) Describe the situation for Turks in Germany since 1989.

Patterns of world development and population change

EXAM PRACTICE

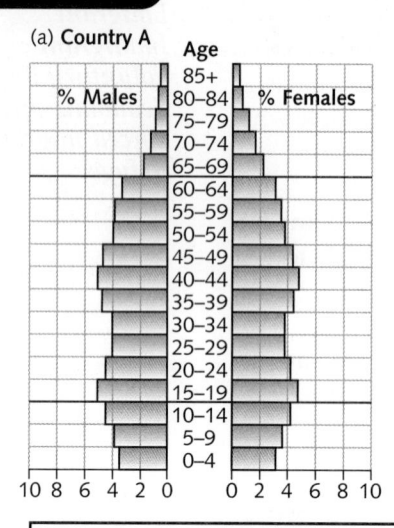

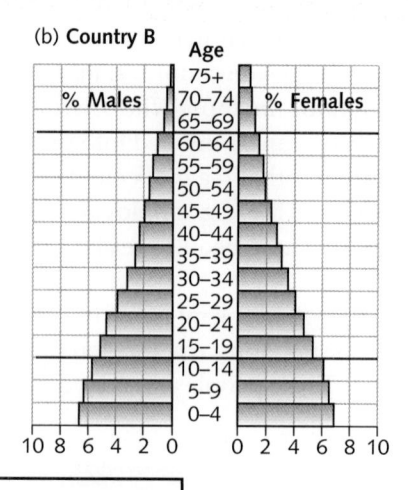

Figure 13.10 Population pyramids for Country A and Country B

a Study the population pyramids in Figure 13.10.

  i Compare the proportion of:
  1. young dependants in countries **A** and **B** (1)
  2. people over the age of 65 years of age in countries **A** and **B**. (1)

  ii Give **two** reasons for the shape of the population structure in country **B**. (2)

  iii State which country has a typical MEDC population structure. Give reasons for your answer. (3)

  iv What does 'life expectancy at birth' (Figure 13.11) indicate about a country? (1)

  v Which social indicator in Figure 13.11 do you consider to be the most useful indicator of development? Give reasons for your answer. (2)

b Population structures are useful to help a country plan for future services.

  i Which country **A** or **B** needs to concentrate on:
  1. building homes and hospitals for the elderly
  2. providing a new clean water supply? (2)

  ii Describe **one** other concern resulting from population structure for an:
  1. LEDC
  2. MEDC. (2)

c i Describe the differences between short-term (emergency) aid and long-term aid. (2)

  ii Give **one** example of **each** of the two types of aid. (2)

  iii Long-term aid can be in the form of large projects or smaller-scale sustainable aid. Which type of long-term aid do you think is the most effective? Give reasons for your answer. (2)

Figure 13.11 Some social indicators	Infant mortality	Life expectancy at birth	Population per doctor
Country A	4	81	600
Country B	70	61	2439

Back to ...
The New Wider World website to check your answers to the Exam Practice question.

EXAM TIPS

You may be asked to 'compare' as in question ai – show how two or more things are similar and/or different. Do not write two separate accounts but use words such as A is bigger than B, whilst C is older than D.

> *The New Wider World*, pp70–73; 144–146; 152–153; 186–189; 192; 194

14 Global communities

1 What are the different patterns of trade in the world?

World trade

No country is self-sufficient in the full range of raw materials (food, minerals and energy) and manufactured goods that are wanted by its people. To try to achieve this, countries must trade with one another.

- **Trade** is the flow of goods from producers to consumers, and it is important in the development of a country.
- **Imports** are the goods and services bought by a country.
- **Exports** are the goods and services sold by a country.

The **trade balance** is the difference between a country's imports and exports. A country can grow more wealthy by selling more than it buys. Some countries have a **trade surplus** – they export more than they import. Others have a **trade deficit** – they import more than they export.

KEY QUESTIONS

1. What are the different patterns of trade in the world?
2. Why is the world becoming an increasingly global community?

Key words to know

Trade
Imports
Exports
Trading balance
Trade surplus
Trade deficit

Patterns of world trade

Trade of LEDCs, e.g. Kenya	Trade of MEDCs, e.g. Japan
Most exports are bulky primary products, the result of former colonial economies where a mineral or a crop is exported in its 'raw state'	MEDCs are industrialised countries which export manufactured goods
Often only two or three items are exported. If production of one of these collapses, e.g. disease spoils a crop, there is a major effect on the economy.	A wide range of items are exported. The economy can withstand changes in demand of some products.
Prices of, and demand for, these products fluctuate. Prices have risen slower than manufactured goods. The result is a widening trade gap with MEDCs.	Prices of, and demand for, these products tend to be steady. Prices have risen considerably in comparison with raw materials.
The volume and value of trade is small	The volume and value of trade is large
Most exports come from transnational companies which send profits to the parent company, based in an MEDC	Profits are kept by the exporting country
There are poor internal transport networks, which makes movement of goods difficult	Trade is helped by good internal transport networks
Trade is severely hit at times of world economic recession	Trade is affected at times of world economic recession
As the trade gap widens, many LEDCs fall further into debt	
Typical LEDC exports, e.g. Kenya: • foodstuffs 59 % • minerals 22 % • machinery 9 % • chemicals 4 % • manufactured goods 3 % • other 3 %.	Typical MEDC exports, e.g. Japan: • manufactured goods 71 % • machinery 11 % • chemicals 6 % • minerals 1 % • foodstuffs 1 % • other 10 %.

Figure 14.1 Differences between trade of LEDCs and MEDCs

Global communities

MEDC	NIC	Middle income LEDC	LEDC
Japan, 3378	Thailand, 1004	Brazil, 346	Kenya, 93

Figure 14.2 Examples of values of trade per capita, US$

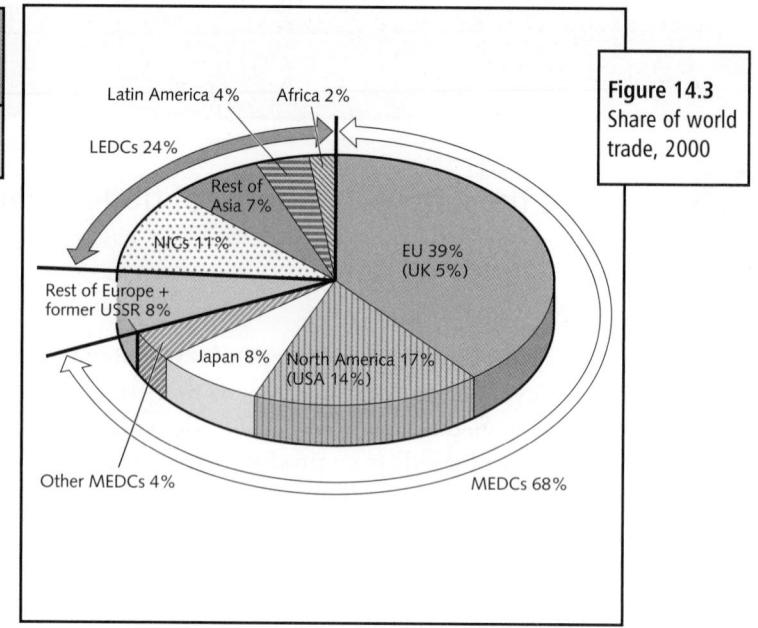

Figure 14.3 Share of world trade, 2000

- Latin America 4%
- Africa 2%
- LEDCs 24%
- Rest of Asia 7%
- NICs 11%
- Rest of Europe + former USSR 8%
- Japan 8%
- EU 39% (UK 5%)
- North America 17% (USA 14%)
- Other MEDCs 4%
- MEDCs 68%

Key words to know

New industrialised country (NIC)
Trade barrier
Tariff
Quota
Trading bloc

- In the late twentieth century, the older industrialised countries of the USA and western Europe faced increasing competition, initially from Japan but later from the **newly industrialised countries (NICs)** of Asia's Pacific Rim.
- LEDCs have 82 per cent of the world's population, but only 24 per cent of the world's trade.
- Over 60 per cent of LEDC trade is from 8 middle income LEDCs, e.g. Brazil.
- The oil-exporting countries (OPEC) have seen their share of world trade decline since 1990 due to the Gulf War and a world recession.
- World trade is now dominated by the increasing number of large, powerful transnational companies.

Trading blocs

MEDCs have tried to control trade by creating **trade barriers** which they hope will protect jobs and industries within their own country.

There are two ways of controlling trade:

1. **Tariffs** are taxes paid on imports. The price of imported goods is increased to make them more expensive and thus less competitive, than home-produced goods.
2. **Quotas** limit the amount of goods that can be imported. Quotas are often placed on primary goods and so work against LEDCs.

Trading blocs are where several countries group together to try to increase the volume and value of their trade. Stopping tariffs reduces the price of products sold between member countries. The larger the internal market, the greater the number of potential customers.

The European Union (EU) is an example of a trading bloc. Germany can sell cars to the UK at a cheaper price than cars from Japan. However, Japanese car manufacturing is now located in the UK to allow trade within the EU without tariffs. It is difficult for LEDCs to import into the EU. Within the EU many of the potential customers are wealthy and can afford to buy numerous high-valued goods.

NAFTA — North American Free Trade Association (3): Canada, Mexico, USA

EFTA — European Free Trade Association (5): Iceland, Liechtenstein, Norway, Sweden, Switzerland

EU — European Union (25): Austria, Belgium, Cyprus, Czech Republic, Denmark, Estonia, Finland, France, Germany, Greece, Hungary, Ireland, Italy, Latvia, Lithuania, Luxembourg, Malta, Netherlands, Poland, Portugal, Slovakia, Slovenia, Spain, Sweden, UK

ASEAN — Association of South East Asian Nations (7): Brunei, Indonesia, Malaysia, Philippines, Singapore, Thailand, Vietnam

Mercosur (5): Argentina, Brazil, Paraguay, Uruguay, Chile

(25) = number of member countries

African Union (53)

OPEC — Organisation of Petroleum Exporting Countries (12): Algeria, Gabon, Indonesia, Iran, Iraq, Kuwait, Libya, Nigeria, Qatar, Saudi Arabia, United Arab Emirates, Venezuela

Figure 14.4 World trading groups 2002

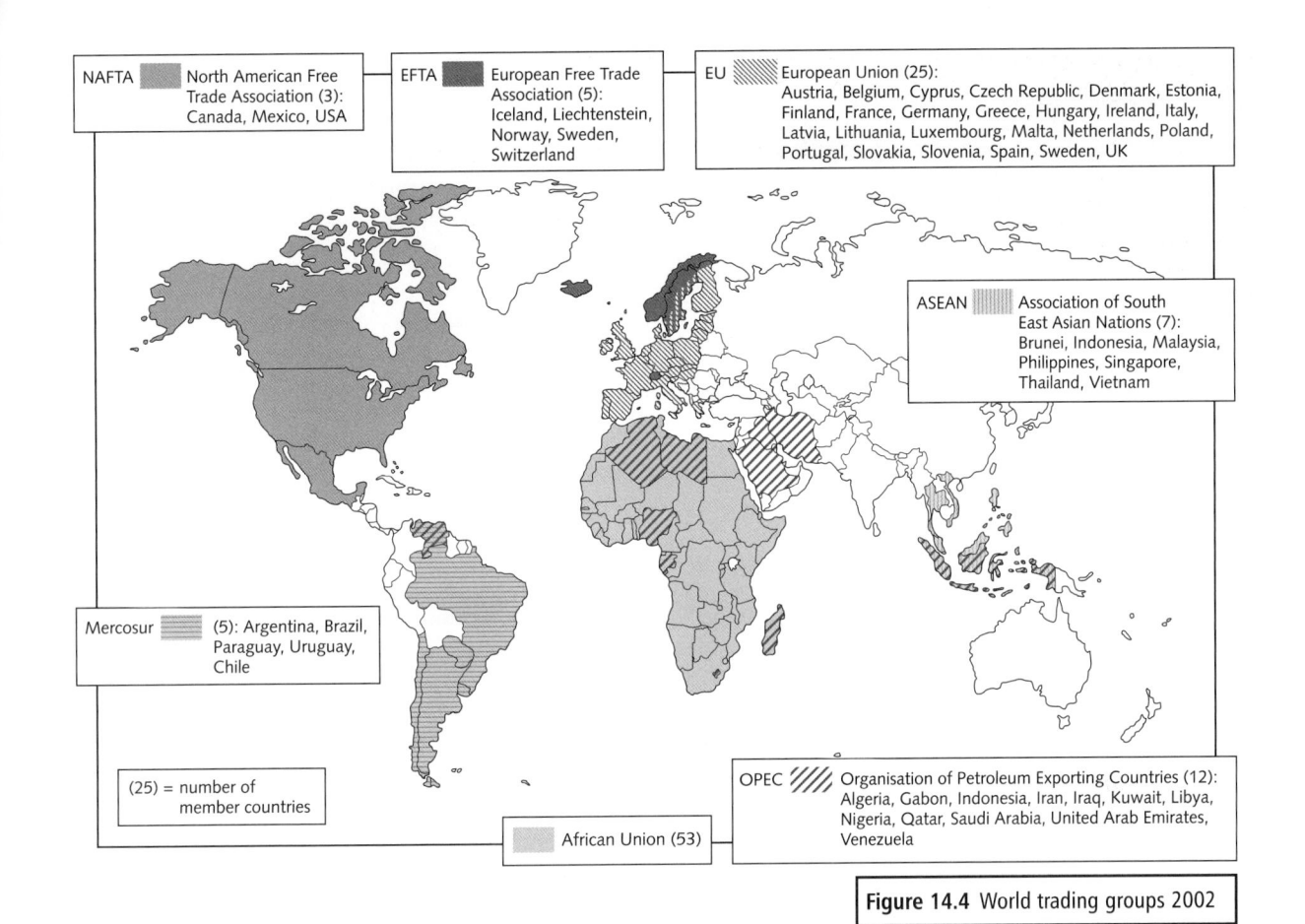

In 1995 the **World Trade Organisation (WTO)**, with over 120 members, was set up to supervise trade agreements and to settle trade disputes.

Key words to know

World Trade Organisation (WTO)

Check this!...

1 Explain the difference between trade surplus and trade deficit.

2 Give reasons for the widening trade gap between MEDCs and LEDCs.

3 Using Figure 14.1 draw two pie graphs to show the difference in trade between Kenya, an example of an LEDC, and Japan, an MEDC.

4 Britain's trade within the EU was 32 % in 1973 and 57 % in 2001. Explain why Britain's trade with the EU has increased.

Global communities

Case Study

Why is Japan a major contributor to world trade?

Back to ...

The New Wider World pp70–73, 146, 152–3, 192 and 194 for a case study of Japan.

Using your case study

Japan can be used to answer exam questions on why one MEDC is a major contributor to world trade. The 'Back to ...' references bring together a wealth of information about Japan. Use the information to describe the trade of Japan, its exports, imports and trading partners, p194 of *The New Wider World*.

Japan is the second most wealthy and industrialised country after the USA and the third highest trading nation. How did it achieve this?

Use the information to describe how Japan has few natural resources (p146) and explain how it turned to transforming low cost products, e.g. oil, into high cost exports, e.g. camcorders (pp152–153). Describe the problems (pp70–71) that have been overcome to achieve this and the solutions (pp72–73).

Include other ways in which Japan achieves a high trade surplus, p194 of *The New Wider World*.

Case study links

This case study has links with Chapter 9 – Japanese industry in South Wales.

Update

For more information on Japan's trade use the link on *The New Wider World Coursemate* website.

Learn it!

a) Describe the value, types of import and export and partners of Japan's trade. Use Figures 11.25, 11.26 on p194 of *The New Wider World* to help you.

b) Explain why Japan has grown into such a successful major trading nation. Illustrate your answer with a map based on Figure 9.24, p146 of *The New Wider World*.

2 Why is the world becoming an increasingly global community?

What are transnational companies?

Transnational companies (TNCs), or multinational companies, operate in many countries. The headquarters and main factory are usually in an MEDC with branch factories and workshops in LEDCs.

TNCs employ approximately 40 million people around the world and control over 75 per cent of world trade. TNCs controlled over half of the world's manufacturing by the late 1990s. Several of the largest corporations have a higher turnover than the total GNP of Africa.

The largest TNCs are car manufacturers and oil corporations but these have recently been joined by electronic and high-tech firms. One predicted change is an increase in the number of TNCs based in the Pacific Rim.

What are the advantages of globalisation for TNCs?

- In industry, labour costs have become one of the major production costs. Wages in LEDCs are much lower than in MEDCs, e.g. Indonesia 30 pence per hour, USA £6.80 per hour.
- Large volumes of goods allow cheaper bulk transport, so for big companies it costs less to manufacture goods in an LEDC and transport them long distances to the MEDC market.

For example, the clothing industry has become a global industry because most of the cost in the fashion industry is in making the clothes. Many sportswear companies have moved production from the USA and Europe to Indonesia and Bangladesh.

Economic and social effects on the host LEDC country

Allowing TNCs to locate in the country brings both advantages and disadvantages for LEDCs.

Advantages to the country	Disadvantages to the country
Brings work to the country and pays local labour	Does not encourage development of own industries
Attracts other TNCs to set up	Local labour force usually poorly paid
Improves the levels of education and technical skill of the people	Very few skilled workers employed
Brings some investment and foreign currency to the country	Most of the profits go overseas
Companies provide expensive machinery and modern technology	Increasing mechanisation means fewer workers needed
Increased personal income can lead to an increased demand for consumer goods and the growth of new industries	GNP grows less quickly than that of the company's headquarters
Improvements in factories, roads, airports and services	Money may be better spent on improving housing, diet and sanitation
Some recent improvement in standards of production, health control, and environmental control	Influences government decisions
	Decisions are made outside the country, and the firm could pull out at any time
	Insufficient attention to safety and health factors and the protection of the environment

Figure 14.5 Effects of locating TNCs in an LEDC

Case Study

Ford, a global car corporation

Back to ...

The New Wider World pp144–145 for information on Ford.

Using your case study

Use the information on the Ford case study to answer questions on the production structure and global locations of one named transnational company.

- Describe the origin of Ford and the global location of the production of Ford cars today
- Describe the location of:
  a) component manufacture
  b) assembly
  c) head office and the type of jobs found there. Jobs are also located where the cars are sold, e.g. sales, mechanics.
- Describe the advantages of globalisation for the corporation by mentioning the reduction of strike risk, assembly in trade bloc areas of the EU and NAFTA, designing and building cars with the specific needs of a region, e.g. India where a high-tech plant was opened in 1999 to supply the 35 Indian Ford dealerships.

Case study links

This case study has links with Chapter 9 – car industry and other TNCs located in South Wales.

Update

For more information on Ford use the link on *The New Wider World Coursemate* website.

Learn it!

a) Describe the global locations and production structure of Ford. Use Figure 9.20 on p145 of *The New Wider World* to help you.

b) Describe the advantages of globalisation for Ford.

c) Use Figure 14.5 to give the economic and social effects of Ford plants on the host countries, e.g. South Wales, India.

Check this!...

1 Use the information in the box to draw a flow diagram on a world map to show:
   a) where the assembly took place
   b) the journeys made by the components to the place of assembly
   c) where the jeans were sold.

2 Write an account of your day and every time you use something, eat something, watch or listen to something state where it/they come(s) from.

3 Study Figure 14.5. Do you think it is a good or bad thing for TNCs to expand into LEDCs? Give your reasons.

Sewn in Tunisia using thread from Hungary.

Stonewashed in Tunisia using pumice stone from an extinct volcano in Turkey.

Designed in the USA.

Cotton for denim grown in Benin.

Denim cotton woven and dyed in Italy.

Brass made from copper, Namibia and zinc, Australia.

Brass wire made in Japan.

Zip made in France from brass wire.

Brass buttons made in Germany.

Pocket lining from cotton woven in Pakistan.

Pressed and sent to the UK.

Lorry to Bangor where they are sold.

EXAM PRACTICE

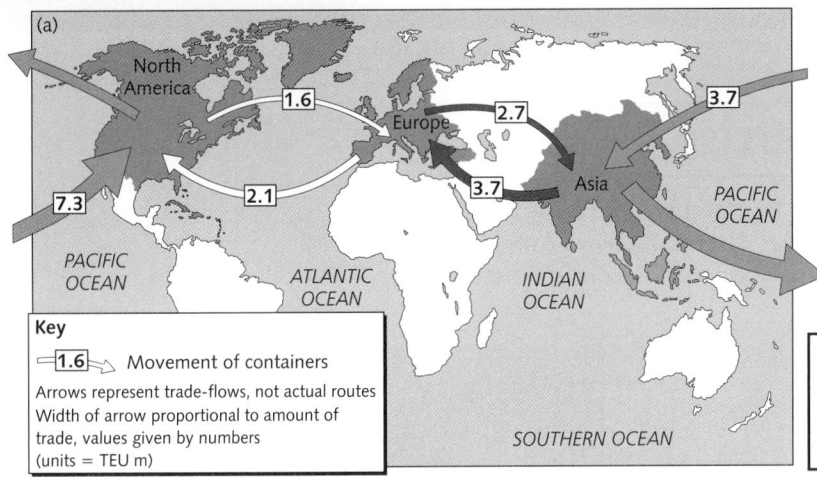

Figure 14.6 (a) The movement of shipping containers between the USA, EU and Asia, 2001 (TEU = 20ft equivalent units)
(b) Trade of two countries

Key: Movement of containers (1.6). Arrows represent trade-flows, not actual routes. Width of arrow proportional to amount of trade, values given by numbers (units = TEU m)

Map values: North America–Europe 1.6; Europe–North America 2.1; Europe–Asia 2.7; Asia–Europe 3.7; Asia–North America 7.3; North America–Asia 3.7

(b)

Country 1 Trade per capita = 25 US$ Exports	Country 2 Trade per capita = 3809 US$ Exports
Foodstuffs 28 %	Foodstuffs 10 %
Minerals and fuels 42 %	Minerals and fuels 8 %
Manufactured goods 30 %	Manufactured goods 9 %
	Machinery and transport 48 %
	Chemicals 10 %
	Others 15 %

a Containers are the large boxes which can be transferred between ship, lorry, plane and train without unloading. Study Figure 14.6a.

　i Name the route with the largest volume of container traffic. (1)

　ii Suggest which port has the larger container traffic in North America, New York on the east coast or Los Angeles on the west coast. (1)

　iii Suggest why North America (an MEDC), imports more than Asia (LEDCs). (1)

　iv Give the value of the total container flow into Europe. (1)

　v Using your own knowledge, describe **two** methods used by the EU to reduce the amount of imports into this trading bloc. (4)

b Study Figure 14.6b.

　i State which country, 1 or 2 is an LEDC. Give **four** reasons. (4)

　ii Using your own knowledge, explain why the money received from exports by LEDCs may vary widely each year. (3)

c i Describe the global distribution of a transnational company of your choice. (3)

　ii Do you think LEDCs should encourage TNCs to set up in their country? Give reasons for your opinion. (7)

EXAM TIPS

Question aii uses the command 'suggest'. This means the examiner does not expect you to have learned the answer to this question but wants you to think about it and show your understanding of the topic in your answer.

Back to ...

The New Wider World website to check your answers to the Exam Practice question.

Global communities

15 The interdependent world – decisions

Decision Making Excercise 3

IKEA is a transnational company (TNC) founded in 1943 by a 17 year old Swedish boy. By 2003 its sales figure was $US 12.2 billion from 186 stores in 31 countries. It sells 'assemble your own' furniture and other Swedish products.

Figure 15.1a Global distribution of IKEA stores

Key
33 = Number of IKEA shops

Canada 11
USA 20
Russia 5
China 2
Australia 5
Brandt line

Sweden 14
Norway 5
Finland 2
Denmark 4
Netherlands 11
UK 12
Belgium 4
Germany 33
Poland 7
Czech Rep. 3
Slovakia 1
France 13
Austria 6
Hungary 2
Portugal 1
Spain 5
Switzerland 6
Italy 9

a i Use Figure 15.1a to describe the global distribution of IKEA stores. (4)

ii Compare the locations of IKEA stores with the levels of development shown by the Brandt line. (2)

120

Figure 15.1b Some indicators of development

	Population (millions)	Urbanisation (%)	Real GNP/capita (US$)	Wages (£/hr)
USA	290	77	36 000	6.8
UK	60	89	25 000	6.5
China	1287	31	4 700	0.35
Germany	82	87	26 000	8.0
Poland	39	65	9 700	3.0

Figure 15.1c IKEA's top five countries for selling products, top five countries for buying resources

IKEA – top 5 selling countries
- Germany 20%
- UK 12%
- USA 11%
- France 9%
- Sweden 8%
- Other 40%

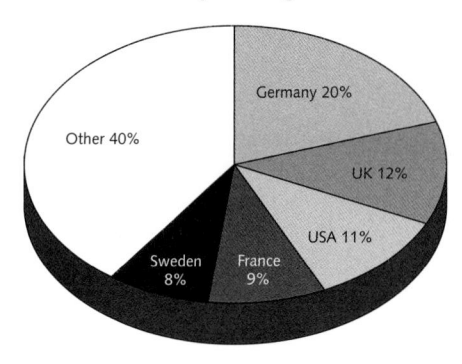

Top 5 countries from which IKEA buys resources
- China 18%
- Poland 12%
- Sweden 9%
- Italy 7%
- Germany 6%
- Other 48%

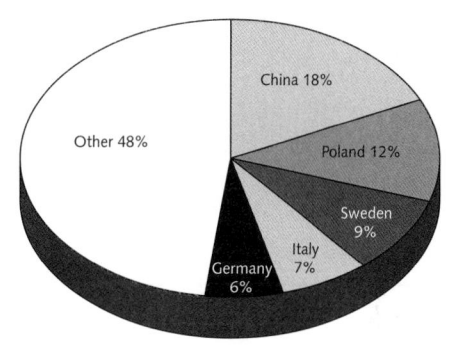

b i You are employed in the marketing department of IKEA and have to recommend a new country in which to build a future IKEA store. Which of the development indicators in Figure 15.1b would you find the most useful for your recommendation? Explain why. (4)

ii Use Figures 15.1b and c to explain why the top IKEA sales regions are different from the regions where IKEA buys its raw materials. (2)

c In 2003 the UK had 12 IKEA stores serving 35 million customers per year. IKEA and Stockport Council applied for planning permission to develop a new store north of the Portwood roundabout shown on Figure 15.2a.

i Use the maps of Figure 15.2a to describe **five** advantages of this site for a new IKEA store. (5)

ii In 2004 John Prescott, Deputy Prime Minister, had to decide whether or not to give planning permission for this development. Using all the information state which decision you would make. Give your reasons. (8)

The interdependent world – decisions

(a)

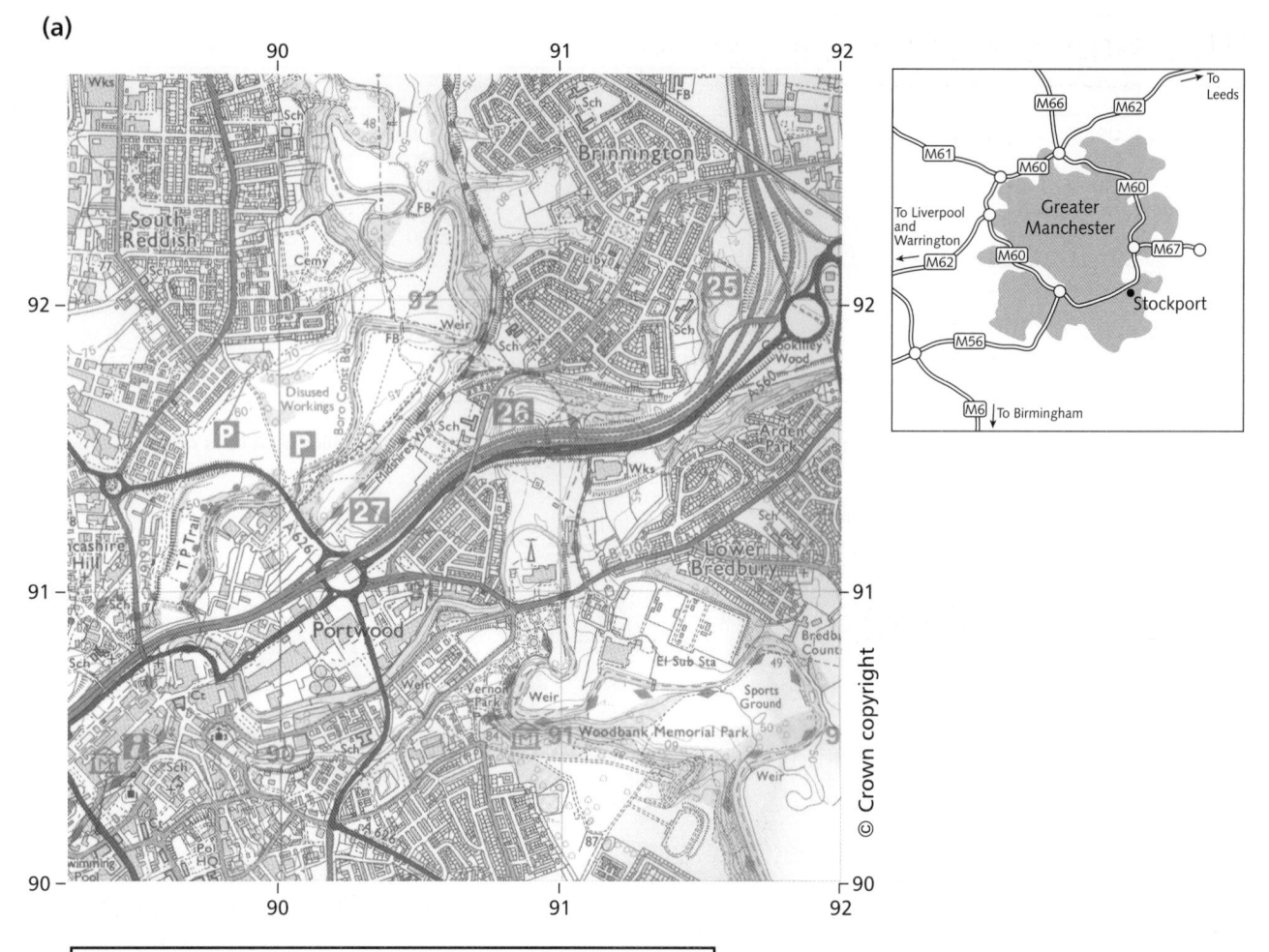

Figure 15.2 (a) OS map and motorway map showing Stockport region (b) Fact file on IKEA

(b) Fact file
- North London store busiest in the world.
- 13 500 visited the Cardiff store on its first day, Christmas 2003, the biggest tourist attraction in Wales.
- The nearest store to Stockport is at Warrington where traffic queues back to, and on, the M62 at weekends.
- Boat trips come to IKEA, Warrington, from Ireland.
- If permission is granted there are immediate plans for another 20 stores in the UK. This will mean:
  - 26 000m^2 floor space for stores
  - size of a small village will be covered with tarmac for car parking
  - £1 billion inward investment
  - 4000 jobs during construction
  - 10 000 permanent jobs within the new stores.

Back to ...
The New Wider World website to check your answers to Decision-making Exercise 3.

EXAM TIPS
When using the evidence from an OS map always give grid references. Show the examiner you can read a map and describe features as they are found on the map in front of you, not as theory you have learned.

Decision Making Excercise 4

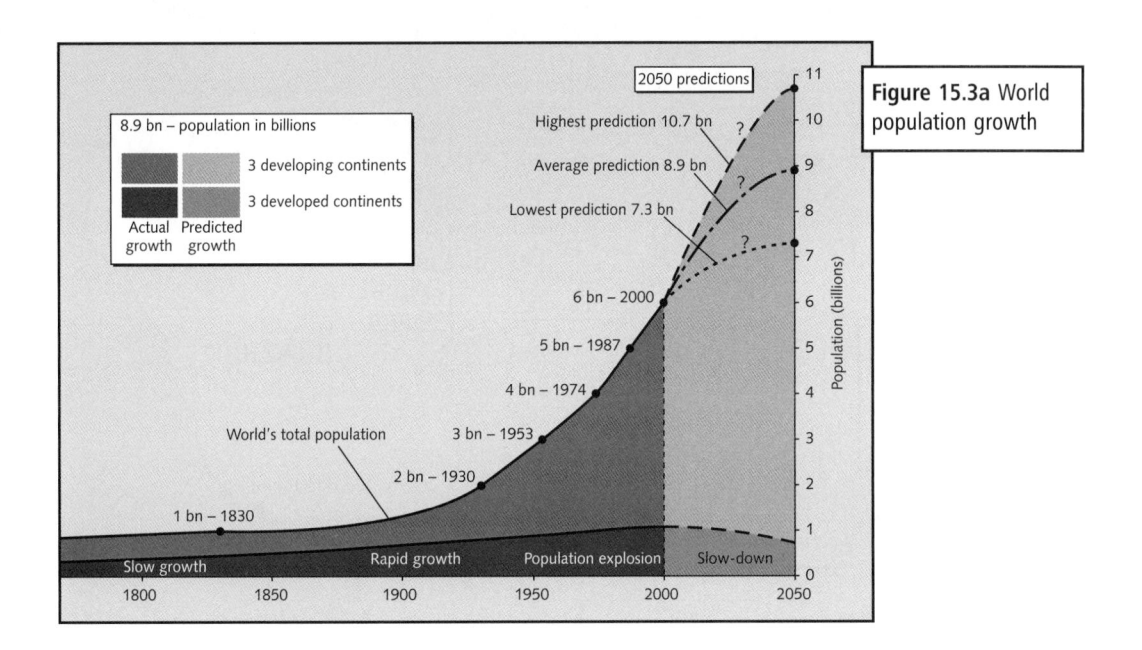

Figure 15.3a World population growth

Region	Population (%)			
	1970	1980	1990	2000
LEDCs	36	26	20	19
The Sahel	35	36	37	42
South America	17	12	12	9
China	46	28	16	14

Figure 15.3b The changing percentage of underfed people in selected parts of the world

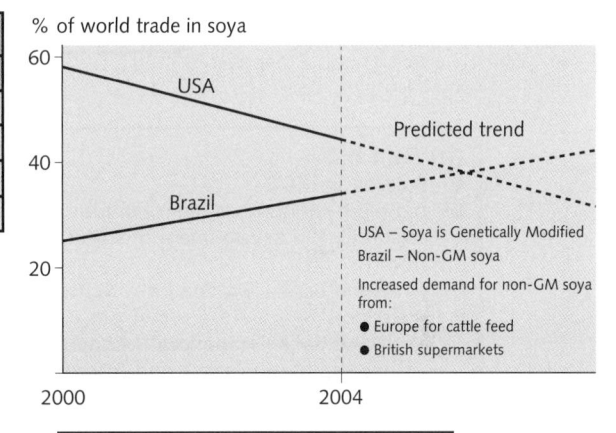

Figure 15.3c World trade in soya, USA and Brazil

a Study Figures 15.3 a, b and c.

  i   Give the world population in 2000. (1)

  ii Give the average prediction for the world population in 2050. (1)

  The increasing numbers of people in the world need to be fed.

  iii Calculate the percentage fall in the number of underfed people in LEDCs from 1970 to 2000 (Figure 15.3b). (1)

  iv Describe the trend of underfed people in the regions shown in Figure 15.3b. (3)

b MEDCs grow surplus food which they export. The biggest agricultural product in world trade is soya.

  i   Use Figure 15.3c to describe the trend for soya exports for the USA and Brazil. (3)

  ii Explain why the pattern in world trade in soya is changing. (3)

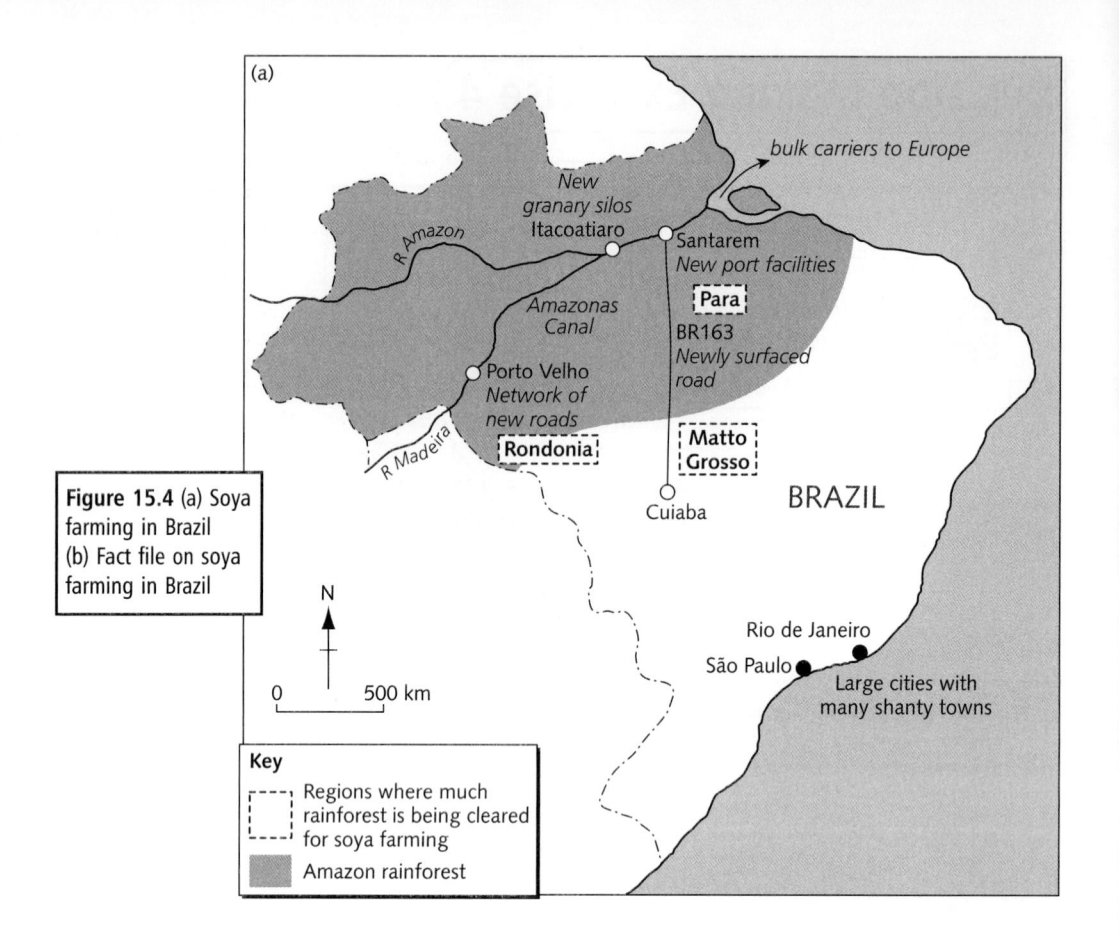

Figure 15.4 (a) Soya farming in Brazil
(b) Fact file on soya farming in Brazil

Map labels: bulk carriers to Europe; New granary silos Itacoatiaro; Santarem New port facilities; Para; BR163 Newly surfaced road; Amazonas Canal; Porto Velho Network of new roads; Rondonia; Matto Grosso; BRAZIL; Cuiaba; R Amazon; R Madeira; Rio de Janeiro; São Paulo; Large cities with many shanty towns.

Key:
- Regions where much rainforest is being cleared for soya farming
- Amazon rainforest

(b) Fact file
- Brazil is an LEDC.
- Aid has been given to the rural poor Amazon region for the development of soya farming from:
  - World Bank – 'Prodeagro' – Matto Grosso region
  - World Bank – 'Planaflora' – Rondonia region
  - Japan – Matto Grosso and Toscantino regions
  - Brazilian government, invesment in infrastructure.
- The US food giant, Cargill, with 98 000 employees in 61 countries, is the biggest exporter of Brazilian soya. It exports 7 million tons per year from 90 buying stations from within Brazil.
- Most soya is produced for export. Soya farming has been taken over by large companies using plantation farms which employ 1.7 workers/hectare. Family farms employ 30 workers/hectare.
- Brazilian rainforest the size of Wales was cut down in 2001. The amount is increasing each year mainly due to the spread of soya farming. Soya cultivation – 7500 hectares in 2004, predicted 35 000 hectares in 2005.
- The intense farming of non-genetically modified soya involves pesticides and fertilisers. Many of the farms are near the River Amazon and its tributaries.

c Study Figure 15.4.

  i Describe **three** improvements in transport for the benefit of soya farming. (3)

  ii Describe the environmental effects of soya farming. (3)

  iii Should there be an increase in soya farming in Amazonia, Brazil? Make your decision by weighing up the arguments for and against any increase. Use information from Figures 15.3 and 15.4 to help you. (7)

EXAM TIPS

There are two types of mark schemes: points marking, where you are given a mark for each point you make, and levels marking used in extended answers. In the latter, the examiner reads your complete answer and then awards a single mark based on both factual content and the way you present your answer. There are three levels of answer:
- lower, if your answer has little correct information and has not adapted material to answer the question
- middle, if you have covered the answer but not in sufficient depth or have only answered part of the answer correctly
- higher, if you have included detail across all the answer and have used geographical terminology to present a clear argument.

Back to ...

The New Wider World website to check your answers to Decision-making Exercise 4.

16 Skills

1. Map skills.
2. Interpreting photographs and observing landscapes.
3. Graphical skills.
4. Looking for patterns.

1 Map skills

Map scales

All maps should include a scale. This shows how distance on the map (in cm or mm) relates to real-life distance on the ground.

On a map, scale is shown in two ways (see Figure 16.1). Whenever you use a map you should try to use the scale to get an idea of the real-life distance between places.

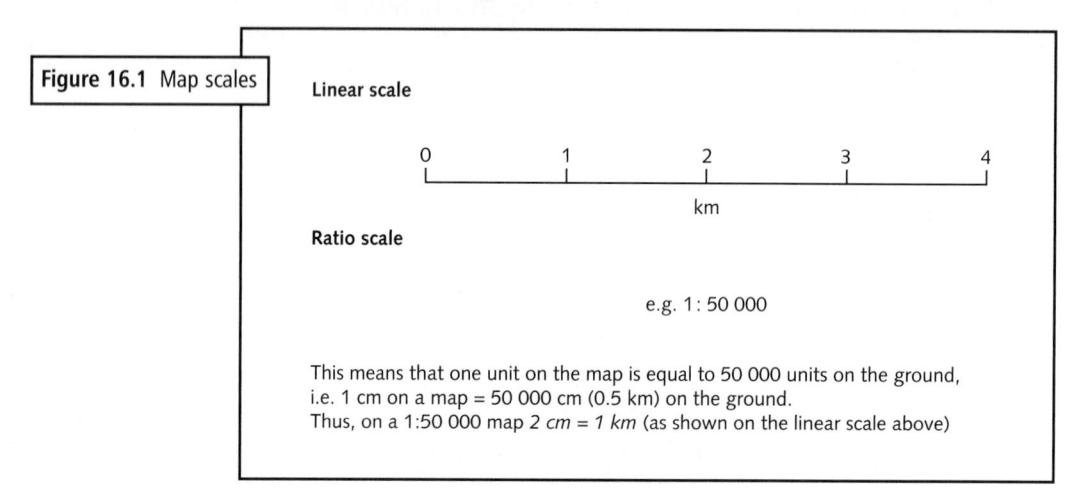

Figure 16.1 Map scales

Linear scale

0   1   2   3   4
km

Ratio scale

e.g. 1: 50 000

This means that one unit on the map is equal to 50 000 units on the ground, i.e. 1 cm on a map = 50 000 cm (0.5 km) on the ground.
Thus, on a 1:50 000 map *2 cm = 1 km* (as shown on the linear scale above)

Back to …

The New Wider World **pp41, 292** and **320** for examples of 1:50 000 OS maps.

The New Wider World **inside back cover** to see a copy of the 1:50 000 OS map key.

There are many different scales of map. The larger the scale (e.g. 1:10 000), the more detail is shown; the smaller the scale (e.g. 1:1 million), the less detail is shown. Large-scale maps can show road layouts in towns, individual buildings and fields. Small-scale maps, like country maps in atlases, cover huge areas but give very little fine detail.

At GCSE you will come across two scales of Ordnance Survey (OS) maps: the 1:50 000 (2 cm = 1 km) and the more detailed 1:25 000 (4 cm = 1 km). You should take time to learn how to use both of these scales.

Ordnance Survey map symbols

Maps contain a huge amount of information. This is made possible by using symbols instead of written labels, which would take up far too much space. Many symbols are clear in their meaning but they are always explained in a key. The key is usually found at the base or to the side of a map.

Key word to know

Eastings

Finding grid references

OS maps have gridlines drawn on them to enable locations to be given. The lines that run 'up and down' and increase in value from left to right (west to east), are called **eastings**. Those that run across the map and increase in value from bottom to top (south to north), are called **northings**.

To locate a grid square on a map, we use a **four-figure grid reference**. The first two digits refer to the easting value and the second two digits to the northing value.

To locate a point rather than a grid square, each grid square is split into 'tenths' to give a **six-figure grid reference**.

When giving a grid reference it is perfectly reasonable to estimate the 'tenths' but you can always use a ruler to be more precise.

Giving compass directions

Figure 16.2 shows the compass directions. Usually on a map the direction north is 'straight up', but it is very important that you check the key when examining maps and diagrams. This is why it is also good practice to include a north point on all maps and diagrams that you draw.

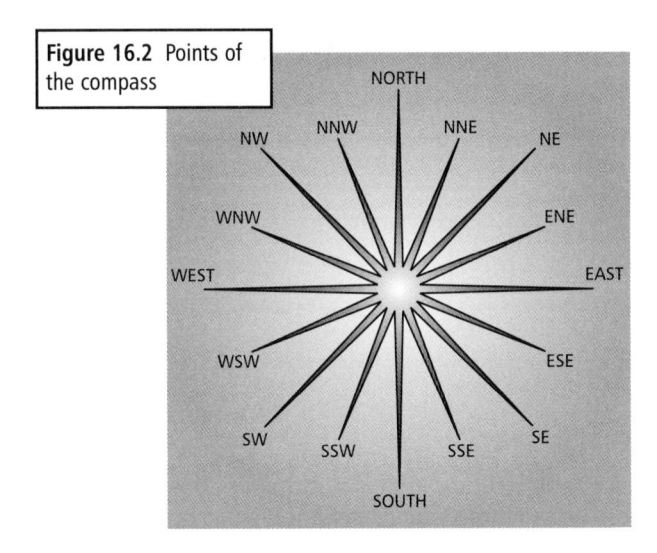

Figure 16.2 Points of the compass

Measuring distances

Every map should have a scale, usually in the form of a measured line (called a *linear scale*) with distances written alongside. To calculate a straight-line distance, you simply measure the distance on the map between the two points in question, using a ruler or the straight edge of a piece of paper. You then line up your ruler or paper alongside the linear scale to discover the actual distance on the ground in kilometres or miles.

A curved distance takes rather longer to work out. The best technique is to use the straight edge of a piece of paper to mark off sections of the curved line, effectively converting the curved distance into a straight-line distance. Look at Figure 16.3 to see how this technique works.

Remember to always give the units, for example kilometres, when writing your answer.

Key words to know

Northings
Four-figure grid reference
Six-figure grid reference

Back to ...

The New Wider World **p41** Figure 3.18: find the village of Thorngumbald. Most of the village is in grid square 2026.

The New Wider World **p41** Figure 3.18: locate the Post Office (P) in the village of Thorngumbald. Its six-figure grid reference is 208266. Notice how the eastings value is represented by the three digits 208 and the northings value is represented by the digits 266. It is the third digit of each set that is the 'tenths' value. Thus, the eastings value is 20 and 8/10ths and the northings value is 26 and 6/10ths.

The New Wider World **p41** Figure 3.18. When answering an exam question, be sure to express a compass direction carefully and precisely. For example, on this OS map Thorngumbald is to the south-east of Hedon, and Hedon is to the east of Salt End.

Skills 127

Figure 16.3 Measuring a curved distance

1. Place the straight edge of the paper alongside the route. Mark on the start (S). Look along the edge of the paper and mark off the point where the curved line no longer runs alongside the paper.

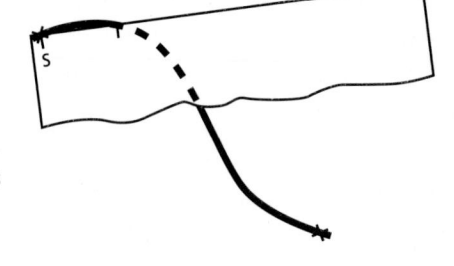

2. Carefully pivot the paper at this point until the curved line once again runs alongside. Continue along the curved line marking off the straight segments until you reach the finish. Mark this on the paper (F).

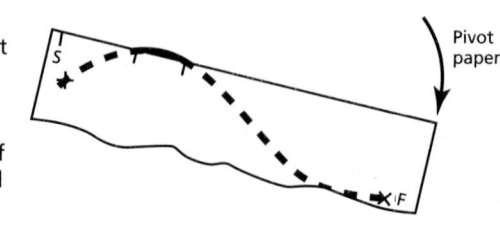

3. Measure the total straight-line distance using a ruler and convert to kilometres using the linear scale on the map.

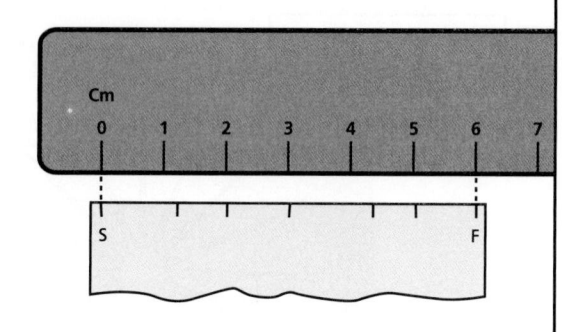

Key words to know

Sketch map

Drawing sketch maps

A **sketch map** is a simplified map that is not drawn absolutely to scale. However, it is important to add a scale even if it is just an approximation.

A sketch map is very useful because the person drawing it can decide what to include and what to leave out. It may be that only information about the physical landscape is needed or, alternatively, just the settlements and roads.

A sketch map can be drawn from any kind of map, including OS maps, maps taken from atlases, or those based on maps seen on the internet.

To draw a sketch map you should follow these steps:
- Start by drawing a frame. Make sure that the shape of the frame matches the shape of the area on the original map. It might be a square or a rectangle. Make your frame bigger or smaller than the original if you want to enlarge or reduce it.
- Now carefully transfer the information that you require from the original map on to your sketch map. You could use grid lines to help you – this is easy if your original map is an OS map – or simply draw one or two major guiding features, such as roads or rivers.
- Once complete, you can use colour and shading if you wish, although black-and-white sketches are often the most successful.

- Label and annotate as required (see below), and don't forget to include an approximate scale, a north point and a title.

Labels

Labels are often single words identifying, for example, physical features or names of places.

Annotations

Annotations are usually short sentences giving a description or explanation. They are more detailed and often more useful than labels.

> **Key words to know**
> *Labels*
> *Annotations*
> *Cross-section*

Drawing a cross-section

A **cross-section** is an imaginary slice through a landscape. It is very useful because it helps you to visualise what a landscape actually looks like.

To draw a cross-section you need a piece of scrap paper, a sharp pencil, a ruler and an eraser. The stages of construction are shown in Figure 16.4.

Figure 16.4 Drawing a cross-section

① Heights in metres

②
- Place the edge of a straight piece of paper along the line of section and mark off the contours and other details.
- Place the paper along the horizontal base of a graph.
- Choose an appropriate vertical scale.
- Mark off contours on to the graph.

③
- Join points with a curved line and continue to the axes.

Skills

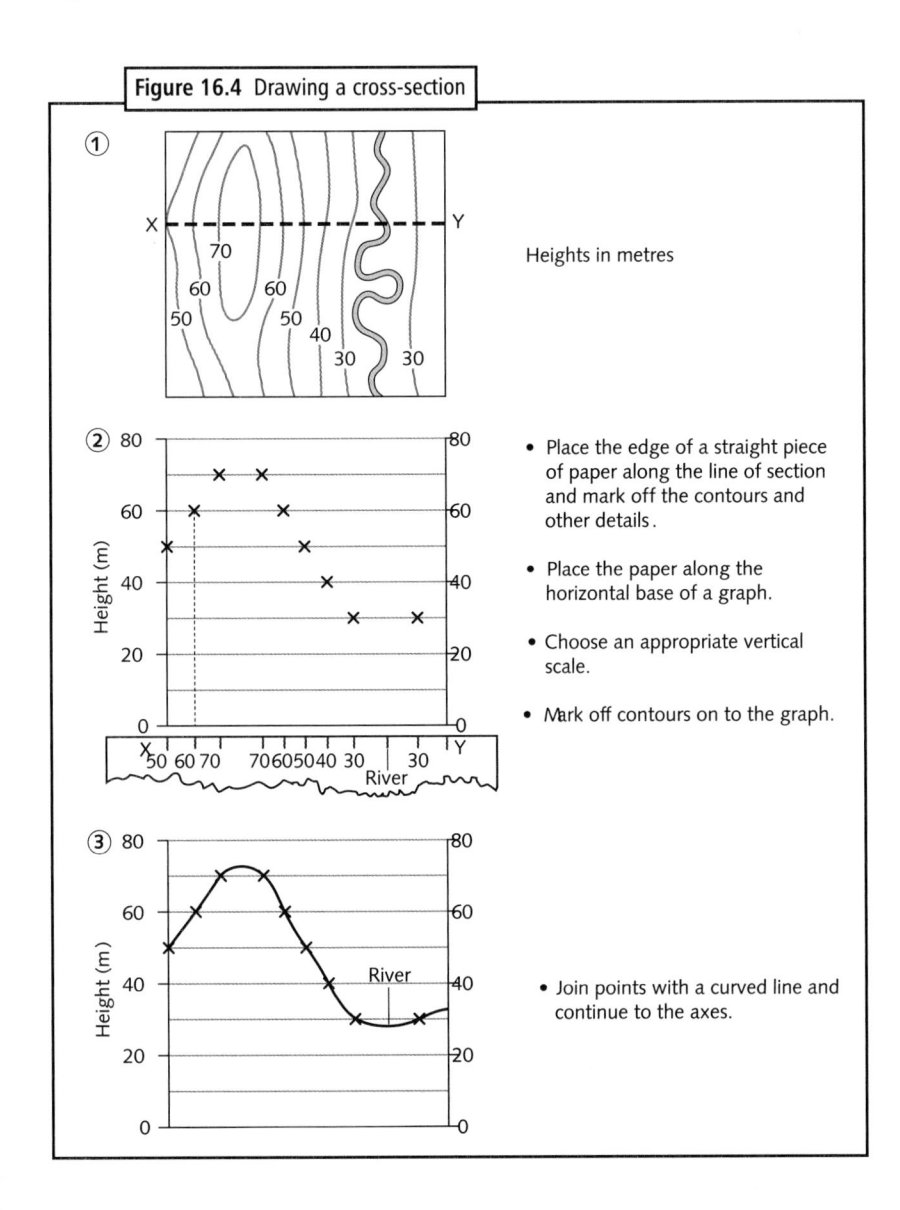

As you complete your cross-section, bear in mind the following points:
- double-check that you have written down the correct height values
- make your vertical scale as realistic as possible – don't exaggerate it so much that you create a totally unreal landscape
- complete the cross-section to both vertical axes by carrying on the trend of the landscape
- label any features
- complete axes labels and give grid references for each end of your cross-section
- give your cross-section a title.

A *long profile* is very similar to a cross-section, although it usually involves marking off contour values along a curved distance (see 'Measuring distances' on p127). Long profiles are most commonly drawn to show changes down a river valley.

Describing the physical landscape

Key words to know
Relief
Drainage

It is very likely that you will be asked to describe aspects of the physical landscape on an OS map. Mostly this involves describing the relief and drainage.

Relief is the geographical term used to describe the lie of the land. To gain the most marks in an exam you should comment on:
- The height of the land, using actual figures taken from contours or spot heights to support your points. Using words like 'high' and 'low' is fairly meaningless, without the use of actual figures. Refer to different areas or parts of the map using compass directions to enable you to be precise.
- The slope of the land – is the land flat, or sloping? Which way do the slopes face? Are the slopes gentle or steep? Are there bare cliffs exposed? Again, it is important to give precise supporting information such as grid references, compass directions, etc.
- The presence of features such as valleys, etc. Refer to names and use grid references.

Drainage is all about the presence (or absence) of water. When describing the drainage of an area try to comment on the following:
- Are there rivers on the map and which way are they flowing (look at the contours)? Is there a dense network of rivers?
- Are the rivers single or multi-channelled? Give names of the rivers, and use distances, heights and directions to add depth to your description.
- If there are no surface rivers, it may well be that the rock is permeable and that water has passed underground. If this is the case look for evidence of springs or wells.
- Can you see a pattern to the rivers (see Figure 16.5)?
- Are there any lakes, artificial or man-made?
- Is there evidence of the influence of people on drainage channels, for example straightened channels, built embankments, etc? Straight channels are rare in nature and usually indicate human intervention.

Back to ...

The New Wider World **p278**
Figure 17.2: the River Exe drainage basin is a very dense network.

The New Wider World **p291**
Figures 17.36 and 17.37 which show what happens when rivers are artificially straightened.

Describing the human landscape

Ordnance Survey maps contain a lot of information about aspects of human geography, for example roads, settlements, functions and industry.

- **Roads** Different colours are used to show the various types of road. When describing road networks, refer to the type of road and use road numbers whenever possible. For example, the main road passing through Thorngumbald (2026) is the A1033. Use compass directions when describing the pattern of roads. Look out for roads that might be intended to act as by-passes, such as the A1033 to the south of Hedon. Road networks are clearly visible in settlements and it is possible to identify patterns.
- **Settlements** The pale pink/brown colour on the map shows the extent of the built-up areas. This is where the houses and shops are. The white spaces in between are areas of open ground, such as parks. Some important buildings such as schools – you can see several of these on the outskirts of Hull – are shown separately. The shapes of settlements can be readily identified.
- **Functions** There are several functions and services shown on the map. In Preston just to the north of Hedon, there is a Post Office, a public house, several places of worship, a school and a sports centre. Not all functions, particularly shops, are shown on OS maps.
- **Industry** Industrial buildings are usually large and are often arranged in a regular pattern. A good example is the Works to the south of Salt End in grid squares 1627 and 1628. It has easy access to main roads and, in this case, has a jetty into the river. You can see other industrial buildings alongside the A1033 to the west of Salt End.

Describing patterns on specialist maps

In addition to OS maps, there are many specialist maps, e.g. geological maps, weather maps, etc.

- Geological maps show the different types of rock below the ground surface.
- Weather maps (synoptic charts) show weather information.

To interpret specialist maps you should make good use of the key, which will tell you the meaning of the symbols. In describing what the maps show, apply all the principles of good practice described above. Refer to specific locations, give facts and figures, refer to distances and compass directions, etc. You may be asked to relate a specialist map to an OS map.

2 Interpreting photographs and observing landscapes

Interpreting ground photographs

Ground photographs are photographs taken by someone standing on the ground. They show what a place looks like as we would see it if we were standing on the ground.

> **Back to ...**
>
> *The New Wider World* **p41** Figure 3.18: study the roads, settlements, functions and industry.

> **Back to ...**
>
> *The New Wider World* **pp205–206** Figures 12.13, 12.15 and 12.16 which are all examples of weather maps.
>
> *The New Wider World* **p305** Figures 18.17 and 18.18. A geological map appears alongside an OS map. In an exam you may be asked to relate the rock types to the landscape. In this case, notice, for example, that The Foreland (a geographical feature known as a headland) corresponds with the resistant rock chalk.

Skills

Back to ...

The New Wider World **p150**
Figures 9.33–9.34, which show some features of recycling and appropriate technology in LEDCs. In an exam, you could be asked to describe in detail what the people are doing.

The New Wider World **p88**
Figure 5.26, which is an oblique aerial photograph of the new town Barra di Tijuca near Rio de Janeiro.

To interpret a ground photograph you need to look at it closely and look for clues to help you understand what is happening. For example, if trees are in leaf and people are wearing shorts then it was probably taken in the summer.

Interpreting aerial photographs

Aerial photographs give us much the same view of an area as we would see when looking out of an aeroplane window. Vertical aerial photographs look directly down on an area much as a map does. Oblique aerial photographs look down at an area at an angle.

Aerial photographs are excellent in showing what an area looks like. They can help us understand and bring to life the detail shown on a map.

You may well be required to relate an aerial photograph to a map extract. Usually you will be asked to work out which way the camera is pointing. To do this, you first need to locate on the map extract some of the features shown at the bottom, middle and top of the photograph. This gives you a line of sight. Then use the compass directions on the map to help you work out which way the photograph faces.

Interpreting satellite images

Back to ...

The New Wider World **p216**
Figure 13.13, which is a satellite image of a hurricane to the west of Florida.

Satellites can provide us with very accurate and detailed images often covering large areas of the Earth's surface. Many modern maps are produced using satellite images because they are so accurate and up to date.

Computers can create satellite images that use false colours to help identify features of interest, for example, green crops, surface water or settlements.

Drawing a sketch from a photograph

Key word to know

Sketch

It is important to realise that the purpose of a **sketch** is to identify the main geographical characteristics of the landscape. It is not necessary to produce a brilliant artistic drawing; clarity and accuracy are all that is needed. Examiners reward accurate labels and annotations.

To draw a sketch, you first need to draw a frame to the same general shape of the photograph. Then draw one or two major lines that will subsequently act as guidelines for the rest of your sketch. You could draw the profile of a slope or a hilltop, or a road or river, for example. Consider what it is that you are trying to show and concentrate on these aspects; it may be river features or the pattern of settlements. Don't take time drawing a lot of detail that is not required and only serves to confuse.

Always use a good sharp pencil and don't be afraid to rub things out as you go along.

Finally, remember to label or annotate (detailed labels) your sketch to identify the features, and give your sketch a title.

Figure 16.5 Annotated sketch of a photograph of Flamborough Head

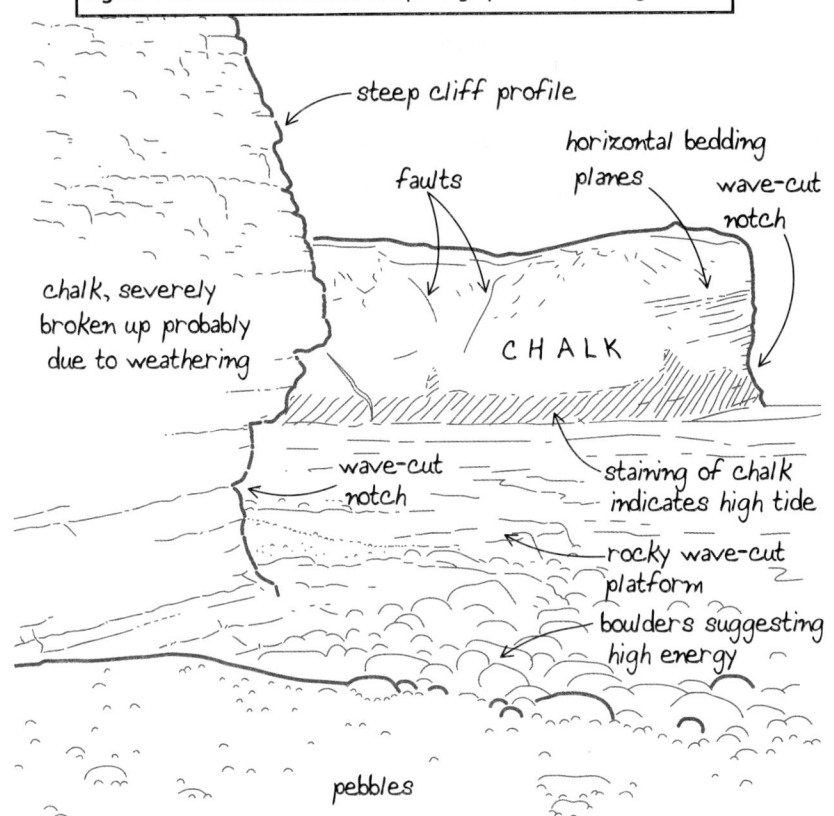

- steep cliff profile
- faults
- horizontal bedding planes
- wave-cut notch
- chalk, severely broken up probably due to weathering
- CHALK
- wave-cut notch
- staining of chalk indicates high tide
- rocky wave-cut platform
- boulders suggesting high energy
- pebbles

Back to ...

The New Wider World **p300** Figure 18.5, which shows several features of coastal erosion. Figure 11.6 is an annotated sketch of this photograph.

Drawing field sketches

A **field sketch** is a sketch drawn outside (in the field) to show a particular view. Field sketches are often used to show aspects of the physical landscape, for example a waterfall or cliff. However, they can also be used to show features of the human landscape, for example aspects of village architecture or farming land use.

To draw a field sketch, you should follow the guidelines in 'Drawing a sketch from a photograph' on p132. Decide how large an area you wish to sketch and draw a frame to the appropriate size and shape. Take time to represent the landscape accurately within your frame but avoid the temptation to strive for a work of art! It is the labels and annotations that are most valuable.

3 Graphical skills

Drawing line graphs

A **line graph** shows continuous changes over a period of time, for example stream flow or population change. It is a very common and effective technique to use, but it is important to remember that time, which is shown on the horizontal axis, must have an equal spacing, for example from year to year.

Keys words to know

Field sketch
Line graph
Bar graph
Histogram
Pie graph

Skills

Back to ...

The New Wider World **p10** Figure 1.10, which is a line graph showing the growth in world population since 1800. Notice that the points have been joined up with a freehand curve, which is usually the case with such graphs.

The New Wider World **p164** Figure 10.15, which is a rainfall climate graph and is an example of a histogram. The monthly rainfall values form part of the total annual rainfall, so they can be drawn as 'touching' bars.

The New Wider World **p14** Figure 1.17 which is a composite bar chart showing the differences between male and female life expectancy in selected countries.

Drawing bar graphs and histograms

Bar graphs and histograms are one of the most common methods used to display statistical information. However, they are not exactly the same.

- A **bar graph** is used to show the frequency or amount of a number of different categories, such as types of goods bought from a supermarket. The bars are drawn with a gap between them and they are coloured or shaded differently because they are unconnected (see Figure 16.6).

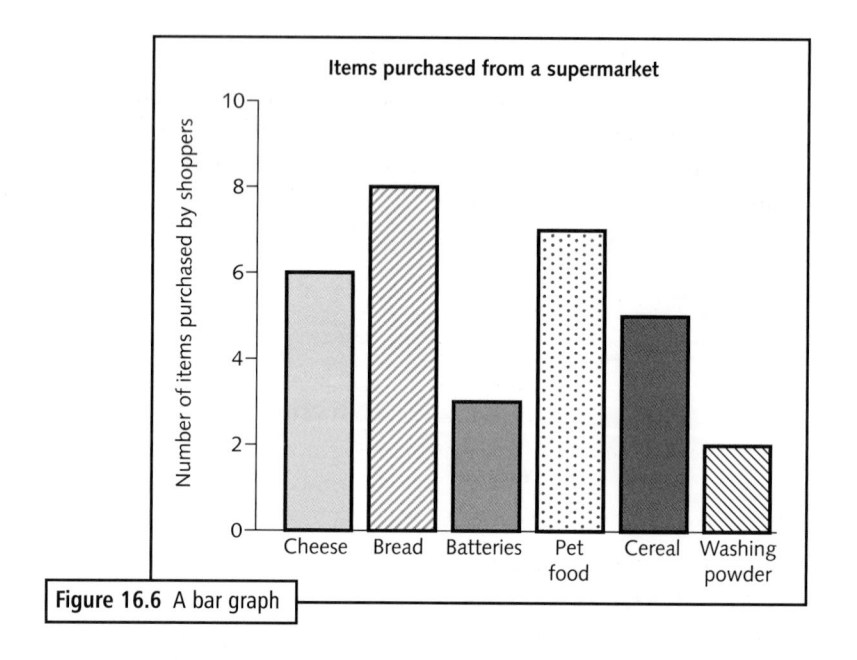

Figure 16.6 A bar graph

- A **histogram** also uses blocks but with no gaps between them. This is because a histogram is drawn when there is continuous data (such as daily rainfall values over a period of a month) or the values are all part of a single survey, for example the sizes of particles in a sediment sample. As the bars are effectively connected, a single colour or type of shading is used.

It is possible to use multiple bar charts and 'split' or composite bar charts to show two or more pieces of information at the same time.

Back to ...

The New Wider World **p173** Figure 10.36 which uses pie graphs to show statistics for the Lake District National Park.

The New Wider World **p186** Figure 11.11 which compares types of trade for a number of different countries.

Drawing pie graphs

A **pie graph** is quite simply a circle divided into segments, rather like slicing a cake! It is usually drawn to show the proportions of a total, for example the number of shoppers visiting a supermarket each day during one week. Pie graphs work best when they have between 4 and 10 segments; pie graphs with only one segment are a waste of time and those with many segments become too confusing.

When drawing a pie graph, remember to convert your values into degrees (for percentages multiply by 3.6).

Drawing scattergraphs

If you think that two sets of data are related, then the information can be plotted on a graph called a **scattergraph**. To complete a scattergraph you should do the following:
- Draw two graph axes in the normal way, but try to put the variable that is thought to be causing the change in the other (called the *independent variable*) on the horizontal (*x*) axis. In Figure 16.7, the wealth of a country (GNP) is thought to be responsible for the number of cars owned by a family.
- Use each pair of values to plot a single point on the graph using a cross.
- Use a **best-fit line** to clarify the trend of the points if there is one (see Figure 16.7). Your best-fit line should pass roughly through the centre of the points so that there is approximately the same number of points on either side of the line. Use a ruler to draw a straight line. The best-fit line does *not* need to pass through the origin. The resultant pattern can now be described.

Key words to know
Scattergraph
Best-fit line

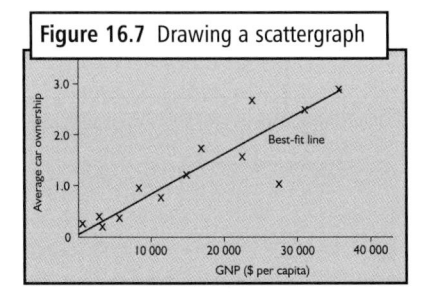

Figure 16.7 Drawing a scattergraph

Drawing flow lines

Flow lines are an excellent way to show movement, for example where people visiting a particular country have come from. Each line is drawn with its width proportional to its value, for example 1 cm = 10 million tourists. Flow lines are most effective when drawn on a base map.

Key words to know
Flow lines
Choropleth map
Isopleth map

Drawing choropleth maps

A **choropleth map** is a map that uses different colours or density of shading to show the distribution of data categories.

Notice the following key features in Figure 1.2 on p5 of *The New Wider World*:
- The base map shows regions or areas, in this case countries.
- Data is divided into a number of groups or categories. Ideally there should be between four and six categories. Notice that the category values do not overlap.
- The darker the shading, the higher the values.
- The map has a powerful and immediate visual impact; it is an effective form of mapping.

Drawing isopleth maps

An **isopleth map** is a map that uses lines of equal value to show patterns. Contours are a good example of isopleths, and are usually drawn at intervals of 10 metres.

Some of the most common isopleth maps are drawn to show aspects of weather and climate, e.g. isobars show pressure, and isotherms show temperature.

Whilst isopleth maps are rather difficult maps to draw, they are very effective at showing patterns, particularly when they are superimposed on a base map.

To draw an isopleth map, you need to mark your observed data on to a base map or sheet of tracing paper/acetate. You then need to consider how many lines to attempt to draw and at what intervals you will draw them. This decision is largely 'trial and error' and you may need to have a go in rough first.

Back to ...

The New Wider World **p178**
Question 4 which includes a flow map showing the numbers of tourists travelling to Spain. Notice that the largest number of tourists come from France.

The New Wider World **p201**
Figure 12.3 which uses isotherms to show average July temperatures in the UK. Figure 12.4 on the same page uses isotherms to show January temperatures.

Skills

Look at Figure 16.8 to see how isopleths are drawn. Notice how they pass between values that are higher and lower than the value of the line. Just remember that all values to one side of a line will be higher, and all those to the other side will be lower.

There is a degree of individual determination and decision-making, so do not worry if your map turns out to be slightly different from those of your neighbours.

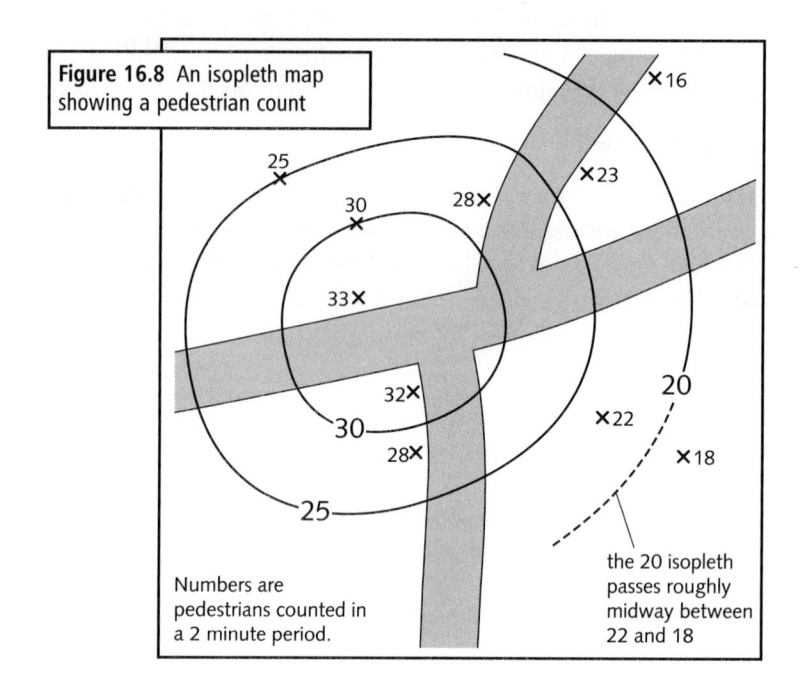

Figure 16.8 An isopleth map showing a pedestrian count

Numbers are pedestrians counted in a 2 minute period.

the 20 isopleth passes roughly midway between 22 and 18

Key words to know

Describe
Compare and contrast
Explain

Back to …

The New Wider World **p4** Figure 1.1: a description of the distribution of world population as shown here might be as follows:

'World population is unevenly distributed. In some parts of the world, for example north-west Europe, India, eastern China and south-east Africa, there is a dense population distribution. However, large parts of the world have a relatively low population density, for example Canada, much of the Russian Federation, north Africa and much of Australia.'

4 Looking for patterns

How to 'describe'

To **describe** a map, photograph or diagram you need to put into words what it shows. Start by describing the overall picture or pattern. Refer to the information available on the map, photograph or diagram and give actual facts and figures to support your statements. Then, if appropriate, look for any exceptions (called *anomalies*) to the general pattern. The most important thing is to be as precise and detailed as you can. Also, avoid giving reasons unless you are specifically asked to 'explain'.

How to 'compare' and 'contrast'

To **compare** or **contrast**, you need to write about similarities and differences, for example between two areas on a map. It is essential to make comparisons all the way through your answer, so you should use words like 'whereas' or 'compared with'. Avoid the temptation to write separate paragraphs on the two areas under discussion.

As with making a description, you should refer to places and data wherever possible.

How to 'explain' or 'give reasons'

To **explain** patterns on maps or diagrams you need to try to think of reasons why they exist. This is much more difficult and will test your understanding of geography. You may need to refer to other maps and diagrams to help you. Log on to *The New Wider World Coursemate* website. This gives examples of answers which 'explain' and 'give reasons'.

How to 'analyse'

An analysis is very similar to an explanation except that it usually involves more detail and a much greater use of facts and figures. When conducting your coursework you will probably be required to **analyse** your data.

How to 'synthesise'

A synthesis involves the 'pulling together' of a variety of different forms of information to give a general overview. It is a kind of conclusion, pulling together all the different aspects that have been studied.

> **Key words to know**
>
> *Analyse*
> *Synthesise*

A
ageing population   110
aid   103–5
air masses   26
anticyclones   27
arêtes   4

B
bar graphs   134

C
CBDs (Central Business Districts)   77–8, 78–80, 85
choropleth maps   135
cliffs   18, 19
climate   29–30
coasts   17–3
Common Agricultural Policy (CAP)   68
compass directions   127
conservation   49
continentality   30
corries   4
cross-sections, drawing   129–30

D
demographic transition model   107
dependency ratio   109
deposition
   by rivers   8–9
   coastal   17
   glacial   3–4
depressions   27
desertification   51–4
development of countries   102–5

E
energy, sustainable development   43–5
erosion
   by rivers   8
   coastal   17, 17–18
   glacial   3
estuaries   11, 21

B
farming   66–9
field sketches   133
fishing industry   46–9
flooding
   coastal   21–3
   river   12–15
floodplains   10–11
flow lines   135

G
glaciers   3–6
global warming   55–8
globalisation   115
graphs   133–5
green belts   88
greenhouse effect   55
grid references   126–7

H
hanging valleys   5
headlands and bays   18
hill sheep farming   66–9
histograms   134

H
industry   70–4
inner cities   78, 83–4, 85, 90
interlocking spurs   9
isopleth maps   135–6

L
landscape, describing   130–1
LEDCs (less economically developed countries)
   flooding in   12
   population   106, 107, 108
   trade   113, 114
   transnational companies and   116–17
   urban growth   94–101
line graphs   133

M
maps
   describing   136–7
   map skills   126–31
   types of   131, 135–6
mass movement   2
meanders   10
MEDCs (more economically developed countries)
   population   106, 107, 108
   trade   113, 114
   transnational companies   116
   urban growth   94–5
migration   111
moraine   5

O
ox-bow lakes   10

P
photographs   131–3, 136–7
pie charts   134
population   106–10

R
resources, sustainable development of   42–9
ribbon lakes   6
rivers   8–15
rural areas   90–2
rural-urban fringes   86, 89, 90
rural-urban migration   95, 100

S
scales, map   126, 127
scattergraphs   135
scree slopes   1, 2
shopping   77–80
sketch maps, drawing   128–9
sketches   132–3
soil creep   2
spits   19–20
suburbanisation   90–91
suburbia   78, 85–6, 89–90
sustainable development
   of countries   103–5
   of resources   42–9

T
tourism   34–6
trade, world   113–17
transnational companies (TNCs)   116–17
transport, urban   89
transportation
   by rivers   8
   coastal   17
   glacial   3

U
urban areas
   global development   94–101
   land use patterns   82–6
   shopping within   77–80
   urban change   86–90

V
valleys   5, 9

W
waterfalls and gorges   9
waves   16
weather   25–31
weathering   1–2
wind farms   45